Fifty Hikes in the Adirondacks

Scott's Clearing

Fifty Hikes in the Adirondacks

Short Walks,
Day Trips, and
Backpacks Throughout
the Park

Barbara McMartin

Photographs by the author

Backcountry
Publications
Woodstock, VT

An Invitation to the Reader

Trails change continually. New logging roads are cut, and old ones grow over. Woods reclaim abandoned fire tower trails, and hiking clubs reroute sections of eroding paths. Occasionally landmarks, highways, and trailheads are relocated or renamed. If you find conditions along the trails in this book changed from their description here, please let the author and publisher know so that corrections may be made in future editions. Address comments and suggestions to:

Editor, Fifty Hikes
Backcountry Publications
PO Box 175
Woodstock, VT 05091

International Standard Book Number: 0-942440-00-5
Library of Congress Catalog Card Number: 79-92569

©1980 by Barbara McMartin. All rights reserved.
Published by Backcountry Publications
Woodstock, VT 05091

Printed in the United States of America
Design by Wladislaw Finne
Back cover photograph and those on pages 56 and 61 by Alec Reid. Photograph on page 117 by Ken Hokenson; page 157 by Glen Nichols; page 170 by Peter Gloo; page 185 from DEC; page 206 by James Lenney. All others by the author.

Acknowledgments

While good trails seal the bonds of friendship, good friends and great companions are essential to great hikes. I hiked the majority of the trails in this guide with Alec Reid, who also helped print my photographs; or with Erwin Miller, who, with his wife, also provided shelter close to the northernmost trails.

James Lenney, Willard Reed, Peter Gloo, Jill Parker, Courtney Young, Jr., William Potter, Larry King, Maryde King, William White, Judy Aldinger, Howard Ulman, Bruce Coon, and the Mohawk Valley Alpiners either helped or accompanied me on many hikes.

These people are not just close friends; they are also among the most knowledgeable hikers in the Adirondacks. I am grateful to them for making the hikes more enjoyable for me and for providing insights that make this a better book for my readers.

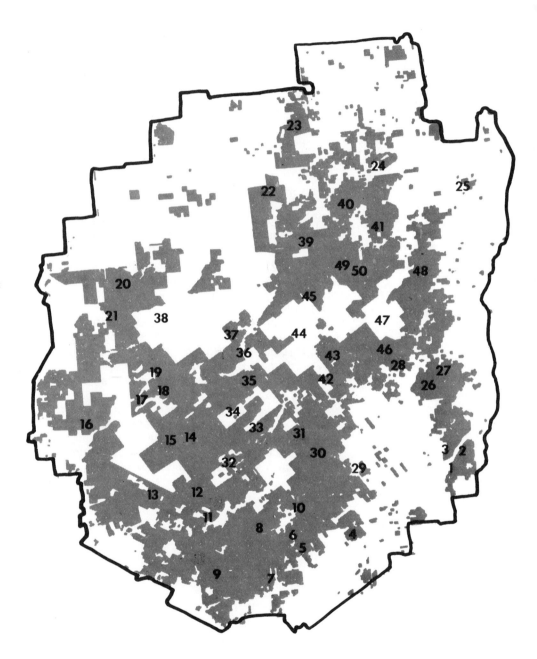

Adirondack Park
(shaded areas are public lands)

Contents

Introduction

The Adirondack Park is surrounded by a magical Blue Line that sets it apart from the rest of New York State. With 5.6 million acres, this park is larger than either Massachusetts or New Jersey. Calling the area a park is confusing, for the Blue Line in fact delineates a hodge-podge of public and private lands.

The public lands inside the park's boundary have been gradually incorporated into a body known as the Forest Preserve, which was established in 1892 and was initially intended to protect forever the state's water resources. At present, the Adirondack Park Agency oversees all of the land within the park, both public and private. The public lands are divided into Wilderness, Wild Forest, and Primitive Areas, categories that reflect the amount and type of use with which they are ecologically compatible.

Forest Preserve lands, roughly one-third of the area inside the Blue Line, are managed by the New York State Department of Environmental Conservation (DEC), which has responsibility for all public trails. The Forest Preserve is managed in a way that permits hunting throughout, but prohibits any cutting of timber.

I have selected these fifty hikes to represent as many of the Adirondack's regions, both political and natural, as possible. The guide covers the major trailheads in each Wild Forest Area and in all but two of the designated Wilderness Areas. Even so, it covers only a small fraction of the hiking trails that course through the Forest Preserve's 2.4 million acres.

This guide describes every type of hiking trail, from those well known, to those visited by only a few people. The trails lead you up the tall peaks of the northern mountain ranges as well as up the gentler mountains surrounding the central Adirondack dome. They follow abandoned logging roads and chains of uninhabited lakes. On them you meet wild rivers and distant waterfalls, discover caves and cliffs, and reach a few of the fire towers that still survive. In short, this guide acquaints you with a cross-section of trails available to Adirondack hikers.

Of course, I hope this guidebook does more than introduce you to the 360 miles of trails and 60,000 feet of climbing outlined in the fifty hikes. It should make you aware of the geological structures that underlie the trails and their relation to the various types of forest vegetation. It should lead you to observe alpine summits and broad plains, virgin forests and quaking bogs, ferns and wildflowers, birds and wild animals.

Equally important, you should become acquainted with a few of the early settlers who pioneered in the mines and forests, the trappers, lumbermen, and guides whose footsteps echoed on the woodland routes that are today's hiking trails. I have also included a selection of books that can increase your knowledge and appreciation of the trails' history. These books are chosen not necessarily because they are the most scholarly, but because they have most vividly recreated the past for me. I want this guide to locate where specific historical events occurred.

All the details I have tried to weave into this trail guide are still no more than hints of what you will find. Enrichment is the most important part of this guide. If you let it take you on a true voyage of discovery, you will enjoy much more than the pleasures of hiking. You will come to know the land and to develop a sense of love and reverence for all that it embraces. That is what I want to share with you.

Before You Start

The majority of these fifty hikes are just that—hikes. This guide is designed to acquaint you with extended walks throughout the Adirondacks. Strenuous hikes are usually associated with the High Peaks Region in the northeastern part of the Adirondack range, but you can also find them everywhere in the Forest Preserve. To give everybody a chance to discover the wonders of this vast area, however, I have included a few shorter, easy walks. Many more exist,

described in my regional guide series (see the final section of this introduction, Books About the Adirondacks).

While all these excursions are dayhikes (although you must pack in and camp overnight to reach the start of one hike), you should be well prepared and well equipped before starting the longer walks. If you are new to hiking, it will be best to join a hiking group and learn from those with experience. The more experience you have in the woods, the greater will be your enjoyment and your safety. Do not count on this summary of what you need to know to prepare you for every situation you are likely to encounter. This guide was not written primarily for novices, and this introduction is not a primer for beginning hikers. Treat it as a checklist and a set of reminders.

The Weather

Whenever possible, wait for a sunny day. The pleasures are much greater, and the problems more predictable. But even on sunny days you should be prepared for the worst; downpours and cold fronts can occur almost unannounced. The hiking season in the Adirondacks generally extends from May through October, but this does not mean you can't see snowflakes in July. In May, for instance, the temperature may range from a sweltering 92 degrees Fahrenheit on a trail not yet sheltered by leaf cover, to a frigid 22 degrees Fahrenheit on a mountain path smothered in a foot of new snow. June is no less variable, and by then the black flies, scourge of the north, are out in full force. July and August can be severe on the tops of the higher mountains, and by mid-September you should again be prepared for snow. Of course, preparing for the worst does not mean the worst will happen. Remember, the greatest advantage in planning day trips is that you can wait until a good day comes before setting out.

Preparations

Even with the best of forecasts, your watchword should be to *plan for the unexpected.* Possible changes in temperature mean you should take extra clothing, of which at least one layer should be wool—yes, wool, even in the heat of summer. It is the one material that keeps you warm when wet. In addition to changes of warm clothing, you may also want to carry a change of socks and a shirt, even on a day hike. Experiment with a combination of layers of light waterproof gear, warm wool shirts, thermal underwear, and cool, long-sleeved cotton shirts. Your pants should be sturdy and comfortable. If you are modest you might want to carry a bathing suit in your pack. Gloves and a hat usually also find their way into my pack.

Changes in terrain mean you need a sturdy, lightweight, waterproof, over-the-ankle pair of boots. And, you need a pair that fits perfectly and is well broken-in. You need to wear two pairs of socks, an inner lightweight pair and a heavy outer pair that is at least partly wool.

Of course you want a sturdy daypack, large enough to hold your needs. The separate pouch along the side of my pack always contains a whistle, a case with dry matches, a jackknife, a small can-opener, chapstick, and a space blanket. I have used them all.

Carry a map and compass (more of that later), a flashlight in case you are delayed beyond dusk, and a watch so you do not panic if that happens. You also need a small first-aid kit, containing a few bandages, first-aid cream, and moleskin for the unexpected blister.

Buy a small squeeze bottle of insect repellent. Carry it all summer long, for the black fly season in spring stretches into the mosquito season of early summer. Deer flies and horse flies follow, and many years see a resurgence of black flies in autumn. If you plan ahead, the bugs are not all that bad. If it is warm and dry enough to walk in early May, you can enjoy a few weeks before the bugs start. They first appear at lower elevations and in the south, so try a few higher or more northern hikes until the black flies catch up with you. Most years there is about a week in early June—the timing and length may vary—when you should simply stay home. That week invariably occurs the week the trout fishing is best. Although modern science has made great improvements in repellents, nothing really seems to work during this one short period.

I fill a ziplock bag with toilet paper so it stays dry. I also throw in a few 'wash and dries' to use before lunch on those dry mountain tops.

All wise hikers are likely to carry these basic items, but my personal list has additional items you should consider. I always wear unbreakable glasses. Overhanging twigs and branches have a way of poking eyes. Even if you do not need them for vision, carry dark sunglasses for bright days and a lightly tinted pair for the duller light.

There is always a magnifying glass in my pack for resolving the contour lines on maps and for identifying plant specimens. I would not be without my lightweight pair of binoculars. Distant mountain tops and birds are an important part of what I see. For pure fun I carry a small, lightweight, and inexpensive altimeter that works according to barometric pressure. On relatively stable days, it is a good clue to my progress up a mountain, and on an unstable day, it can alert me to sudden changes of weather.

Managing water has become a problem in the Adirondacks. The appearance of Giardia cysts in once pure mountain streams means that the hiker can no longer drink with impunity. As a general rule, the day hiker ought to carry enough water for his needs. The camper must use other methods, and though there is a variety of opinions about the best methods of water purification, certain filters do work. These can be bulky and expensive and I suggest you consult the latest techniques available in camping equipment stores.

The day hiker may find, as I do, that the lightweight aluminum fuel bottles, used, of course, only for drinking purposes, are the most indestructible and leak-proof water carriers. The introduction of individual cardboard juice cartons has solved the juice and pick-me-up problem for me. They are sturdy, safe, and offer a variety of natural juices, perfect for the hiker.

Remember, hiking should be fun. If you are uncomfortable with the weather or tired, turn back and make the complete hike another day. Do not create a situation where you risk yourself or your companions.

And, *never walk alone.* Be sure someone knows your intended route and expected return time. Always sign in at the DEC trailhead registers where they are available. The unexpected can occur. Weather can change, trail markings can become obscured, you can fall, and you can get lost. But you will not be in real danger if you have anticipated the unexpected.

Behaviour in the Woods

So now you are safe in the woods, but what about the woods? The Adirondack environment that can threaten you can be just as fragile as you are, and you are the only one who can protect it.

Walk dry. Wet soil is more easily compacted, making roots more susceptible to damage, so try to hike when the trails are dry. Stay on trails or rock surfaces, especially on higher summits. Avoid wet places, or walk through them with extreme care. This guide does point out a few bogs; enjoy them without altering them.

Camp at designated areas where they exist or in places where a campsite will leave no trace, always away from water or trailsides, and at lower elevations.

Bury your wastes at least 200 feet from water and from a trail or path. If possible, select a leaf- or duff-covered area where a suitable hole can be easily scraped aside. With the appearance of Giardia in some locations, it is imperative that hikers manage human wastes to prevent the spread of this hikers' scourge.

Do not bathe with soap in lakes or streams; when picnicking or camping carry wash water as well as dish water back from the shore. Keep lake or running water pure for drinking and swimming.

If you are camping, carry a stove for cooking, and do not build fires unless they are needed. Then use only dead downed wood, and build your fire on dry stone or on gravelly or sandy soil surfaces, surrounded by a fire ring of stones to protect duff, leaf mold, or organic soils from burning.

Burn organic trash if you can. Otherwise, carry out everything you carry into the woods.

Respect the rights of others—the property rights of private landholders, as well as the privacy of fellow hikers and the wilderness rights of future hikers.

Notes for Using This Guide

Summaries at the beginning of each hike list the hiking distance, vertical rise, time on the trail, and the United States Geological Survey (USGS) topographical map or maps for the area the hike traverses. If the hike is in one of the official Wilderness Areas, that fact is noted. And if the hike climbs a mountain with a fire tower that is still open, that fact is noted along with the days that the observer is not on duty.

Unless otherwise indicated, distances are for the round trip or circuit. Distances have been derived from either state trail markings or measurements made from the USGS sheets. The latter are correct to within 10 percent. Errors and inconsistencies in the state signing system are described in the text.

Distances are given in miles, feet, and yards. Unless you are an experienced hiker, you probably have little sense of distance. You might want to

Queen Anne's lace

practice 'guestimating' 100-yard intervals on the level and pacing them out to check. Because the difficulty of a hike can be so affected by elevation changes and the condition of the trail, time is as important as distance in estimating a segment of a trip.

Vertical rise refers to the total rise in elevation for the hike. In cases where the terrain is relatively level a numerical figure has not been used.

Hiking time is given for the total time for a leisurely pace, but it is simply the minimum needed to walk the trail as described. The text often tells you to allow more time for sightseeing, and the difference is a good indication of the special things you might encounter on the way.

The maps, the USGS topographical sheets mentioned in each heading, are not absolutely necessary equipment, because the maps in this guide are based on them. (The hike route is shown by a dashed line, and the walking direction of any loop by an arrow.) However, you will have more fun on a mountain top if you can identify some of the surrounding countryside, and the maps enable you to do this.

If you do not know how to read a map you should learn to do so before hiking all but a half-dozen of the simplest trails in this guide. Spend time walking with someone who does know how to read a map. The same instructions are appropriate for the use of a compass. If you are not proficient in the use of a compass, get help, or work with a good book on compass reading or orienteering.

The skillful use of maps and a compass is only developed with practice.

This book is a guide to fifty great hikes, not a course in using map and compass. Almost all of the routes described are on marked trails, but markings have a way of changing.

You cannot always depend on them. Furthermore, bridges wash out, beaver build new ponds, and mountain tops become so clouded in fog that visibility beyond your fingertips is impossible. None of this should bother you if you have developed map and compass skills.

Other Helpful Information

Adirondack Association, Inc.
Adirondack, NY 12808

This group publishes several useful brochures, among them: "The Adirondack Adventure," "Adirondack Fishing Water," "Adirondack Area Map and Information Guide," "North Country Craft Trail Map," "Off-the-Beaten Path (Scenic Roads)," and "The Historic Adirondacks."

Adirondack Mountain Club
172 Ridge Street
Glens Falls, NY 12801

The club (ADK) is active in Adirondack conservation efforts, and its many chapters throughout New York State offer group outings and hikes. ADK publishes regional guides. Membership is currently $22 per year.

City Street Directory, Inc.
35 Sandi Drive
Poughkeepsie, NY 12603

This company publishes "Adirondack Region Atlas," the best road map for locating trailheads in the Adirondacks. The map sells for $3.75.

New York State Department
of Environmental Conservation
50 Wolf Road
Albany, NY 12233

The Department of Environmental Conservation (DEC) is the source of all DEC booklets, trail maps, and campsite information. Some specific titles are: "Nordic Skiing Trails in New York State," "Lake George Islands Map," "Moose River Recreation Area," "Pharaoh Lake Trails Map," "Trails in the Lake George Region," "Trails in the Cranberry Lake Region," "Trails in the Old Forge-Big Moose Region," and "Trails in the Schroon Lake Region."

The DEC operates regional offices throughout New York State. Addresses and telephone numbers for offices in Region 5 are: Lands and Forests Headquarters, Ray Brook, NY 12977, 518-891-1370 (covering Clinton, Essex, and Warren counties); Lands and Forests Headquarters, Northville, NY 12134, 518-863-4545 (covering Hamilton and Fulton counties); and Lands and Forests Headquarters, Hudson Street Extension, Box 220, Warrensburg, NY 12885, 518-623-3671 (covering Saratoga, Warren, and Washington counties).

For Region 6, which also extends into the Adirondack region, offices are: Lands and Forests Headquarters, Route 26A, P.O. Box 3, Lowville, NY 13367, 315-784-0100 (covering Jefferson and Lewis counties); and Lands and Forests Headquarters, 225 North Main Street, Herkimer, NY 13350, 315-866-6330 (covering Herkimer and Oneida counties.

New York State
Department of Commerce
Office of Tourism
99 Washington Avenue
Albany, NY 12245

Among the publications this office issues are the "I Love New York" brochures, camping guides, a tourism map, and the "State Travel Guide."

Branch of Distribution
U.S. Geological Survey

1200 South Eads Street
Arlington, VA 22202

If you are ordering USGS topographical maps by mail, write to the above address and ask for the index and price list for New York State.

Books About the Adirondacks

Aber, Ted and Stella King. *The History of Hamilton County.* Lake Pleasant, N.Y.: Great Wilderness Books, 1965.

Adirondack Mountain Club. *Guide to Adirondack Trails: High Peaks Region and Northville-Placid Trail.* Glens Falls, N.Y.: Adirondack Mountain Club.

Beetle, David H. *Up Old Forge Way and West Canada Creek.* Lakemont, N.Y. and Old Forge, N.Y.: North Country Books, 1972. (One-volume reprint of two books composed of articles published by the *Utica-Observer Dispatch,* Utica, N.Y., 1946 and 1948).

Carson, Russell M.L. *Peaks and People of the Adirondacks.* Glens Falls, N.Y.: Adirondack Mountain Club, 1973. (Reprint of 1927 edition).

Donaldson, Alfred L. *The History of the Adirondacks.* Vols. I and II. Harrison, N.Y.: Harbor Hill Books, 1977. (Reprint of 1921 edition).

Dunham, Harvey L. *French Louie: Early Life in the North Woods.* Saranac Lake, N.Y.: North Country Books, 1970.

Fox, William F. *History of the Lumber Industry in the State of New York.* Harrison, N.Y.: Harbor Hill Books, 1976.

Gallos, Phil. *By Foot in the Adirondacks.* Saranac Lake, N.Y.: Adirondack Publishing Company, Inc., 1972.

Grady, Joseph F. *The Adirondacks, Fulton Chain-Big Moose Region: The Story of a Wilderness.* Old Forge, N.Y.: North Country Books, 1966. (Reprint of 1933 edition).

Graham, Frank, Jr. *The Adirondack Park: A Political History.* N.Y.: Alfred A. Knopf, 1978.

Hyde, Floy S. *Adirondack Forests, Fields and Mines.* Lakemont, N.Y.: North Country Books, 1974.

Jamieson, Paul F. "Adirondack Eskers." *Adirondack Life,* November/December 1978, p. 20.

_____. *Adirondack Canoe Waters: North Flow.* Glens Falls, N.Y.: Adirondack Mountain Club, 1975.

_____. *Adirondack Reader.* Second Edition, Glens Falls, N.Y.: The Adirondack Mountain Club, 1982

Ketchledge, E.H. *Trees of the Adirondack High Peak Region.* Glens Falls, N.Y.: Adirondack Mountain Club,1967

Masten, Arthur H. *The Story of Adirondac.* Syracuse, N.Y.: Adirondack Museum and Syracuse University Press, 1968. (Reprint of 1923 edition).

McMartin, Barbara. *Caroga: The Town Recalls its Past.* Caroga, N.Y.: Town of Caroga, 1976.

_____. *Discover the Adirondacks, 1: From Indian Lake to the Hudson River/A Four-Season Guide to the Out-of-Doors.* Somersworth, N.H.: New Hampshire Publishing Company, 1979.

_____. *Discover the Adirondacks, 2: Walks, Waterways and Winter Treks in the Southern Adirondacks.* Somersworth, N.H.: New Hampshire Publishing Company, 1980.

_____. *Guide to the Eastern Adirondacks.* Glens Falls, N.Y.: Adirondack Mountain Club, 1981

_____. *Old Roads and Open Peaks.* Glens Falls, N.Y.: Adirondack Mountain Club, 1977.

Murray, William H.H. *Adventures in the Wilderness.* Syracuse, N.Y.: Adirondack Museum and Syracuse University Press, 1970. (Reprint of 1869 edition).

Newland, D.H. and Henry Vaughn. *Guide to the Geology of the Lake George Region.* Albany, N.Y.: University of the State of New York, 1942.

O'Kane, Walter Collins. *Trails and Summits of the Adirondacks.* Boston and New York: Houghton Mifflin Company, 1928.

Pilcher, Edith. "Nehasne." *Adirondack Life,* September/October 1979, p. 14.

Rickett, Harold William. *Wild Flowers of the United States, Volume I: The Northeastern States.* New York: The New York Botanical Garden and McGraw-Hill Book Company, 1966.

Simms, Jeptha R. *Trappers of New York, or a Biography of Nicholas Stoner and Nathaniel Foster.* Harrison, N.Y.: Harbor Hill Books, 1982. (Reprint of 1857 edition)

Street, Alfred B. *The Indian Pass.* Harrison, N.Y.: Harbor Hill Books, 1975. (Reprint of 1960 edition).

Van De Water, Frederic F. *Lake Champlain and Lake George.* The American Lakes Series. Indianapolis and New York: Bobbs Merrill, Co., 1946.

Van Diver, Bradford C. *Rocks and Routes of the North Country, New York.* Geneva, N.Y.: W.F. Humphrey Press, 1976.

Wherry, Edgar T. *The Fern Guide: Northeast and Midland United States and Adjacent Canada.* Philadelphia: The Morris Arboretum of the University of Pennsylvania, 1972.

1

Buck Mountain

Distance (round trip): 6.6 miles
Vertical rise: 2,000 feet
Hiking time: 4½ hours
Map: USGS 15' Bolton Landing

Buck Mountain lies on the southeast shore of Lake George, and it is a perfect introduction to the Adirondacks. Pick a bright day in May, and start your Adirondack hiking with a great climb.

The views from Buck Mountain's summit encompass thousands of square miles of the Adirondacks to the north and west, parts of Vermont's Green Mountains to the east, and two large bodies of water that have figured significantly in the settlement and military histories of this region and indeed the United States. Lake Champlain and Lake George were major water highways connecting the Hudson and its river settlements to the south with the St. Lawrence and its settlements in French Canada to the north. Both lakes were important military routes, as the number of old forts and battlefields along their shores attest.

Lake George was christened Lac du St. Sacrement by its European discoverer, Father Jogues, in 1609. From that date until the end of the War of 1812, the lake was the scene of many bloody battles among the Indians, French, English, and American patriots. During that entire period, no peaceful settlement graced its shores, although there was a military presence after 1755, when Fort William Henry was erected on its southern shore. Much of the lake is still bordered with stands of solemn evergreens, so that in places it looks very much as it did to the first white men who visited it.

Buck Mountain is only one of Lake George's mountains. Those planning additional hikes in this long-favorite resort region should investigate some of the area's state campsites. Three range along the lake's western shore, all accessible from NY 9N: Lake George Battleground Campsite is southernmost near Lake George village, the Hearthstone Point State Campsite is just 2 miles north of the village, and Rogers Rock Campsite is near the north end of the lake. Perhaps the most beautiful campsites are those scattered among the many state-owned islands in the lake. All of the Lake George island campsites are accessible only by water. The required permits may be obtained from island caretakers on Glen, Long, and Narrow islands, or through Ticketron.

You will also want the campsite recreation circular, available from the DEC (see introduction).

Like Buck Mountain, many of Lake George's mountains are within the public lands of the New York State Forest Preserve, and several have excellent trails, the majority of which were constructed as horse trails in the 1930s by the CCC. The trail on Buck Mountain is one of the best designed in the Adirondacks. Spring comes early here, so any of these mountains is ideal for that first spring hike. Fires have swept most of the summits, leaving bare rock promontories with great views. Because of the sparseness of the cover near the summits the trails are hot and dry in summer, so you will probably find spring or fall preferable for hiking here. You must be sure to carry water. Finally, rattlesnakes inhabit the rock crevices on many of the mountains. Their infrequent presence on trails should not deter you, but do wear sturdy, high boots, and watch where you place your hands.

To reach the start of the trail up Buck Mountain take Adirondack Northway (I-87) to either Exit 21 or Exit 22, head into Lake George village, and pass Fort William Henry and the Minnehaha Boat Landing. Continue east around the south end of the lake .4 mile to NY 9L. Turn left on that highway, which follows the eastern shore of Lake George north for 6.8 miles and forks. The way left is marked "Pilot Knob, 4 miles." The state parking turnout for the Buck Mountain trailhead is 3.3 miles along this dead-end road on your right and is well marked.

You begin walking along an abandoned roadway at the east end of the parking lot. The trail is marked with yellow DEC hiking trail signs and light blue horse trail signs. The trail is raised and dry as it immediately plunges into a hemlock bog with many osmunda ferns, their huge root clump masses rising from the soggy ground. As the forest changes to tall hardwoods, the heavy vines of fox grapes are reminiscent of typical Hudson Highland cover.

At this lower elevation, the trail intersects several logging roads: at the first fork turn right, and at the second, left. You will begin to hear a stream on your left, and after you pass another old woods road forking left, you cross the stream, Butternut Brook, and continue beside it, climbing a slope beneath a deep hemlock-covered ledge. The trail zigzags as it climbs seriously, and if you look down on your right you should see a picnic table beneath the hemlock and beside the stream.

Another indistinct woods road coming from the left will remind you that this area was once farmed and logged. You are now climbing moderately and are already high enough to see the blue water of Lake George through the trees. Rock ledges rise on your left where the trail has been carved into the hillside. After walking for about a half-hour you pass an old stone fence. It leads to a promontory with a small opening and a view of mountains to the south. Beyond that you walk through an open field and cross a small stream on a slippery log. The stream cascades in a pretty series of small waterfalls down to Butternut Brook. Follow the stream for 100 yards to an intersection, where a sign says it is 1.5 miles back to Pilot Knob trailhead. (Pilot Knob itself is privately owned and inaccessible.) You probably walked that distance in forty minutes.

At the intersection the blue trail

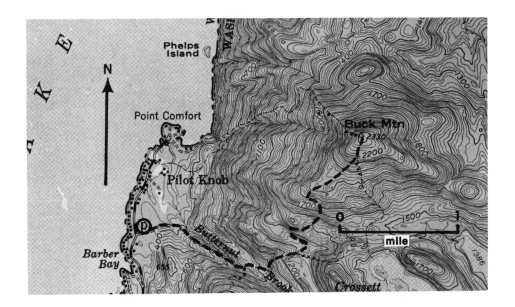

bears right to Imman Pond, 3.1 miles away. Take the left fork, which heads north to the summit of Buck Mountain, 1.8 miles distant. Here the trail is deeply cut into the hillside, with high banks on either side, and the route is somewhat boulder strewn. You begin a gradual but steady climb with gentle switchbacks into a scrubby deciduous forest. Refreshing level stretches curve between the steepest segments. About twenty minutes from the intersection, a logging road joins from the left, and you turn sharply right, uphill. At this point there are so few trail markers that you may be misled.

A couple hundred yards past the logging road, water pours from a spring-fed pipe to the right and spills across the trail to join the small stream on the left. Be sure your canteen is full. About twenty minutes beyond the logging road you cross the stream again. The forest cover of small maple, beech, and birch is home to a multitude of birds, and you

may even spot a nesting pair of scarlet tanagers. About ten minutes from the second stream crossing, in a level between climbs, the trail has been widened to avoid a wet seep. This is the only place where the route might be confusing. Look for the yellow markers on your left to show you where to begin the climb again, with the steepest grades so far encountered. Even the stretches between switchbacks seem steeper now. The forest is more open, with scrubby oak indicating the summit is near.

You soon reach the first real overlook, with views southeast to Crosset Pond. Beyond it the trail climbs and then flattens out, heading north across a shoulder of the mountain. Pine, hemlock, and tall birch fill the level ground below the last rise. The path, narrow here, crosses a boggy area lush with wild iris, clintonia, spring anemones, bunchberry, golden thread, putty root orchid, *corallorhiza trifida,* and huge clumps of

Buck Mountain **19**

20 *Buck Mountain*

polygala, or gay wings. As open rock and the summit appear ahead, you realize you still have a way to walk. Yellow arrows painted on the bare rock direct you between scrubby patches of cherry, maple, birch, popple, and blueberry. The view begins to unfold, and after two and a half hours of walking, you reach the summit. In a cleft filled with garnet sand near the summit, a sign indicates that the trail continues northeast toward Shelving Rock Road, 2.5 miles away.

Buck Mountain rises steeply from the deepest part of Lake George. From the summit you will not only enjoy views of the lake, which lies in a deep fault valley whose ends are blocked by glacial debris, but you will meet some of the other peaks described in this guide. Crane Mountain (Hike 29) lies almost due west, and Gore Mountain with its tower and ski slopes is to its north. Just north of Gore on the horizon is the distinctive flat-topped hump of Blue Mountain (Hike 36). In the distance between Crane and Blue lies Snowy Mountain (Hike 33). It is 43 miles away and distinguished by the jagged knob whose cliff face reflects white, prompting the name.

On the north-northeast beyond Little Buck Mountain lies Sleeping Beauty, with Erebus to its left and Black Mountain (Hike 2) just peeping up behind. If it is a clear day in summer, when there is little definition between rocks and trees, the cliffs on Sleeping Beauty may not show up in such a way that they reveal the form of a reclining female stretched like a romantic billboard across that mountain's southwestern slopes. Pharaoh

Mountain rises almost 21 miles away in the direction of magnetic north. Beyond it and more than 40 miles distant, range the Adirondack's High Peaks, with Giant (Hike 48) to the right of Pharaoh, and the cluster that includes Nippletop and Marcy to the left.

Northwest of Buck, lying against the western shore of Lake George, is Green Island, with the huge nineteenth-century Hotel Sagamore. Look beyond it to the hills on the horizon. South of a line to Green are the cliffs on Moxon Mountain, which mark the route toward Vanderwhacker (Hike 43). Sight above the middle of the island to Hoffman Mountain, whose western notch makes a great day's trek (Hike 46). From the eastern promontories you can enjoy the sweep of the Champlain Valley with the Green Mountains behind.

When you start your return, retrace your footsteps, being careful to follow the designated route on the open summit. That way you will not disturb the fragile plants that have managed to find niches in cracks along the open rock.

The long sweep of the shoulder you traverse points to Pilot Knob Mountain on the south. Your zigzag descent to the shoulder and the trek across it should take no more than twenty minutes; you then begin the series of switchbacks that will bring you within forty-five minutes to the piped spring. When you reach the trail intersection, less than a half-hour beyond, most of the steep descent is finished. Native columbine and sweetfern shrub edge the route. The rest of the walk is so easy that a half-hour will suffice for the last 1.5 miles, unless you pause to look at wildflowers.

View south from Buck Mountain toward Lake George village

Black Mountain

Distance (around loop): 8.5 miles
Vertical rise: 1,100 feet
Hiking time: 6 hours
Map: USGS 15' Bolton Landing
Fire Tower; closed Thursday, Friday

Black Mountain, at 2,646 feet, is the highest peak in the two ranges of mountains that shelter Lake George, and the views from the summit are more than proportional to its height. One of the trails to its summit rises steeply from the shore of Lake George, but it is accessible only by water. Your route on Black Mountain is a loop that requires a bit less climbing, but it still traverses part of the reputedly more handsome trail from the lake. This loop also allows you to visit a series of charming ponds that lie south and east of the summit.

There is a fire tower on Black Mountain, and although you might appreciate the fire observer's help in identifying distant mountains, Black's summit is mostly open rock so overlooks in every direction can be found at ground level.

Black Mountain is about halfway along the eastern shore of Lake George. You reach the trailhead from NY 22. From the north and west, take Exit 28 off the Adirondack Northway (I-87) to NY 74, and follow that route east to NY 22 at Ticonderoga. Head south on NY 22 to Clemons. From the

south, pick up NY 22 at Fort Ann and continue north to Clemons. This latter route takes you on a beautiful drive through the Champlain Valley and across the South Bay of Lake Champlain above Whitehall.

At Clemons drive 2.6 miles west toward Huletts Landing on County Route 6, and then bear south (left) on Pike Road for .8 mile to the trailhead. Signs at the trailhead indicate that the Black Mountain tower is 2.8 miles away, and that the Lapland Pond Lean-to, which you pass on your return leg, is 2.5 miles distant.

On the drive from Clemons west, you will have views of Black Mountain as well as of Knob Hill and Sugarloaf, two unusual small mountains whose distinctive shapes you will be able to identify again clearly from Black's summit.

The trail begins along a gravel road that leads to a private residence. Red trail disks on telephone poles, which you will follow all the way to the summit, mark the route. A splash of the wildflowers that make every walk in the Lake George region special brighten this otherwise dull roadway. Trillium, blue cohosh, crinkleroot,

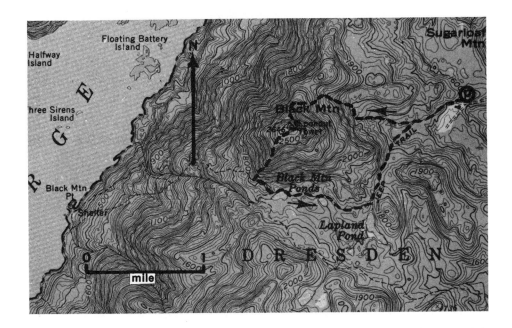

twisted stalk, Solomon's seal, and clintonia are only a few of the flowers you may see.

You reach an intersection in .9 mile. Across the field of the nearby farmhouse the tower still looks a long way away. The trail follows the right side of the field and continues gently uphill through a more mature and taller woods, making pleasanter walking. You should spot the rattlesnake fern, which will remind you to be watchful of rattlesnakes on this mountain, as on all of Lake George's mountains.

After a half-hour or so, in just over 1.2 miles, the trail to the Lapland Pond Lean-to and the ponds to the south forks left, marked with blue disks. You take the right-hand trail, still marked with red disks. It leads to the tower in 1.55 miles (in this case the preciseness of the DEC sign appears accurate). The trail continues to follow an old roadway, which has

stretches of corduroy. Look to the edges for trailing arbutus and foamflower. A snowmobile trail forks right at a second intersection. It winds toward the summit by a more circuitous route, with a lower grade than the hiking trail. You will meet it again just below the last pitch on the summit.

For the hiking trail, go left, on the less obvious route. Fortunately a plethora of red disks marks the intersection. The trail quickly takes you across a little stream where water falls over a series of small horizontal ledges. This is your last source of water.

The trail turns sharply left uphill and really begins to climb, following the little watercourse to a rock ledge. The trail heads straight up the ledge, so steeply that you will probably have to pause and catch your breath. Beyond, the trail, wide enough that vehicles once used it, is worn to bedrock. The forest is fairly open, and within an hour you can look back toward Knob Hill. You pass through an area of heavy blowdowns where winter has taken its toll of many treetops, leaving a scene of destruction. Then you continue climbing through spruce forests with some hemlock, low balsam, and striped maple. The underbrush becomes thick before finally opening by moss-covered ledges near the summit.

It will probably take you a little over an hour and a half to reach the open, windswept summit, which picnic tables, two cabins, and the tower share. A sign points south where the red-marked trail continues to Black Mountain Point on Lake George, some 2.7 miles away.

From the tower you can't help noticing first the Tongue Mountain Range (Hike 3) on the opposite shore of Lake George. The Range Trail and Fivemile Mountain, Fifth Peak, and French Point Mountain are easily identified. You will appreciate from this vantage the lumps and valleys on the Range Trail that make it so challenging and difficult: the deep valley to the south of Fifth Peak, the height of the two unnamed knobs to its south, and the deep valley between French Point Mountain and First Peak reveal how much climbing there is.

Elephant Mountain lies northeast of Black on the east shore of Lake George. Sabbath Day Point, Silver Bay, and The Hague stretch north on the lake's western shore, with the slopes of Rogers Rock silhouetted beyond. Slightly south of Rogers Rock, on the east shore, Anthony's Nose raises its unmistakable profile. In the distance to the northeast Lake Champlain is visible, with the Green Mountains beyond.

If it is a really clear day, you can identify the mountains on the horizon that lie between the northern end of the Tongue Mountain Range and Catamount, the long mountain northwest of Sabbath Day Point. Sight beyond Catamount to Giant Mountain. Dix rises directly over Fivemile Mountain, and continuing to the left, you see McComb, Nippletop, Basin, Haystack, Marcy, Skylight, and Redfield. Pharaoh Mountain, just to the left of Nippletop, is much nearer. Still in the closer range, Hoffman Mountain is farther left, with Santanoni to its left on the horizon. Vanderwhacker is next left, its steep cone standing isolated. This panorama occupies the skyline defined by Fivemile Mountain and the valley between it and Fifth Peak. Over that valley is the flat top of Blue Mountain.

Once you have climbed back down the tower, the views south are best as you begin your descent, continuing along the red trail. At the end of the promontory, ledges to the right overlook Erebus Mountain and the islands that fill the narrows of Lake George. This is the best place from which to appreciate the deep trench of the down drop fault, or graben, that forms the lake. Here the bent forms of wind-shaped trees frame the views, and clusters of misshapen cherries, maples, and elderberries provide little shelter from the sun. The trail, built up with rock, hugs the steep slopes and begins its twisting, turning descent, dropping rapidly and without views below many cliffs and ledges. The switchbacks (I lost track of the count after twenty) allow you to descend quickly to a magnificent lookout southeast to the chain of ponds you are about to visit, as well as southwest to Lake George.

Lapland Pond

Below the overlook, the trail becomes less steep and the woods become deeper, changing to a high, open forest of huge birch. You have passed the imaginary line that separates the sharp knob of Black Mountain's summit and the valley below. On the upper slopes, which rise 800 feet in .5 mile, rock work was necessary to build the trail against the mountain, but here it is beautiful, soft, and wide. After walking only a few minutes on the wider trail, a total descent of forty minutes (if you did not pause too long for views) you reach an intersection. The well-used, red-marked trail turns right toward Black Mountain Point, but you turn left on the yellow-marked trail. This little-used route will take you .3 mile to Black Mountain Pond, .7 mile to Round Pond, and a bit over 1 mile to Lapland Pond.

You begin beside a boggy swale with handsome birch. Next, climb to a hemlock knoll above Black Mountain Pond, which is hardly visible at first below the ledge on which you are walking. Descend to the muddy shore of the marshy little body of water, complete with beaver house and bog plants. Continue up another knoll topped with huge paper birch, and walk on high ground to Round Pond. The trail dips to its shore beside a hemlock-covered hillside that makes a great place to camp.

Just east of Round Pond you intersect a snowmobile trail. Your yellow-marked route continues east, winding alongside a hemlock marsh, and reaches a three-way junction fifteen minutes from Round Pond. (The sign indicates it is .77 mile from Black Mountain Pond. You will notice that distances vary in the Adirondacks according to the sign markers.) The entire walk between intersections takes no more than thirty minutes, unless of course, you could not resist stopping at one of the ponds. The yellow-marked route heads right (south) toward Millman and Fishbrook ponds. You take the blue-blazed trail left, which the sign indicates heads toward Pine Brook Road. Walk along it for no more than five minutes, about .2 mile, to another intersection, where a spur trail heads back southeast along Lapland Pond's eastern shore to a lovely lean-to high on a rock slide.

Lapland is the largest and deepest of the three ponds and has beautiful shores. You will surely stop here for a rest or swim before continuing north. The trail north is marked both with blue hiking trail disks and orange snowmobile trail disks. It follows a long level valley on an old road, and although the woods are handsome, the walking is dull compared to earlier stretches. It goes quickly, though, and within ten minutes you begin a long descent, first following a stream and then continuing through the saddle high and dry above the stream, which you ultimately cross. Thirty minutes probably suffices for the walk from Lapland Pond to the last trail intersection and the end of the blue-marked trail. You fork right on the red trail to retrace your steps for the final 1.2 miles to your car.

Tongue Mountain Range

Distance (around loop): 12.4 miles
Vertical rise: 3,000 feet
Hiking time: 8 hours
Map: USGS 15' Bolton Landing

The Tongue Mountain Range is a great block fault thrust up in the midst of the fault valley that Lake George has filled. On this loop hike you first climb its ridge, then follow the backbone of the Tongue that thrusts south into the lake, and conclude with a walk back north along the shore of Northwest Bay. From countless vantage points along the ridge, views of Lake George and The Narrows are superb. French Point Mountain, halfway along the portion of the Range Trail you hike here, lies just far enough out of line with the rest of the Tongue Range to have long, interrupted views both north and south. Because the lack of tree cover on the ridge permits a completely different range of flowers from those found in the deep woods that fill the slopes along Northwest Bay, this hike also introduces you to an amazing variety of Adirondack flora.

The Tongue Mountain Range is a good choice for spring hiking. The trail is among the first to dry out enough to walk, and in May the cover of wildflowers is magnificent. The long stretches of open ridge that are a plus in spring discourage hiking in

summer months, when a canopy of shade trees is more desirable. The abundance of hardwoods make it a spectacular fall hike.

This is a most strenuous trip, however, so if you plan to go in early spring be sure you are up to it. The hike is long, and the vertical rise is equivalent to that on Giant or Algonquin mountains, the two highest peaks described in this guide. You rise 1,560 feet directly from lake level to Fifth Peak, and then snake across the peaks to the south as if you were following the Great Wall of China, soaring to each summit from a deep intervening valley.

For the easiest route to the trailhead from the Adirondack Northway (I-87), exit at Interchange 24 and follow County Route 11 east, toward Bolton Landing and NY 9N. After descending the long hill toward the lake, head north on NY 9N. From the intersection you will see the Tip of the Tongue and a portion of the ridge you will walk.

Drive north on NY 9N for .4 miles, past signs for a boat launching site and the Tongue Mountain-Clay Meadows trailhead, to a parking area

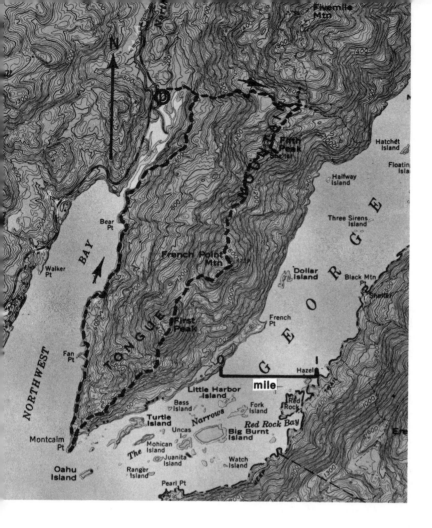

beside an old quarry on the east side of the road. If you have allowed enough time for a full day of hiking, take a few minutes now to cross the road just south of the parking area and walk about 100 yards along the evergreen-covered promontory above Northwest Bay Brook to a handsome little falls in the deep hemlock-shrouded gorge.

Signs at the trailhead direct you east toward the Tongue Mountain Range. You begin at the blue markers by walking through a tall red pine

reforestation stand—the site of the old farm that gave the area the name Clay Meadows—and then crossing the marsh beside a small inlet of Northwest Bay. The marsh sports many ferns and in spring brilliant yellow clumps of marsh marigolds.

Within ten minutes and .3 mile, you reach a junction. You will return later in the day by way of the trail to the right. For now, go straight ahead on the red-marked trail (there are few visible markers). The trail follows a small stream that flows from Fifth

Peak on your right. Although you hardly ever see it, you can almost always hear it. Five minutes from the intersection you may want to leave the trail to walk right toward the stream at the top of its plunge down a deep, shaded gorge.

The well-worn trail climbs steeply, crossing three bridges, two over intermittent streams. Watch as ledges appear along the trail on your left; one of these is manmade and is the clue to turn sharply left for a switchback that covers the last steep pitch before a plateau. This is the only place where the relative absence of trail markers might cause confusion. You then round the hemlock marsh that fills the plateau and cross the stream that feeds it, here without benefit of a bridge. You climb steeply again, a pitch covering about 160 vertical feet, before reaching a second plateau and the major intersection with the Range Trail. It is 1.9 miles from Clay Meadows to this spot, and the climb should take nearly an hour and fifteen minutes.

Here the red route continues straight ahead and down to the shore of Lake George. The left, or north, branch of the blue trail leads to Fivemile Mountain and Deer Leap. (A trailhead farther north on NY 9N offers easier access to these peaks in the Tongue Mountain Range.) Your route is right on the blue trail, south to the Tip of the Tongue.

The roller-coaster trip along the ridge begins mildly enough with a .5-mile climb of under 300 feet toward Fifth Peak. You leave the blue trail on a yellow-marked, .2-mile-long spur to reach the actual peak and its nearby lean-to. Note that there is no water at all on the peak. Hikers who detour to the peak often bushwhack southwest from there, descending a few tricky ledges to intersect the blue trail farther along, rather than retrace steps along the spur.

Beyond Fifth Peak, the trail shows much less use, and the trail markers are more numerous and definitely necessary. In places under the leaf cover the footpath is hardly visible, although the trail shows signs of its superior CCC construction.

There is a second lookout on Fifth Peak from a shoulder .2 mile south of the summit. Just beyond it the trail crosses the ridge to afford a view straight down Northwest Bay. Then it starts to drop into the valley south of the peak. "Drop" is scarcely the word for the long rock slide with several extremely steep pitches. You will lose almost 350 feet in elevation in .2 mile. As you descend, look back to the cliffs behind you. And while you are grappling for handholds on the descent, you might be amused to learn that Robert Moses, the master road-builder, had plans to build a highway that would encircle Lake George's shores. The prospect always conjures images of a huge flying span across the gulf between Fifth Peak and the unnamed knob to its immediate south.

You no sooner hit bottom than you immediately start climbing again, heading up that knob. It is just short of 1 mile from Fifth Peak to the top of the first knob. There is a view back to the cliffs on Fifth Peak, but the trail leads you immediately on, plunging down the next southern slope. Here you turn sharply, below the cliff, and head away from the lake. Another steep drop takes you to a hemlock swale where you must look carefully for the turn left to head up a second knob.

Again, you will make a short, sharp descent before continuing on the ridge without the aid of many trail markers. Your route gradually heads southeast to French Point Mountain. It takes a good hour to walk from the south shoulder of Fifth Peak to the summit of French Point Mountain, because of the scramble over and around the unnamed knobs.

Your hike has lasted about three hours so far, and you have covered 4.6 miles. That makes French Point Mountain the perfect place to stop for lunch. You will find a perch suspended almost 1,400 feet above the lake, with fantastic views northeast up the lake and south toward The Narrows, which are choked with tiny islands, just a few of the 200 that grace Lake George. The DEC map for the island campsites of Lake George (see introduction), which shows the campsites and day-use areas on the islands below you, is the best guide to their names. Opposite your perch lies Paradise Bay whose deep green, gem-clear waters are visited by the steamer *Mohican* on its regular trips on the lake. During your lunch stop you will certainly see one of the steamers, successors to those that plied the lake as long ago as 1817. Black Mountain is a little north of east across the lake, and Erebus, Sleeping Beauty, and the Buck Range are to the south.

If you have been keeping count, you should tally the wildflowers you have seen on the way. A list that exceeds thirty-two is not unusual and in season probably will include: pale corydalis, four kinds of violets, twisted stalk, red trillium, dwarf ginseng, wild oat, foamflower and myterwort, toad flax and Canada mayflower, lady's slippers, clintonia, Dutchman's-breeches, bluets, saxifrage, early buttercup, cucumber root, pipsissiwa, three-toothed cinque-

foil, wood betony or lousewort, and the amazing fields of trailing arbutus for which the Tongue Mountain Range is famous.

After leaving French Point Mountain, cross over the ridge, guided by blue paint daubs on the bare rock, for another view of Northwest Bay. You can now almost see the Tip of the Tongue, or Montcalm Point. Imagine the scene during the French and Indian War when Montcalm's army of attacking French rounded the tip toward Northwest Bay. You head down toward the bay in as steep a descent as that which followed Fifth Peak. Walk along the vertical side of the mountain with cliffs below, and then turn away from the bay, still descending, in a switchback heading toward Lake George. The scrub cover of beech, butternut, shadblow, white pine, ash, oak and hop hornbeam is not thick enough to block the views. The drier, sparser cover contrasts with the deep rich woods of the western slopes. Most of the time now you are walking right at the exposed edge of the cliffs overlooking Lake George.

After climbing another small promontory you will see that First Peak, your next destination, is maddeningly far away on the opposite side of another deep valley. Here, the talus slopes make rugged walking.

When you reach First Peak, a forty-five-minute walk after lunch, you are rewarded with a view back to French Point Mountain. You can appreciate the magnificence of the cliff that falls away from it, dropping to water level. The reason for your difficult walk is clear, for looking back north is like viewing the ridges of a dragon's back. Someone said the trail was laid out along the teeth of a giant saw.

The sawblade continues southwest

to the very Tip of the Tongue. Green Island is opposite the tip, and Dome Island lies farther south in the middle of the lake. From First Peak the trail drops steeply at first and then levels out, as it twists and turns along the top of the ridge on a fairly well-marked route. From an outcrop a spectacular cliff drops away to Turtle Bay, and you overlook Turtle Island and Shelving Rock across The Narrows. The trail continues into a narrow slot between ledges where the talus provides very difficult footing.

You have been walking for almost two hours since lunch, and you haven't reached the Tip yet. After still more rock outcrops with views and one last knoll to climb, you descend nearly to lake level and reach a junction. Continue straight ahead on a .2-mile spur to the Tip and a well-earned rest soaking your feet in the cooling waters of the lake. The sign says you have traveled 2.5 miles from French Point Mountain, descending 1,426 feet. It doesn't say how much you climbed in that "descent." After returning from your detour to the Tip, you will have walked 7.6 miles, but you still have 4.8 miles left to reach Clay Meadows again.

The blue trail along the shores of Northwest Bay is level at first, but before you have time to enjoy the flatness, you have to climb around a small piece of private land. Beyond it, the trail continues at lake level, sometimes wet underfoot, and usually close to the water, but shortly the steepness of the shoreline forces you to climb again.

You cross a small creek and then turn sharply left, to edge a small bay. About forty minutes from the intersection, you cross a stream with a waterfall; ledges beside it drip with mosses and maidenhair spleenwort.

View from French Point Mountain across Lake George

For those who count ferns, this could be the twentieth species you have seen along the hike.

Rock work edges the trail, which was originally constructed as a bridle path. The walking is easier as you cross two bridges in a beautiful deep hemlock stand, but only briefly. You climb again, now around the marshes that edge Northwest Bay Brook. When you reach a final bridge, you are just 200 feet short of the trail intersection you passed at the outset. Here you head left to the highway and your car.

By the end of your trip you will certainly have walked for eight hours, but if you have paused to enjoy the spectacular scenery you will probably have been on the trail for at least ten hours. Look up at the Tongue Mountain Range when you leave to drive south along the highway. You will have a great respect for the sinuous route that the trail takes along the bumps and ridges of the Tongue Mountain Range.

Hadley Mountain

Distance (round trip): 4 miles
Vertical rise: 1,550 feet
Hiking time: 2½-3 hours
Map: USGS 15' Lake Luzerne
Fire Tower; closed Thursday, Friday

With a summit of only 2,700 feet, half the height of Mount Marcy, Hadley might not sound like much of a mountain. This just proves how little elevation can figure in the true pleasures of mountain climbing. Views from the fire tower on Hadley or from its open summit are among the most spectacular in the Adirondacks. In the north you can see many of the eastern High Peaks; in the south, the major summits of the Catskills; and in the east, an open panorama of the hills beyond Lakes George and Champlain ranging to Vermont's Green Mountains and the edges of the Berkshires in Massachusetts. The view southwest is across Great Sacandaga Lake and northwest to a multitude of southern Adirondack mountains. Once I climbed Hadley on a perfectly clear day, and I remember the trip as one of the most beautiful I have ever had in the mountains.

Hadley is near the southern end of a chain of summits that together comprise West Mountain, a ridge in the southeast corner of the Adirondacks. There are many open spots along the ridge's north-northeast to south-southwest ranging axis, and

you should plan to extend your visit to Hadley by walking along it, watching the perspectives change. The lichens growing in niches between open rock make a multicolored carpet and easy crunchy walking through the scrub. Here, moving from open rock ledges to scrubby promontories can hardly be called bushwhacking.

The only difficult part about climbing Hadley is locating the trailhead; no markers point the way, and there are few road names to assist in the search. If you are driving from the west, along the shores of the Great Sacandaga Lake, the signs are pretty clear. The north shore road is County Route 4. Just before the Paul River Hardware Store turn north onto Hadley Hill Road. The intersection is in Day Center, almost a thirty-minute-drive east of Northville. Follow Hadley Hill Road for 5.2 miles to Tower Road, on the left. The parking turnout for the tower is 1.4 miles north on Tower Road.

From the south, east, or north, take NY 9N, which passes through Lake Luzerne. Turn left in Lake Luzerne to Hadley, and then go north on Stony Creek Road. Hadley Hill Road is a left turn at a marked intersection just over 3 miles north of Hadley. Drive west on Hadley Hill Road for nearly 3 miles and turn right on an unnamed road. Follow the road for .8 mile to a Y where the macadam road bears right. Go straight ahead on the dirt road. After 1.7 miles, a small sign on the right indicates the parking lot for the Hadley tower. This will probably be the first sign you see for the tower.

At the trailhead a sign states: "Successive fires in 1903, 1908, 1911, and 1915 severely burned 12,000 acres of the surrounding forest land." In response to fires in the late nineteenth and early twentieth centuries, the state erected a series of fire towers across the entire Adirondacks. From early spring to snowfall, these towers were manned by dedicated observers who often trudged long distances with heavy packs to supply their week-long stays on the mountain top. The men were dependent on fragile telephone lines for communication and usually had to maintain both the lines and the trails to

their towers. From the earliest days, each tower was assigned the days its ranger could take off; since the territories of adjacent towers overlapped, the pattern established meant the area was continually under the watchful eye of one or another fire observer during the dangerous months.

Most of the southern Adirondack mountain tops are heavily wooded, so the towers provide the only opportunities for views from their summits. The fire towers have long been favorite hiking destinations, and the recent closing of a substantial number is mourned by many. The daily plane flights that took their place may provide adequate fire surveillance, but they deprive hikers of many fine views. Fortunately, Hadley's tower remains open, although there are great views from the summit, even without the tower.

Fires alone did not create the bare peaks. As recently as ten thousand years ago, advancing glaciers scraped the mountain tops and left huge boulders and glacial erratics

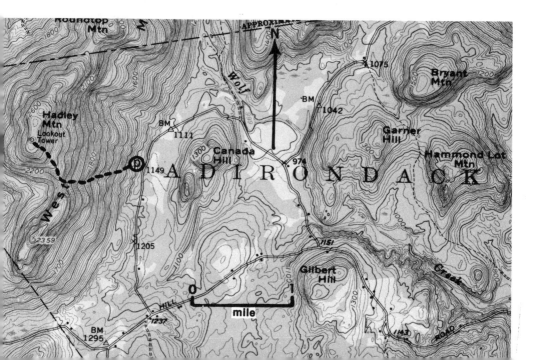

View from Hadley Mountain

perched precariously on even the highest summits. What little organic soil had accumulated in the geologically short interval since the last glacier was quickly consumed by the raging fires.

What caused these great fires? When settlers first advanced into the Adirondacks, cutting the huge pine and hemlock for building lumber and later harvesting hardwoods for pulp, little thought was given to the methods of harvesting timber. Tops and slashes were left in huge, loose piles across the once-forested hills and valleys. The early years of the twentieth century were unusually dry, and the tinder piles were easily ignited by lightning and careless sparks. Nearly a million acres of New York's forest land were burned. Charred stumps and bare soil can still be found on many mountains, and the soil's ability to retain water has been completely disrupted. Only the vigilance of fire observers prevented further burning, and although many dry, bare summits persist, the forests have begun to recover.

Enough of background, history, and directions to the trailhead—the directions along the trail are quite simple, and the trail needs almost no description, even though it is sparsely marked by red disks. It is simple and direct and so wide and open that the present-day observer can drive a jeep to the summit. Much of the route is over exposed bedrock. The high cover of beech and birch soon gives way to smaller trees. The route is fairly consistently steep.

Three-fourths of the way to the summit, the road turns sharply left. Telephone lines angle right through a cliff-lined draw. Those with youngsters may prefer to scramble to the summit under the telephone lines, the little ledges and cliffs providing a bit of sport. Going down, though, it is safer along the road.

On the summit you can spend hours playing "name that peak." Among the features you should spot is the edge of the Helderberg escarpment over the Great Sacandaga Lake. North beyond Roundtop, which is a part of West Mountain, you can see Baldhead, Moose, and Crane mountains. To their left lie Bearpen and Mount Blue. Further left, the knob of Snowy's summit rises above the line of mountains on the horizon. Nippletop and Dix are easily identified in the High Peaks fifty miles away. Pharaoh Mountain can be spotted in the north-northeast, and the peaks surrounding Lake George in the northeast. You will have no trouble at all filling a day with things to do on this lovely mountain top.

Murphy, Middle and Bennett Lakes

Distance (one way): 7.2 miles
Vertical rise: 500 feet
Hiking time: 4 hours
Maps: USGS 15' Lake Pleasant, USGS 15' Harrisburg

During the early nineteenth century, settlers traced a network of roads into the valleys of the southern Adirondacks. These routes were used after the Revolutionary War to reach the rich stands of timber in the northern wilderness and to establish new settlements in the Adirondack interior.

Today some of these old roads are the routes of modern highways. Others remain concealed in the wilderness, completely forgotten. And a few are the trails we now follow. The hamlets of Hope, Hope Falls, and Pumpkin Hollow, on the Sacandaga River and East Stony Creek, were established by settlers who built roads north from Northville immediately after 1800.

One road started near Hope Falls and headed north past several homesteads, a paint mine, and a string of small lakes. Today that road is a fine trail, short enough for a one-day, one-way trek if you spot a car at each end, and interesting enough for an extended camping expedition. There are several good camping sites and a lean-to near the lakes.

The northern end of the trail is the easiest to find; I suggest you arrange to leave a car there. Distances are given from the NY 30 bridge over the

Sacandaga River, about 3 miles north of the fork to Northville. From the bridge, drive north on NY 30 for 7.2 miles to Pumpkin Hollow Road, which is on the right, or east. A snowmobile trail signboard also marks the turn. The northern end of the trail is 1.6 miles along Pumpkin Hollow Road and is marked. There is parking off the road near the trailhead.

There are two ways to reach the southern end of the trail by Hope Falls. Just over 3 miles north of the Sacandaga Bridge turn right, or east, from NY 30 onto Creek Road, and drive east for 2.5 miles to the trailhead, which is on the north side of the road and marked. A prettier approach is from Northville on the Hope Falls Road, which approximates the route used by early settlers. Follow Hope Falls Road north to Creek Road and then bear left for .5 mile to the trailhead. The Hope Falls Road and its extension north make a nice drive along East Stony Creek.

The trail has been marked with both yellow hiking and orange snowmobile trail disks, although the colors are worn. The old road is so easy to follow, you should not be bothered by the indistinct markings. The first mile north is through private

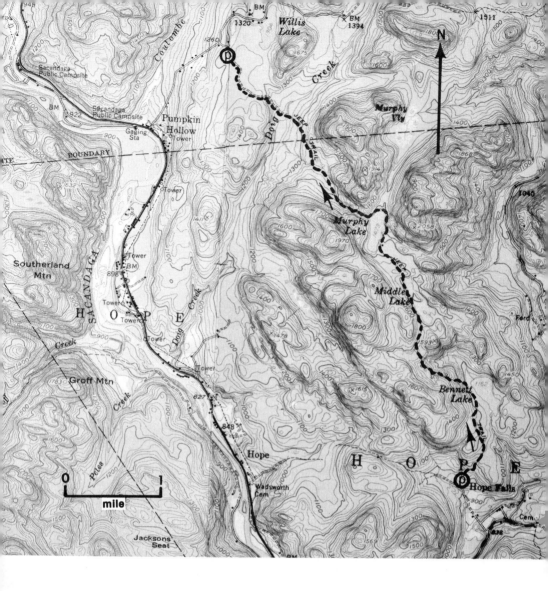

land along a road that has been recently used for logging, with hemlock, sugar maple, and beech remaining. The route is uphill, and the road has eroded and washed out. As you approach a height-of-land, white pine and yellow and gray birch appear. After about twenty-five minutes, you will notice that the forest cover changes to a small, dense population of pine, birch, and beech. You can

see the old stone wall of one of the nineteenth-century farmsites on your left. Just beyond, a cable marks the boundary of state land.

No more than five minutes beyond the cable you arrive at the old paint mine, now hardly more than a depression in the ground. The red-stained rocks and soil indicate a low-grade hematite, the color that made barns and homes deep red. Imagine using this road to walk to school, as children did in the late 1800s, and coming home by lantern light after dark every evening.

The trail continues through a mature mixed forest around the side of the hill. Less than 1.5 miles and forty minutes from your start, you will glimpse Bennett Lake down through the trees on your right. Within 200 yards an unmarked path forks right toward the lake. Follow it down a relatively steep grade for 150 yards to a flat place along the shore, where there are several good camping spots, an outhouse, a fireplace, and a sandy beach.

Returning to the main trail, continue west, climbing a small hill. You will pass an unmarked loop that quickly rejoins the main route and reach a small brook at the top of the rise. This inlet of Bennett Lake is a good source of water.

Approximately ten minutes after you pass the creek, you will have your first glimpse of Middle Lake. The distance between Middle and Bennett lakes is 1.6 miles, and the walk between them should take about forty minutes. The trail continues on the hillside, about 50 feet above the lake. The lake is .6 mile long and very narrow, with steep, evergreen-covered shores and several small islands. One side path leads 100 feet to a camping spot, and shortly beyond that fork the main trail approaches the lakeshore and follows it past many campsites. The remains of an old foundation are

Middle Lake from the cliffs on the unnamed hill

visible on the lakeshore. There are impressive views of the cliffs on the mountain to the north.

At the northern end of Middle Lake the trail turns left and enters a small, thick, wet forest. Only fifteen minutes is required for the .5-mile walk between Middle and Murphy lakes. The approach to the latter is signaled by a mature hemlock stand. As you come to the lake there are spectacular views of cliffs on the small knob to the north as well as those on the mountain to the east. Adventurous bushwhackers will want to find a route to these cliffs for a view of the lake (see *Old Roads and Open Peaks* for descriptions).

A lean-to and several campsites border the trail at its southern approach to the lake. Continue along the trail, north to a huge boulder on the shore. You can enjoy both a great view of the lake and a swim from the boulder.

The footpath around the lake is not always easy to follow, but for .6 mile you stay close to the shore until you reach the northern inlet, crossing that small brook on a dead log. Continue along the shore, heading southwest, for .2 mile to the outlet. From here it is 2.8 miles northwest to the trailhead via the snowmobile trail. The first part of the route beside Murphy Lake outlet is the prettiest. Then you cross the creek, pass a beaver flow with views east to the cliff-faced knob, recross the creek, cross Doig Creek, and end with a rather ordinary and level stretch on the old logging road.

Moose Mountain

Distance (round trip): 3 miles
Vertical rise: 850 feet
Hiking time: 3 hours
Map: USGS 15' Lake Pleasant

While many northern Adirondack peaks are covered by scrubby Alpine flora and many in the east have been burned over, exposing bare rock summits, most mountains in the southern Adirondacks are so heavily wooded that hikers can find views only from isolated cliff tops. Unfortunately, marked trails lead to discouragingly few of those cliffs. Hikers in the southern Adirondacks solve the problem by bushwhacking to the cliffs where there is no trail, navigating by the use of map and compass. Bushwhacking is a skill you develop with long practice.

There is no trail in the traditional sense on Moose Mountain, but for years its cliffs have enticed hikers with views south along the valley of the Sacandaga River and west to the Silver Lake Wilderness. A route often used by bushwhackers was flagged recently in an experiment to find out if hikers would gradually wear a footpath along the prescribed route, just as fishermen traditionally wear paths to their favorite pools. The "marked footpath" is flagged with red ties, and a visible footpath is gradually appearing. The route is not as safe to walk as a trail, but neither is it as difficult as a bushwhack.

Take the USGS map and a compass with you, and treat this hike as an exercise in route finding. The flags should help you, but they will not prevent you from becoming lost. The trek is fairly short, and the navigation is easy, so it is a good trail for Adirondacks newcomers to use to practice bushwhacking.

The marked footpath begins on the east side of NY 30, 7.8 miles north of the bridge over the Sacandaga and almost .5 mile south of the entrance to the Sacandaga Campsite. The pine-covered campsite lies between the highway and the Sacandaga River and is perfect if you are planning to spend the night in the area.

No sign marks the beginning of the path, but it can be identified by a deer crossing sign beside a small rock outcrop. As soon as you duck into the woods to the south of the outcrop you should see a small swampy area, which is fed by an intermittent stream. The recommended route starts up the mountain to the left of the stream.

Before you begin, stop and notice

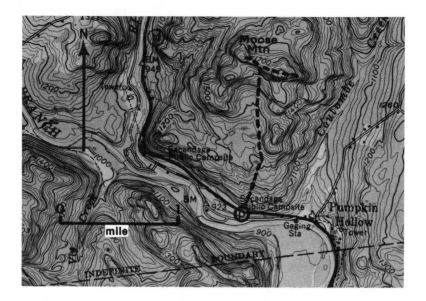

the ferns in the wet area. Rivaling the views from the cliffs in making this route special are the ferns and flowers that grow along it. I have counted at least twenty-four ferns and fern allies, lycopodia, and you can identify almost half of these, including goldies fern, within the first 100 yards. As you climb you will discover distinctly different plant communities. The oak of the lowlands gives way to hemlock, then a magnificent stand of huge maple, and finally to the pioneering birch and spruce that cling to the cliff tops and exposed ledges. Near the summit, the dry crevices on the granite cliff face are filled with the small hairy fern, rusty woodsia.

The path starts by climbing the valley of the intermittent stream, heading a little east of north. It then crosses the stream and continues to a level stretch on the shoulder of the mountain, 350 feet higher than the road. The route is then due north, on

the east side of a depression filled with sphagnum and tall hemlock. You will surely want to stop and explore the bog for ferns and flowers.

Continuing north through a short stretch of hardwood forest, you reach a second bog. Again, stay east of it. Beyond it the path swings to the left, a little west of north, to round the bog and enter a draw that leads toward the summit of Moose Mountain. The distance traversed so far is about 1 mile, and you will have been walking close to forty-five minutes. Remember that stopping to check your compass route adds significantly to hiking time.

Your route is now due north through the draw, climbing 300 feet before angling left, west, to a midpoint on the cliffs that face the mountain on the south. Here a draw, a continuation of the one you have been following, provides a climbing route up the cliffs. The footpath has been laid out in several short traverses to prevent erosion of the steep, over-100-foot climb. This is the only place where you can easily climb the cliffs that ring the summit and rise sharply on either side of the draw.

When you attain the draw saddle, west of the principal summit, the path splits. The left fork leads 250 yards west along the wooded top of the cliff to an overlook that surveys the West Branch of the Sacandaga River, with Finch Mountain to the south of the valley and Mount Dunham on the north. The right fork heads east back from the cliff tops, past two partial overlooks from sloping rock promontories that face southeast. Your hike culminates at the southern and highest end of the cliffs. The view is south along the Main Branch of the Sacandaga.

Sight a little to the west of south, beyond the river, and you can spot Cathead (Hike 7), which is identified by its tower. Wallace and Three Ponds mountains follow to the west, with Silver Lake and Sugarloaf mountains coming after them. From this vantage, you can also see beyond Mount Dunham to Hamilton and Speculator mountains in the northwest. Also, from the easternmost overlook, you can see the cliff-faced hills beside Murphy and Middle lakes (Hike 5).

By the route described you can reach this cliff top in an hour and forty-five minutes: allow thirty minutes to the first level, fifteen for the trek past the bogs, fifteen to the draw, thirty to explore the western cliffs, and fifteen to reach the easternmost cliff. The return takes less than an hour and fifteen minutes, so give yourself time to enjoy a picnic with the views from this seldom-visited mountain.

View from the cliffs on Moose Mountain

7

Cathead

Distance (round trip): 2.5 miles
Vertical rise: 1,100 feet
Hiking time: 1½ hours
Map: USGS 15' Lake Pleasant
Fire Tower; closed Thursday, Friday

Cathead may be a small mountain at the southern edge of the Forest Preserve, but it is the threshold to a great green wilderness that stretches north almost unbroken for twenty miles. No other area is as dense and trailless as the Silver Lake Wilderness to the north and west of Cathead. To the north and east are the gentle mountains that rise beyond Great Sacandaga Lake. And to the south lies the civilization hikers are anxious to escape. From the summit of Cathead you can spot the Helderberg escarpment that rises beyond the Mohawk Valley, edging the plateau that becomes the Catskill Mountains farther south. On a really clear day and with strong binoculars you can even define buildings in the state capital of Albany.

To reach the trailhead, drive north on NY 30 from the southern border of the Adirondack Park. At the intersection 3.2 miles past the bridge to Northville, turn left, or west, toward Benson. The intersection is marked with a sign designating the road as the Northville-Placid Trail. The narrow macadam road immediately climbs away from the Sacandaga Valley

through an old farming community where many homes have been converted to seasonal dwellings. Two miles from NY 30 you pass a bridge and Chartier Road, and .7 mile farther you reach dirt North Road, on the right. Turn here. A sign at the intersection points to the Cathead Mountain Fire Tower. Just before you reach this intersection you will see the mountain itself with its tower ahead and to your right. The dirt road can be rough after a bad winter, but it is usually smoothed in early spring by the Town of Benson.

Land on both sides of the 1.1-mile-long road is posted and private. A sign warns you that the trail is also on private land, that no vehicles are permitted, and that dogs must be leashed. The trailhead parking area before the barrier at the road's end is small, so you must be careful not to block the fire tower road or the adjacent driveway.

This is a good place to emphasize that the Adirondack Park is in reality a confusing mosaic of private and public lands. It is most important to respect private property here and elsewhere. Many landowners who have granted public access across their land have seen it abused by a few careless hikers and other outdoor people. There is a great need to preserve the good will that permits this and other important accesses to public trails.

The road on which the trail begins leads to a logging operation. One hundred yards past the barrier, a sign points left away from the roadway. The Cathead fire tower is just over 1.2 miles from here along a blue-marked trail that follows telephone lines to the summit. The trail winds in a narrow footpath through the wide swath that is cleared below the lines.

A second route to the tower heads left from the telephone line trail within 50 yards of its beginning. It has a gentler grade and has been used as a vehicle route to carry materials to the tower. While it is easier than the first route, it is becoming quite overgrown, so the marked trail is preferable.

Using a series of three log bridges, the trail at first traverses a wet area grown over with royal fern. The third bridge, just before the trail begins its upward course, crosses a running brook, a possible source of water. The brook also marks the edge of the recently logged area; beyond, the tree cover becomes taller, covering patches of strawberries, bluets, violets, trillium, foamflower, wild oat, twisted stalk, cucumber root, and dwarf ginseng. A few tall hemlock mingle with the hardwoods of the

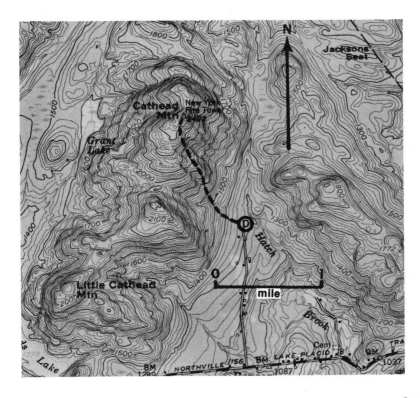

46 *Cathead*

dense forest. Within a half-hour you are climbing steadily. Only a few battered trail markers denote the route, which is so obvious the shortage is not even noticeable.

The lower slope of the hill contains a few particularly tall and straight maple. The tall, arched cover makes a cathedral ceiling over the trail, which begins to traverse the first of the series of small, open rock ledges. These giant stepping stones continue all the way to the summit. The tread becomes all rock.

The trail is particularly straight, heading north-northwest, right up the hill, with the emphasis on up. You climb most of the 1,100 feet in under a mile. You will probably pause often for breath, and if you are hiking in late spring, your pause will have to be brief. The plague of the Adirondacks, hordes of black flies and mosquitoes, will descend on you in swarms and make you wonder what they would find to attack if you were not there.

Within an hour the forest cover becomes shorter, ledges begin to edge the trail, and you emerge in a tiny opening by the ranger's cabin and a sign reminding you to carry out what you carry in. The tower is 200 yards ahead up the rock slope. A hint of roadway leads to the left through a depression below rock ledges on the same level as the cabin. It is the end of the alternate route. If you follow it about 150 feet you will notice a covered spring, and you may spot an alternate footpath to the tower. No matter, for the most obvious route is still below the telephone line.

The rocky summit is filling with blueberries and small cherry trees, but there are some views even if you

Cathead fire tower

do not climb to the tower. Below the mountain to the west is Grant Lake, which is nearly filled with a marsh. Beyond it rise Wallace, Three Ponds, and Silver Lake mountains. To the north you should be able to figure out which of the foreground hills are Finch, Hamilton, and Speculator. You will have no trouble detecting Snowy's white face shining on the horizon, but you need a really clear day to discern the mountains to its north.

Part of Great Sacandaga Lake stretches to the southeast, and beyond it the skyline is almost flat, rising only with the edge of the Helderberg escarpment. Part of the Capital District is visible on an exceptionally clear day, but for that field glasses are essential.

Almost none of the mountains you see have trails to their summits, and almost all the summits are heavily wooded. You see a few cliffs and steep hillsides, but most of your view is filled with the soft, gentle mountains of the southern Adirondacks. The skyline varies little, for the foothills are not spectacular. But the view is deceptively benign, for the soft green hides one of the Adirondacks' most impenetrable wildernesses, where you could pick almost any heading north and not meet a sign of civilization for nearly twenty miles.

After you return to NY 30 by the same route, you may want to head north along the Sacandaga River. The Sacandaga Campsite, south of Wells, is only a short drive north, and it is a lovely place to camp before heading on toward other adventures. Along this part of NY 30 there are several parking turnouts where you can stop for a picnic close to the river.

Falls on the West Branch of the Sacandaga

Distance (round trip): 6 miles
Vertical rise: minimal
Hiking time: 6 hours
Map: USGS 15' Lake Pleasant
Silver Lake Wilderness Area

The falls on the West Branch of the Sacandaga will leave you amazed that such a place can exist so close to the fringes of civilization. The access route is incredibly challenging, the falls themselves are little known, and much around them remains to be explored and discovered. The remote stretch of river by the falls has been known for years to a few hunters and fishermen, but only in recent years have hikers begun to appreciate its beauties.

The West Branch of the Sacandaga uncoils about the Silver Lake Wilderness. The river is formed at the confluence of three south-flowing outlets from three separate ponds; the water flows west, then north, then east, and finally south again, enclosing one of the Adirondack's most secret realms. The gem of that interior is certainly the series of falls on the West River, as natives have called this branch of the Sacandaga since the day when lumbermen and trappers first penetrated its wild recesses.

The trail, path, and bushwhack route described here will take you to the first pair of falls. They are almost 3 miles upstream from Whitehouse,

the site of a lovely old lodge whose chimneys today stand forlornly guarding the spot where the Northville-Placid Trail crosses the river. If you are really adventurous and want a great challenge, you should extend the bushwhack through the deepest part of the West River's gorge to a second pair of falls, past a quiet flow, and to a final falls that are just below the flow formed where the outlet of Piseco Lake joins the West Branch. (See my *Discover the Adirondacks, 2* for a description of that route.)

Your adventures on the West Branch begin when you leave NY 30 at the southern end of the hamlet of Wells and head west on Algonquin Drive. West River Road forks left .7 mile from NY 30 and continues 1.7 miles to Blackbridge. Over the next 1.7 miles west to Jimmy Creek, the road is close to the river and its wild rapids. Then the road pulls away from the river, continuing west for a total distance of 8.6 miles from Wells to Whitehouse, where a parking area now occupies the site of the lodge.

The trailhead for the Northville-Placid Trail is west of the parking

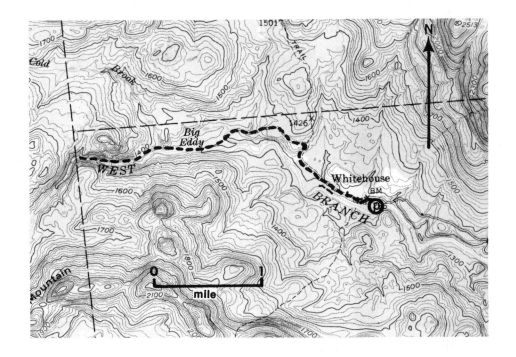

area. Head north on that trail for .8 mile to a fork. The marked trail continues north, but you turn left to continue west. Although the route is unmarked, it follows an abandoned roadway. After .6 mile cross Hamilton Lake Stream on a narrow suspension bridge. Beyond it you head southwest on an increasingly faint footpath toward the river. Your first approach to the West Branch, just below the flow called Big Eddy, will make you wish the entire route had been along the river.

There is a camping spot here at the water's edge. The footpath continues west along the north shore of the river, and you should follow it as far as you can. The majority of visitors here are fishermen whose destination is the pools in Big Eddy, so the foot tread rapidly disappears. A path of sorts exists beside Big Eddy as far as

the crossing of Cold Brook, which empties into the West River with a small waterfall. Look out for poison ivy on the bank beside the confluence of Cold Brook and the river. West of Cold Brook the path really disappears, and you must follow the shore, or, in low water, hop along the rocky stream bed. You pass one more deep pool with an overhanging ledge before reaching the boulder-strewn waterway that leads into the deep gorge.

So far the hike has been relatively mild. You will probably need only a bit more than twenty minutes to hike the section on the Northville-Placid Trail, an almost equal amount to reach Hamilton Lake Stream, and about forty minutes to cover the .8-mile distance to Cold Brook. However, you will need more than forty minutes to trek the next rugged

50 *Falls on the West Branch of the Sacandaga*

.6-mile distance through the deepening gorge to the first falls.

By the time you reach the falls the cliffs of the gorge walls are nearly 400 feet high. The growing mound of boulders and blocks leading up to the falls makes an increasingly difficult walking route.

The level of the water has a great impact on the difficulty of the walk and on the beauties of the gorge. In high water, walking becomes difficult, and you may have to approach the falls by scaling the hill behind the cliffs. In low water you can find a route over the boulders within the narrowing gorge, but then the falls are less dramatic.

The second falls are scarcely 200 yards beyond the first, but since the ravine curves, you can't see them until you are nearly upon them. Even more peculiar than the falls being visually separated is the length of time it takes to walk between them. In high water you definitely must climb the hill behind the cliffs from the east. Even then you will have to be content with a view from above, for descending to the second falls is all but impossible. In low water I have spent at least forty minutes clambering over boulders the size of buses, through openings in the pile of blocks, and leaping across crevices to reach the second falls. If you attempt this section, be careful.

As you climb along the ledge you will notice that the high-water mark is more than 20 feet above summer low point. Swirls of natural foam frost pools of tea-colored water. In dry times the sprays that cascade from the narrow clefts are almost lost in the complex of boulders. In spring, or after periods of heavy rain, the water falling 240 feet through the mile-long gorge creates a roar that barely hints at the brutal force capable of tearing boulders from ravine walls and hurling them into the huge piles that are the West River's falls.

In any season, a trip to the falls is a rough experience. You will remember your day's trip to this dramatic spot as a truly great adventure.

Near Big Eddy

Good Luck Cliffs

Distance (round trip): 4.4 miles
Vertical rise: 700 feet
Hiking time: 3 hours
Maps: USGS 15' Piseco Lake, USGS 7½' Canada Lake

The trek to Good Luck Cliffs is one of the best short hikes in the southern Adirondacks. The route combines a walk along a snowmobile trail with a climb through a small gorge on a "marked footpath." A jumble of easily explored boulders and crevices line the gorge. The marked footpath circles behind the nearly 500-foot-high cliffs to emerge on a small overlook with a dramatic view across the foothills of the Adirondacks to the skyline of hills south of the Mohawk Valley.

The footpath is so well defined that even the disappearance of the temporary orange flags that marked it does not make this informal route too difficult to follow. However, the trek through the gorge is not marked by trail disks, so carry the maps and a compass. The footpath was flagged in an experiment by the state to discover if hikers would create a defined path along marked routes where no trail cutting and grooming was to be done. Here the results are clear, for a footpath has developed and it is a delight to follow.

The trail starts opposite a parking turnout on NY 10, 100 yards north of

a bridge over the Sacandaga and 6 miles north of the intersection of NY 10 and NY 29A.

The trail is marked with a signboard designating the distances to Good Luck Lake, Dexter Lake, and Potters Homestead. Follow it west for just under .5 mile to an intersection. The route to Dexter Lake is straight ahead, but you should turn left on the trail to Good Luck Lake and Spectacle Lake. Here the trail follows an old logging road down a gentle incline for .7 mile, and as it approaches the first low point you can see Good Luck Lake through the trees on the left. This is the closest you can approach the lake via this trail. With a short bushwhack (200 yards) you can quickly find the informal footpath connecting the good campsites on the lake's handsome and dry northern shore. If you do this, you really should stay above the marsh that edges the western shoreline.

As a visit to the lake part of your trek to the cliffs, you will want to know of an alternate approach. A short, informal and unmarked footpath leaves the highway opposite the parking area and 50 yards southeast

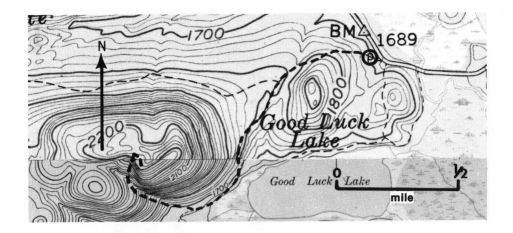

of the marked trailhead. It leads to Good Luck's northern shore in .5 mile.

Good Luck was named not for its good fishing, although fishermen visit it regularly, but because of an incident on its shores that ended well. As Jeptha R. Simms relates in *Trappers of New York,* the party surveying and laying out the roadway, now called the Nick Stoner Trail, through the Sacandaga Valley, were working at Good Luck Lake to hollow out a canoe from the trunk of a tree. The son-in-law of the chief surveyor, Lawrence Vrooman, spotted a loon on the lake and "discharged his gun at the loon, off on the water. The piece burst and scattered its fragments harmlessly in every direction. The accident terminated so fortunately, that the name the lake now bears was entered in the surveyor's field book."

To find the cliffs, continue on the Spectacle Lake snowmobile trail. The trail climbs a small rise and then dips to cross a stream on wooden planks.

You leave the trail at this point, turning right, or north, to follow the right, or east, side of the stream on the faint but clearly defined footpath. The trail stays with the stream for 100 yards, continues straight where the stream comes in from the left, and then meets the small watercourse again in about 300 yards, just above the point where the stream reaches the valley floor. Cross the stream and follow the path to the northwest, alongside the stream.

After 50 yards the path angles left away from the stream to find an easier route uphill, zigzagging as the grade gets steeper. The first pitch up the draw is fairly steep; you attain 300 vertical feet in just 250 yards. The cliffs become visible through the trees on your right, as do the boulders and slabs that have fallen from them to litter the floor of the draw. The trail is never more than 50 yards from the base of the cliffs, but the chasm between the cliffs is sometimes an impenetrable mass of blocks and crevices. Where the path levels off somewhat, a smaller footpath heads 30 feet down a slide to the base of a huge mass of boulders. Stop and explore the area: peer into the 12-foot-deep cave created by overhanging ledges, climb the boulders to observe the cliffs above and the valley below. The perch is

Rock slabs in the gorge below the cliffs

overhung by a thin slab 40 feet tall.

The footpath continues northeast for 50 yards, crosses the stream, and climbs steeply again below the cliffs in a more northerly direction. You walk beyond the cliffs to climb the summit from the west: the last 50-foot climb is quite steep. When you reach the summit ridge, head to the right down a draw and into a small depression, and then climb to the overlook on the opposite side.

You emerge on a small rock crest exposed to the south and west, overlooking Spectacle Lake and the foothills of the Adirondacks as they fade into the Mohawk Valley.

Knowledgeable bushwhackers return from this trip by walking along Good Luck's summit to the northeast, finding two other semiobstructed overlooks, and then heading north around the eastern end of the summit to descend to the Dexter Lake snowmobile trail, thus making a loop on the summit (for more details, see *Discover the Adirondacks, 2*). You should return by the southern route, however. Remember, this is not a marked trail, and you should be prepared to discover some of the route as well as things to see on the way.

10

Pine Orchard

Distance (round trip): 4.8 miles
Vertical rise: minimal
Hiking time: 2½ hours
Map: USGS 15' Harrisburg

Pine Orchard is a gem of a walk wrapped in the deep woods of the southern Adirondacks. Inside Pine Orchard you will discover a treasure that is rare anywhere in the park, yet here very easy to find.

Virgin pine once covered large sections of the Adirondacks. As lumbermen and settlers moved into the mountains after the Revolutionary War these magnificent trees were the first to be felled. They not only made the tall masts for sailing vessels, but their building quality was unsurpassed. The giant pine, some fifteen feet in circumference, are the eastern equivalent of the Olympic rain forests' redwood; a walk among them is equally awe-inspiring.

A few virgin stands remain, and one of them covers a small hill northeast of Wells. You will find larger stands on the Oswegatchie, but none so close to a trailhead. I have been impressed with Pine Orchard for years, but it was not until I had seen many of the other notable Adirondack pine forests that I could truly appreciate its significance.

Fire played an unusual role in the development of the Adirondack forests. Stands of giant hemlock only occur in areas where there have been no fires, but groves of pine only spring up after a fire. Most people are not aware that a pine forest is not a climax forest. Pine seedlings do not sprout beneath their elders. Spruce, balsam, and birch can pioneer below a tall pine stand, and here at Pine Orchard, the pines are so old that maturing yellow birch and maples are filling the niches beneath the remaining giants.

Pine of 5 and 6 feet in diameter were common in the early eighteenth century. Adirondack logs were traditionally cut in 13½-foot lengths, and sometimes the butts, or first cuts, were too large to be moved by man or horse. Charges of black powder in a special splitting tool were used to break the huge ends in two so they could be carried off to mills.

Most of the virgin pine and hemlock forests that survive today are far from roads or railroads. That Pine Orchard was never logged is peculiar and totally unexplained. It was fairly near several sawmills and tanneries. The trek to Pine Orchard is among the most delightful of nature walks, and it is certainly the easiest of hikes, following the relatively level stretch of an abandoned roadway once used by loggers.

To reach Pine Orchard, drive north on NY 30 through Wells, and turn right

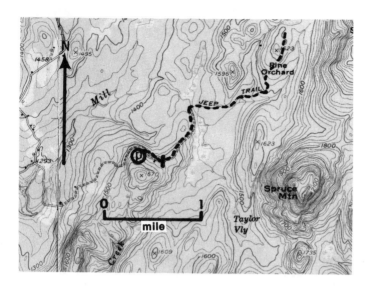

on Griffin Road at the north end of the hamlet, just south of the bridge where NY 30 crosses the Sacandaga River. Follow Griffin Road north along the east side of the Sacandaga for .8 mile and turn right on Windfall Road. A tannery on Mill Creek stood near the road not far from that intersection. Windfall Road parallels Mill Creek for a short distance and then heads north. Follow Windfall Road for 1 mile, and turn at the first road on the right, which is marked only by a sign bearing the name "Doc Flaters," referring to the landowner at the road's end. Drive along that road for 1.9 miles and park on state land at a small turnout, just before you reach the Flater property. Permission is given to walk along the road through the property to the continuing trail to Pine Orchard. But here, as always, you must respect the rights of the private landowner. Do not park on the property, and touch nothing as you walk across it.

You will begin your walk northeast from the turnout and within five minutes cross a cable and return to state land. The continuing roadway is marked as a snowmobile trail and connects with the trail from Willis Lake which comes in on the right, or south, just beyond the cable. The direction you are walking is labeled with a sign showing a destination of NY 8 at Georgia Brook, 8.2 miles to the north.

You start gently downhill, viewing the flow created by a new beaver dam on the right. In twenty minutes and 1 mile from the parking area, you cross a stream. A new snowmobile bridge carries you over the tributary of Mill Creek. A gravel area just beyond has been used as a campsite. So far the trees are not very large, and the mixture of spruce, hemlock, and birch is occasionally quite small and very dense. Ten minutes past the bridge you will see the first big pine.

By the giant white pine

Five minutes later, about .6 mile from the bridge, a washed-out bridge helps you across a small stream that feeds the flow. The trail continues with another little stream on the right and then heads north up a slight rise. More giants greet you as you climb the hill, and a few significant spruce appear among the pine. The trail make a sharp right turn and then circles toward the crest of the hill. Most of the giant pines are near the top, with the highest to the right of the trail. The trail continues north, and as soon as it leaves the crest it enters a grove of enormous hemlock. You reach the hemlock, marking the end of Pine Orchard, after a leisurely, hour-long, walk of 2.4 miles.

You may want to try and find the largest tree in the pine stand. It ap-pears that most of the pine of 15 feet in circumference are doubles, a phenomenon that occurs when blight strikes. The largest single trunk I found was just over 13 feet in cir-cumference or over 4 feet in diameter. Try some elementary trigonometry to estimate the height of the larger trees. Unfortunately, the giants in the orchard crowd so densely together that it is difficult to see the tops of most of the pines, and measuring the base of a right triangle to an estab-lished sighting angle is equally dif-ficult. I calculated a few that ap-proach 150 feet in height. Even without trying to measure the trees, you will enjoy strolling in the parklike open understory beneath these Adirondack giants.

11

Echo Cliffs on Panther Mountain

Distance (round trip): 1.4 miles
Vertical rise: 600 feet
Hiking time: 1⅓ hours
Map: USGS 15' Piseco Lake

Echo Cliffs curve around the western slopes of a shoulder of Panther Mountain overlooking Piseco Lake, and the view from the cliff tops is more than ample reward for this short and easy climb. The mountain is a good destination for a first hike into the southern Adirondacks region.

Piseco lies in the middle of a region of hills and mountains where every valley seems to contain a small and often remote and uninhabited lake. Nearly one hundred hiking destinations in the country of the West Branch of the Sacandaga River, the area just south of Piseco, are described in another of my guides, *Discover the Adirondacks, 2.* A day hike to Echo Cliffs, which offers a sweeping overview of that area, is an excellent introduction to some of those adventures.

The trail begins near the Little Sand Point State Campsite on the western shore of Piseco Lake, the middle of three handsome state campsites offering good camping, boating, fishing, and access to hiking trails.

From the intersection of NY 8 and NY 10 by the southeast shore of

Piseco, head west on NY 8 for 2.8 miles to West Shore Road. Follow that road north for 3.6 miles to an unmarked trailhead, and park along the road's shoulder. The spot is .5 mile south of the entrance to Little Sand Point Campsite.

There are no signs and few trail markers to indicate where the trail enters woods on the west side of the road. The narrow footpath is well used, as the initials carved on the smooth bark of every beech tree along the way indicate. You could almost conclude that the beech dieback was a protest at such desecrations, but the real reason so many beech are dying is that there is a preponderance of mature beech. Those trees were not harvested when local forests were either stripped of their soft woods or culled for their valuable hardwoods. The die-back, which you will observe on this climb, is nature's way of restoring balance, while erasing the tempting slates on which those hikers with no reverence for the woods have left their feeble marks.

The rocky and washed-out stretches also indicate that the trail

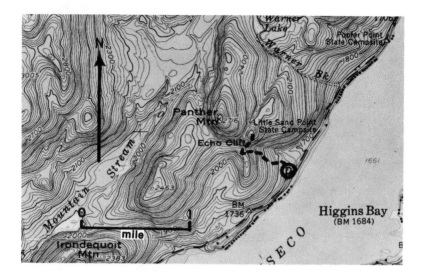

is fairly popular. Many flowers of the deep woods bloom here in their seasons: violets, trillium, jack-in-the-pulpit, dwarf ginseng, and the dog-tooth violets. As you start to climb, magnificent maple line the trail. Then, continuing generally west, you pass through a hemlock glen.

As the trail makes a distinct curve to the right, in the vicinity of one of the few trail markers, look right, northwest through the trees, and you may catch a glimpse of the cliffs. In early spring or late fall their 200-foot vertical rise is easy to spot; in summer you may miss them entirely.

The climb steepens, and boulders line the route where you approach a ledge and turn right below it. You pass a small, intermittent stream with hardly enough flow for a drink in wet weather and then begin a short, steep climb below tall spruce whose roots provide stairs on the sharp incline. Your route is now behind the cliffs. Shortly you have a glimpse of the lake through the trees. Cross the spruce- and hemlock-covered promon-

tory to emerge on the narrow ledge.

The evergreens open to a panorama of the Silver Lake Wilderness across Piseco and Spy lakes. Few tall mountains are visible in the distance, and the dense forest cover is broken only by streams and ponds. Hawks soar in the updrafts above the cliffs. The water of Piseco Lake mirrors cloud patterns.

Summer homes dot the shores of Higgins Bay opposite Echo Cliffs. The narrow strip of land between the bay and Spy Lake was the site of the area's first settlement, which began in the 1820s and was called Rudeston after one Eli Rudes. Several sawmills were built in the vicinity.

In 1838 a village was designed for the north shore of Piseco by Andrew K. Morehouse who envisioned a thriving community with a "grist mill, sawmill, machine shop, a large hotel and boarding house and some half-dozen dwellings." Strong inducements were offered to settlers, but fewer than 200 of them stayed more than a week.

This saga of disappointment in the wilderness is typical of most early nineteenth-century settlers' adventures. Details of many such failures are chronicled in the *Hamilton County History* by Aber and King. Read the chapter on the Town of Arietta to gain insight into the land you survey from Echo Cliffs. Its abandonment explains why so much of the southern Adirondacks was incorporated into the Forest Preserve, creating the largest chunk of state land in the Adirondack Park.

Looking toward the Silver Lake Wilderness from Echo Cliffs

Echo Cliffs on Panther Mountain **61**

12

T Lake Falls

Distance (round trip): 11.5 miles
Vertical rise: 1,200 feet
Hiking time: 8 hours
Map: USGS 15' Piseco Lake
West Canada Lake Wilderness Area

Caution: In the last decade three people have died in falls from the top of T Lake Falls. It can be a dangerous place. This hike is not for pets or small children. Follow the route described, and observe all the cautions.

It is unfortunate to have to preface this hike to such a great place with a caution. Do not let it deter you, for many careful hikers have found the trip to T Lake Falls one of the truly great wilderness treks in the Adirondacks.

The outlet of T Lake drops 350 feet into a tiny pool from the rounded crest of an escarpment. If the falls were a sheer drop of this distance, statisticians would consider the claim that it is one of the highest in New York State. It is the highest in the Adirondacks and tall enough so that Adirondack writers have exaggerated its height to 640 feet, or "twice the height of Niagara." The danger comes when hikers venture out on the smooth rock seeking better views and fail to notice the gradual curve of the rounded, slippery lip until it is too late to turn back safely.

Below the falls, the outlet turns

southwest and joins outlets of several small ponds to form the South Branch of the West Canada Creek. The continuing trail through that valley was used by Indian hunters and early settlers. One of the first descriptions of a visit to the falls was written by Ephraim Phillips in the 1860s. He was Hamilton County's sheriff from 1843 to 1847 and the proprietor of hotels at Lake Pleasant and Piseco Lake.

The trail you follow to T Lake Falls makes a fairly strenuous one-day trip. There is a lean-to at T Lake 1.8 miles from the falls that makes a good spot to stop if you prefer an overnight camping expedition.

The trail begins from the northernmost of the three state campsites on the western shore of Piseco Lake. To reach the start, drive 2.8 miles west from the intersection of NY 8 and NY 10 at the southeast side of the lake, and head north on West Shore Road for 4.9 miles to the Poplar Point State Campsite. If you are coming from the west, the shore road is clearly marked with a sign indicating the three campsites. If you are approaching from the north via NY 8, bear right, or west,

T Lake Falls in summer

toward Piseco and continue around the lake's northern shore.

There is a $2.00 day-use parking fee at Poplar Point. The marked trailhead is 100 yards south of the campsite entrance, where a sign indicates the distance to T Lake as 3.65 miles and to the falls as 5.45 miles.

The first stretch of trail is fairly new. It heads up a southern shoulder of Piseco Mountain after crossing a cement dam for an unused reservoir. The climb into a forest of giant yellow birch with good-sized beech and maple is fairly steep for twenty minutes. Then, in just over .5 mile, you climb into a small boulder-strewn col. Here the trail takes you along a fairly level stretch through the rather rugged valley. In five minutes or so you will see a stream in a draw on your left. After the short rise that follows you will cross a small wet, boggy saddle between a knob on the south and high cliffs that face the mountain proper.

Nearly forty minutes and just over 1 mile into your walk, you cross a ridge and descend a small draw crowded with thick growth that is filling in areas left by dead beech. Walls and ledges continue above on your right, and there is a drop to a deep valley on your left. A small draw at 1.2 miles marks the valley between Piseco and Stacey mountains. Within another five minutes you reach a height-of-land on Stacey and begin the long, gentle descent into the valley that separates it from T Lake Mountain. Shortly the trail picks up the stream that drains that valley, follows it north for 200 yards before crossing it, and then, within 100 feet, crosses a larger stream that flows from the southern flanks of T Lake Mountain. Their confluence is on your right, and the pink feldspar rock lining the streams

makes the spot quite handsome.

Just beyond the stream crossing you should spot old corduroy and other signs that indicate the trail is now following a very old road. This road entered the valley by way of Warner Lake (to the southeast). A field of touch-me-nots, or jewelweed, partially conceals a stand of horse nettles. Watch out! Huge spruce edge the trail, which now begins to climb the eastern edge of T Lake Mountain. Soon the slopes of that mountain drop off to your right, and a rock wall appears on your left. The trail makes a ninety-degree turn left and heads west up a rock outcrop. You are now about 2.5 miles from the start, and you have walked about one hour and fifteen minutes.

If you are clever at spotting old trails, you may see the intersection, about five minutes beyond the sharp turn, where the trail from Mill Stream used to come in from the east. But at this point the trail bends to the left, so most likely you will not spot the old trail until your return, when you should take care not to continue straight on it. Just beyond the intersection a valley opens out on your right; it is the valley of the fault that contains T Lake. The trail begins an up-and-down course, and again, a real woods detective could see where the old trail headed southwest to T Lake Mountain where there was a fire tower. An abandoned coil of telephone wire may be the only real clue; it is amazing how quickly these southern Adirondack forests can conceal old roads and trails.

You can look across the fault valley to unnamed mountains on the north, and you may even notice water from the small arm of T Lake down the slopes on your right. Here walking is easy for the trail is wide, open, and

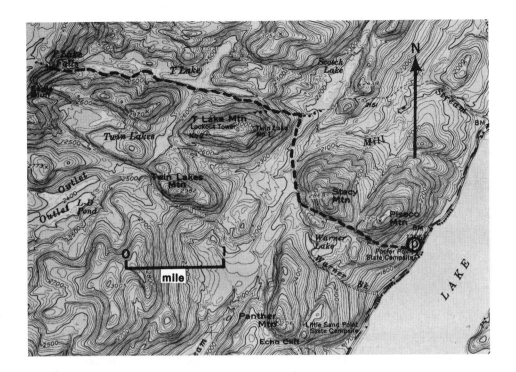

relatively level. After a gradual descent to lake level, you reach the lean-to alongside the small eastern tip of the lake. Rocks east of the lean-to make it easy to get into the water without churning the muddy bottom of the shallow lake.

The best part of the trip starts here. Continuing west, the trail is gorgeous. You first edge the shore in a rich evergreen forest with a deep understory, then pass the end of the bay with its natural rock dam, and walk close to the outlet in a small rock gorge that leads to a beaver meadow. Twenty minutes past the lean-to you will pass a deep water channel created by a beaver dam that tops a second rock ledge. Preceding the dam site the trail has been flooded, and you will have to detour around a small swamp or trust your footing on a fallen log.

Bunchberry and sorrel carpet the woods floor, filling crevices between spruce roots, which make walking difficult on the narrow trail. You pass a twelve-foot waterfall that drops from a small ledge edging a second beaver meadow. This one stretches west for .5 mile. Where the trail skirts the flow you will want to pause to look for birds.

The valley narrows, and the sound of water falling over the rocks at the west end of the flow will make you think you are almost at the falls, but you still have some way to go. Steep ledges rim the hillside above on the south as you drop into a narrow gorge. Cliffs of recently bared slides rim the north.

An hour's walk past the lean-to, or 1.8 miles, the view west opens to reveal the outline of the West Canada Creek valley. Now is the time for caution. A cable that used to make crossing the stream safe is now missing, and without it the ford is tricky. Slippery mosses may make you lose your footing, and most of the smooth rock is just as slippery. Note that you can not see the waterfall from the end of the trail. Do not walk down along the smooth rock, looking for it. There is *no* place on the escarpment from which to see the pool at the bottom of the falls. Instead, cross the stream at least as far upstream as the end of the trail.

North of the crossing there is a camping spot. Continue on a narrow footpath through the woods down the northern side of the falls. From perches well supported by handholds on the side, you can begin to see the sheer rock face.

About 150 feet below the campsite the footpath emerges on a smooth rock that drops into a 30-foot slide down a seventy-degree slope. A cable used to provide a means of safely traversing the slope, but it dangles by a strand from the trunk of a small dead tree. If it has not been replaced, I suggest you walk along the edge of the woods, detouring north around the open rock area. Staying in the woods may make difficult walking, but it is safe. Below the slide the path continues in the woods to the bottom of the falls.

It will take you at least fifteen minutes to climb down beside the falls. From the pool you can look up at the creased and lined rounded slopes over which T Lake Falls tumbles. In wet weather a real torrent splashes into the pool. In dry times you will know how the side of an elephant looks to an ant.

The pool is not quite all the way to the bottom of the valley. If you follow the stream 100 yards farther west, you pass another camping spot, where a sign says it is 6 miles along the old Indian path to Mountain Home, a trailhead in the southwest.

You will need at least twenty minutes to scramble back up the slopes beside the falls. Again, resist the temptation to walk toward the edge of the escarpment. You will have enjoyed just as good views across to the valley from the safety of the trees beside the slope.

The walk back beside the flows is even prettier than the trip out, for the trail east offers better views of the wide expanses of meadowsweet and grasses.

13

High Falls on Honnedaga Outlet

Distance (round trip): 15.2 miles
Vertical rise: minimal
Hiking time: 9 hours
Map: USGS 15' Ohio

The mention of a waterfall always arouses my curiosity. David H. Beetle's book, *The West Canada Creek,* has a tiny note about a pair of waterfalls some 30 feet high on the outlet of Honnedaga Lake that are "of scenic interest." Knowing the marvelous descriptions he has for people and places in the southwestern Adirondacks, I concluded he probably had not seen these falls himself. I queried hiking friends, and although I received lots of information about this part of the Adirondacks, no one I knew had visited the falls.

One day, early in spring when snow melt was still flooding the rivers, I embarked on an expedition to find Honnedaga's falls. The trip turned out to be one of my best adventures in the Adirondacks, and one I am sure you will want to share.

I was able to reach the falls because early in the trip I encountered a native who knew every inch of the ground and whose grandfather, an Adirondack guide, had helped build "High Falls Camp" on Honnedaga's outlet near the falls. Bill Potter, the grandson, walked with me to the falls, which turned out to be

closer to 90 feet high than 30 feet. He filled the entire delightful trek with stories about the West Canada Creek, into which the Honnedaga outlet drains. You can weave these anecdotes into your walk by reading both the Beetle book and Harvey L. Dunham's *French Louie.* That trapper often traveled part of the route you will take.

Honnedaga Lake, owned by the Adirondack League Club, is the highest "big" lake in the Adirondacks. The outlet of that great boomerang-shaped body of water flows south from a level of 2,187 feet into Baby Lake, which is in the Forest Preserve. The outlet, now called Honnedaga Brook, flows east through a broad marsh where the water level is controlled by beaver, and then plunges 90 feet over a wooded escarpment. The rest of Honnedaga Brook's journey southeast to its confluence with Jones Brook, and then through a lovely deep valley into the West Canada Creek, is approximately the route of the unmarked footpath you will follow.

The path heads west from a very rough dirt road that runs north from Nobleboro along the West Canada

Creek and its tributary, the Indian River, to active logging operations and several hunting camps. The roadway can be negotiated by four-wheel-drive vehicles, but even if one is available to you, I recommend that you consider walking much of its distance and then camping along the way. It is much easier to drive this road in summer when it is dry, but if you really want to enjoy the falls at their best, in spring, you should travel when the road is at its worst. You will find numerous clearly marked sections of the state land along the West Canada, many of which are excellent campsites. There are also several desirable spots along Honnedaga Brook. Note that if you don't camp, the route requires a long and full day of hiking.

Before you start your trip north, look at a large map of the Adirondacks to understand the importance of the West Canada Creek as a route north from the Mohawk Valley at Herkimer. Indians made it their route to hunting grounds, and settlers in the eighteenth century also followed the waterway. The vast forest that surrounded the West Canada Creek attracted some of the Adirondack's first settlers. In 1790 Arthur Noble, an Irishman, built a road from Remsen to his patent by the confluence of the creek and its South Branch, where he established a sawmill and small settlement. The West Canada was the ideal highway for floating logs to the mill, and the sawed lumber was then rafted down the West Canada to the Mohawk, and then to Cohoes Falls on the Hudson, where it was transported to Albany for loading on sailing sloops. The first shipment of lumber from the Noble Patent was sent to Ireland.

Nobleboro is located on NY 8 almost 30 miles northeast of Utica and 17 miles west of Piseco. At Nobleboro turn north on Haskell Lane, the only road north from this community, which is even smaller today than it was in the nineteenth century. Haskell Lane follows the West Canada for 16 miles through state and private lands to Miller's Camp, a logging operation on the Indian River, and to Swanson's Dam, on First Stillwater Lake. You follow it only as far as Jones Brook, 9.2 miles north, but you probably can drive no more than 4.6 of those miles.

The road is too far from the river for you to see the Haskell Rifts where many log drivers lost their lives. At about 3.6 miles north look for a footpath to the river, 100 yards east. You may want to stop here and, time permitting, at several other points to view the rapids and the river's giant potholes. Here the potholes are six feet in diameter and more than ten feet deep. They are named for Betty Green, an otherwise unidentified settler who is supposed to have hidden treasures in them. At 4.6 miles a snowmobile trail forks left following the old roadway to Little Salmon Lake. (That lake was surely misnamed, for it has always had the reputation of having no fish at all.) Park here and walk the rest of the way north.

The road heads downhill and immediately fords a small brook that is impassible to vehicles without a very high wheel base. Cross on the small footbridge beside the ford. Within .3 mile you cross Big Brook. There is a campsite just beyond that bridge, but there are better camping places ahead.

This road was used by lumbermen, guides, and trappers on their way to the wilderness around "Big West" in

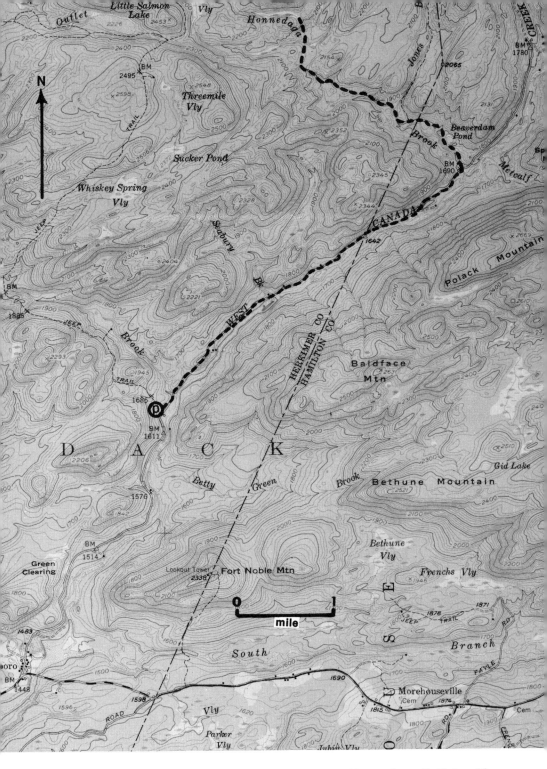

High Falls on Honnedaga Outlet **69**

70 *High Falls on Honnedaga Outlet*

the heart of the West Canada Wilderness. They walked along it loaded with furs to trade for money to splurge on the week-long revels that marked their twice yearly visits to civilization.

The road is close to the marshes that edge the Seabury Stillwater, named for a logging company that once impounded the creek with a flood dam. Here a driving camp housed lumberjacks who risked their lives to speed logs downstream through the notorious log jams. Each point along the road is remembered for its residents from that wild era in the late nineteenth century, all of them friends of the trapper French Louie. Nat Shepard, a lumberman, had a place beside the Seabury Stillwater. Johnny Leaf, an Indian guide, lived here, and for a time French Louie had a camp nearby.

Beyond the Seabury Stillwater, a small hunting camp bears the name Chevarie after the French lumbering company Chevarie and Geandreau, jobbers who worked the area farther north along the West Canada Creek's Second Stillwater. Just past the sign to Haskells, you start uphill and cross the Hamilton-Herkimer county line. You can see "Red Camp" up on the right as you approach Jones Brook. If you have driven this far, park off the road beyond the bridge. The 4.6-mile walk from the snowmobile trail turnout should take no more than 2 hours and a half.

The unmarked path leading to the falls starts on the north side of Jones Brook, climbing .2 mile to Beaverdam Pond. Although the hill north of the pond is known for the number of bear shot there (it is called "the pork-

High Falls on Honnedaga Outlet

barrel"), a spot by the pond makes a good campsite from which to walk to the falls.

The path narrows beyond the pond, still following an old road bed through a hemlock bog to the "rock garden." Here a hunter put "a good-sized cobblestone" into old Jesse Armstrong's wicker pack. He carried it out to Nobleboro where his "friend" tipped up his pack and asked if he intended to start a rock garden.

Open patches of corduroy line the route as it descends a small hill to the level of the brook. In spring this is a handsome stream with flood waters cascading over rapids. You might notice a road turning right. It leads into a spruce swamp so thick "you cannot see in broad daylight," and beyond to a rock cliff that edges Jones Brook.

You take the smaller path left, close to Honnedaga Brook. Beyond this point you have to use your tracking instincts to follow the diminishing path, but if you study the map you will notice that following the proper streams will serve to guide you even if bushwhacking beside them is less desirable than searching for the path.

As you near the confluence of Honnedaga Brook, or Baby Lake outlet as the natives call it, and Jones Brook, the path bears right for 100 yards to a ford across Jones Brook. You can hop rocks except in very high water. The presence of a cable and a cable car used by hunters testifies to the fact the water can be very high.

The Jones Brook crossing marks the halfway point between the West Canada and High Falls Camp. The footpath continues west along Honnedaga Brook, past rapids, and patches of lovely wildflowers. Enormous yellow birch line the valley. Notice the horizontal slashes on trees beside the brook. Several that are six feet above normal stream level attest to the height of the spring ice jam.

Blazes now mark the route, which becomes increasingly less clear. The path climbs a small ridge away from the outlet, and from it you can look beyond the end of "Brushy" Mountain, the big flat-topped hill where many a buck has been shot. The narrow path is hard to follow, but sounds from the brook will reassure you. A deep, dark, tangled, junglelike hemlock bog with sphagnum underfoot fills the top of the ridge. Beyond, along a short rise, the path is routed beside several "sitting rocks" just the right height for resting on if you are carrying a huge wicker pack. The path traverses a steep-sided hill and emerges at a bridge over a dam just below the High Falls Camp.

Across the dam you might spot an abandoned and almost invisible road that heads west to Jock's Lake and on toward Remsen. The Bill Potter who was my guide's grandfather used this route to guide the twelve hunters from the western part of the state who commissioned the camp. The camp was built between 1906 and 1911 by Homer Dugall, Nat Shepard, George Winks, and Bill Potter. The trail to the falls traditionally went up onto and over the cabin's front porch. If you walk around to the back you'll see scratches, claw marks, and other signs of big bear. The state owns all but a small patch of land surrounding the camp, so you do not have to disturb private property to continue almost due north to High Falls.

So far you have gone about 2.5 miles along the path and probably walked for 1 hour and fifteen minutes.

For the last .5 mile the path to High Falls is so little used that it really disappears, and your route is almost a bushwhack. Again natural features guide you. Heading north, stay west of the flooded lands by the brook and just below the hill on the west.

First, cross a little brook north of the camp, then a hemlock knoll, and then Two Mile Brook, which flows toward your right to join Honnedaga Brook. Look for blazes on the far side of the brook, for the path does swing a little west and uphill here. You traverse a second hemlock area, still heading generally north, and emerge in a grassy meadow. Cross the meadow and find the continuing path 100 feet to the east.

Shortly you hear the falls, for they are not more than a twenty-five-minute walk from the cabin. You have to cross a wet area overgrown with shrubs to reach the base of the falls. The path is no longer visible. For the best view of the falls climb onto the stone diversion wall that used to channel logs downstream.

Water cascades from the beaver pond, spilling over a series of ledges. In spring flood, the water splits to form a second falls 200 feet farther north. That one dries up completely after the spring runoff, just as the first shrinks to an insignificant trickle in a dry summer. In spring, though, you will find no more enticing destination. The remote country of the West Canada has a special lure; hikers in search of beauty and new places to explore mingle their footsteps with those of hunters, trappers, guides, and lumbermen, the heroes of the western Adirondacks' wild country.

14

Moose River Plains

Distance (four walks): 5.4 miles
Vertical rise: minimal
Hiking time: 3½ hours
Maps: USGS 15' West Canada Lakes, USGS 15' Indian Lake,
  USGS 15' Old Forge

The Moose River Recreational Area has long been a sportsmen's paradise. In 1963 the state acquired 50,000 acres from the Gould Paper Company, the heart of the region surrounding the South Branch of the Moose River in western Hamilton County. The area is now open to sportsmen, campers, and hikers. You will find that there are many exciting destinations in the recreational area besides those outlined in this hike and in Hike 15, Beaver Lake.

A good dirt road, for which there is a $1.50 use fee, runs almost 24 miles through the recreational area, starting on the east at the Headquarters Gate by the Cedar River Flow and ending on the west by Lake Limekiln Gate, south of Inlet. Over 150 campsites have been designated in several districts along the roadway, so if you prefer camping from your car to carrying a backpack, the Moose River Plains area is for you. The campsites are dispersed along various access roads, well separated from each other. Signs indicate safe springs beside the road. A few campsites are near lovely streams, some are near accesses to ponds, and a few are in

deep woods. Tent camping is allowed on any of the sites or at any undeveloped site in the interior. If you are spending the night anywhere in the recreation area you must register, between 8:00 A.M. and 8:00 P.M., with a caretaker at either end of the access road. You will need a camping permit if you stay longer than three nights. The area opens to the public about Memorial Day, or after the dirt road has dried out. Consult the DEC Moose River brochure for complete details (see Introduction). You will most probably want to visit here later in summer, when the black flies have diminished. But you should go before hunting season begins, when access is limited to cars with chains or four-wheel-drive. And you certainly will want to bring along a fishing pole and canoe. The Moose River's ponds are quite accessible.

One 3-mile-long stretch along the Moose River is natural meadow and open field. These plains are as intriguing to Adirondackers used to unbroken forests as a water hole is to visitors to the desert. The scrub growth infrequently dotted with trees is a natural phenomenon explained by

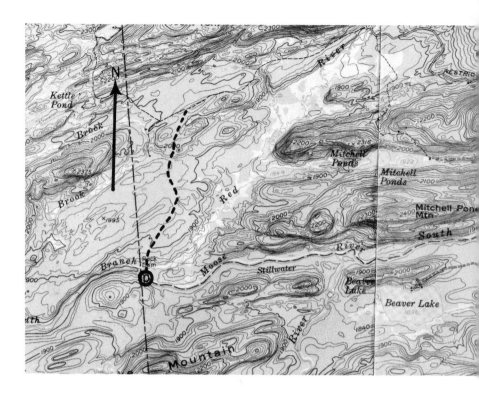

the poor sandy soil remaining from a glacial lake that once covered the area. The vast expanse is so unusual in the Adirondacks that early visitors were convinced the plains were man-made, specifically the work of Indians. They were reputed to have regularly burned the plains to provide a habitat for deer and game. The berries and low browse are natural and attract deer especially. In winter The Plains becomes a huge deer yard.

Because it has been less than twenty years since the last logs were taken from the area, scrub forests, thick with small new growth, cover much of the remainder of the recreational area. However, there are significant stands of large pine and balsam, and magnificent tamarack edge the road. A network of logging roads

covered the area, and those not open to vehicles are now the area's foot trails. All are easy for walking. This "hike" actually takes you on four separate short trails, to give you a general introduction to the Moose River Recreational Area.

Start at the eastern end of the road through the recreational area. To reach that entrance drive west from Indian Lake on NY 28-NY 30 for 2 miles and turn south on Cedar River Road. It is almost 12 miles to the Headquarters Gate near the Cedar River Flow. You pass the trailhead to Wakely Tower (Hike 34) just before you reach the gate.

The Northville-Placid Trail forks left 1.2 miles from the gate, leading to lean-tos by the Cedar River Flow and in the interior of the West Canada

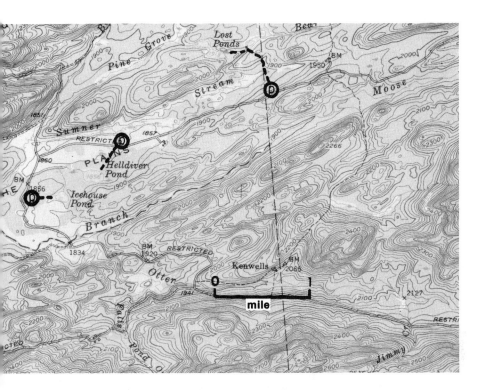

Lake Wilderness. At 1.7 miles you reach a section of private land which continues for 3.3 miles before state-land resumes and the marked camp-sites begin.

South of the road you begin to see Little Moose and Manbury mountains, which rise more than 1,200 feet above The Plains. You will cross several small streams, including Cedar and Bradley brooks, all flowing into the South Branch of the Moose River, which is south of the road. Just beyond, where you cross Silver Run, interesting cliffs overhang a lovely flow north of the road.

At 9.3 miles turn left for a quick look at the Moose River. Several of the nearby camping spots are nicer than most. As you start west again you begin to see in the distance Mitchell Pond Mountain with its interesting cliffs guarding the west end of The Plains.

The preponderance of low cherry, elderberry, birch, and mountain ash explain the area's wildlife, but now a few of the truly giant pine appear. At 10.8 miles you reach a side road that leads north toward Lost Ponds, the first of your destinations on foot. Drive .4 mile from the main dirt road and park. You'll want to pick a few blueberries before you start walking north on the dirt roadway, following the yellow trail markers. The trail is so smooth and easy that fishermen use wheeled carrying devices to transport canoes to Lost Ponds. At an unmarked intersection by a campsite, just before the roadway bridges the outlet of the eastern pond, turn right,

76 *Moose River Plains*

or east, onto a very narrow footpath. It leads 100 yards to the eastern Lost Pond. Its shores are fairly swampy, and the lake is more suitable for exploration by boat than by foot.

Continue on the yellow-marked roadway beyond the bridge and then fork left. (The sign says only "trail," to differentiate this route from the myriad interconnected logging roads.) This path leads to the south side of the western pond, where there are signs that deer have heavily browsed the banks. A rock ledge topped with enormous pine faces the north shore of this very handsome pond. This is brook trout water—no bait is allowed. I am not sure about the fish, but the plants are varied and interesting, with trillium and trailing arbutus, lots of woody bog plants, and, of course, blueberries. If you are just exploring, the 1.2-mile round-trip walk to visit both ponds should take under an hour.

Returning to the main dirt road, continue west for another 1.5 miles to a turnout on the left, or south, for Helldiver Pond. You can drive this side road for .2 mile, leaving but .3 mile to walk to the pond. It is named for the hell divers, or grebes, that have nested here. From the parking area beneath notably tall pines, you plunge into a dense, dark spruce thicket on a yellow-marked trail. The path veers right and emerges in a wet field on a corduroy walkway across the sphagnum mats that ring this boggy pond. You will want a camera. This is one of the great quaking bogs, with bog rosemary, leatherleaf, Labrador tea, mats thick with cranberries and sheep laurel, and painted

View from the road through the Moose River Plains near the Silver Run flow

trillium, creeping white winterberry, and golden thread along the borders. The pond delights naturalists as well as fishermen.

To find your third destination, return to the main road and continue west another .8 mile through the most open part of The Plains to a major intersection. Bear south for .5 mile to a sign for the trail to Icehouse Pond. Park at the roadside, below one of the region's giant pines, which serves as the best signpost for the trail. Head east through fields typical of The Plains: small cherry, popple, shadblow, willows, and birch are dotted with clumps of larger spruce, balsam, or tamarack. Another feast of blueberries awaits summer hikers. This short trail quickly leads to beautiful deep woods surrounding the pond. Clumps of over-sized painted trillium fill the banks beneath tall spruce.

Returning again to your car, head back north toward the intersection, crossing the outlet of the last two ponds you visited .2 mile from the trailhead. Stop and look at the impressive 4-foot-tall, mud-packed beaver dam that stretches for 100 feet across the swamps beside the outlet.

At the intersection head north and then west, following the road past many lovely vistas of bogs, brooks, and ledges for 3.5 miles to an intersection beside the Red River. For your last destination on this day in The Plains, turn left, or south, on a road that takes you to the western boundary of the recreation area, to the edge of the private lands of the Adirondack League Club.

The road follows the meandering Red River for 3.9 miles to a trailhead on the left, or east, side of the road. Here a sign indicates where a very narrow yellow-marked trail heads downhill into the woods, descending to the level of a sphagnum bog. A footbridge carries you dryly across. Notice how much larger the stumps of harvested trees are than anything else growing here.

You reach an intersection with an old logging road and turn right. More bogs and wet places fill the level route. You do need the trail markers, for the foot tread of other hikers is barely visible. There is one exceptional patch where the bright, light greens of sorrel are massed beneath a deep, dark spruce stand. You begin to hear water after only a half-hour, so the trail must be shorter than the 1.9 miles stated on the trailhead sign. Even 1.5 miles seems like a bit of exaggeration.

You have reached the confluence of the Red and Moose rivers. Both are blocked by a smooth natural rock dam, with quiet flows above and rapids below. This is a spot for summer swimming after a day of exploring and hiking. There is a campsite on a spruce knoll beside the dam. You have had a good woods walk to a special place, a suitable finish to a day of discovering the Moose River Plains.

If you wish to follow the main road out to the western gate, return to the major intersection by the Red River and bear left, or north, toward Limekiln Lake and NY 28 at Inlet.

15

Beaver Lake

Distance (round trip): 4.6 miles
Vertical rise: minimal
Hiking time: 2 hours
Map: USGS 15' West Canada Lakes

Beaver Lake is the largest lake in the Moose River Plains. Along the trail to the lake you will find a few giant trees, including pine, like those that once covered parts of the Moose River Valley. The trail is short and easy, so you can extend your day here by exploring two other nearby ponds or walking other short trails in the Moose River Recreational Area described in Hike 14. Read that hike description as an introduction to the area and the regulations governing it, and for general driving directions.

If you enter from the west, registering at the Limekiln Gate, drive southeast on the main dirt road for 10.6 miles to a major intersection. This intersection is 13 miles west of Headquarters Gate at the eastern end of the road. The distances do not sound great, but even when the dirt road is in good condition, travel is slow.

Bear south at the intersection; within 1.5 miles you cross the South Branch of the Moose River. Beyond the bridge turn right, west, onto a dirt road. After .2 mile, at the confluence of Otter Brook and the South Branch, this road is barred to vehicular traffic.

The trail begins here, following the abandoned roadway.

The trail traverses fields of butterflies and meadows that border the Moose, and then begins a very gentle uphill trek into deep woods. A stand of large yellow birch hints at the mature forests that once covered this part of The Plains. The tall, open forest gives way to a dense spruce grove. Within twenty minutes, or about .8 mile from the trail's start, you attain a slight height-of-land in a beautiful forest of spruce, maple, and birch. A soft, spongy layer of needles on top of sand cushions the broad roadway, making walking easy. Ground pine, golden thread, bunchberry, sorrel, foamflower, and sarsaparilla make a marvelous carpet beside the road.

In another ten minutes you see the first of the huge white pine, and beyond, the hollow trunk of one whose diameter exceeded 6 feet. Near it, stretching 120 feet along the south side of the road, lies one of the fallen giants.

The hollow trunk is more than halfway to the lake: only a fifteen-

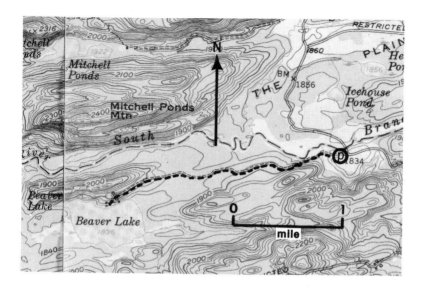

minute-walk beyond it you see water through the trees, and shortly after that you come into a meadow. Cross the meadow heading south, down toward the lake. It is hard to believe that an elegant summer home was built on this spot in 1904.

Beaver Lake is fairly shallow, but it has a sandy bottom. Even the good-sized spruce and hemlock around the shores are dwarfed by the scattering of pine that have survived the logging. There is a lovely campsite here, and another lies along the shore to the east, beyond a spruce thicket, guarded by a few enormous pine stumps.

The lake seems to have a resident loon family, but no beaver. Anyway, it appears that the lake's name did not derive from previous residents, but from its shape. It is a very short-tailed beaver (on the USGS map, his tail extends west onto the Old Forge quadrangle).

When you return to your car, you might want to head south to discover Squaw and Indian lakes. After driving for 1.5 miles, you cross Otter Brook. An abandoned and unmarked trail once headed east from near the bridge to a place marked Kenwells on the USGS map. For ten years after 1891 Wellington Alexander Kenwell ran a hunting lodge on the site. At that time the road from Headquarters on the Cedar River was 19 miles of wagon ruts.

It is difficult to imagine the isolation of these settlers in the wilderness, but Beetle's account of Kenwell in his book *Up Old Forge Way* provides a good illustration. Kenwell was asked to name the worst noise he had ever heard in the woods. Not wolves, not panther, not owls, but a "dreadful scraping sound, Mrs. Kenwell scraping the bottom of the flour barrel, and he knew he had to go 11 miles in a spring thaw to get more."

Beyond the brook, the road angles west for 1 mile to a major trailhead for the West Canada Wilderness Area. A sign 2.4 miles beyond that trailhead marks the start of the .45-mile-long trail to Squaw Lake.

The road continues southwest for almost 2 more miles, passing the flow near Muskrat Lake. The swampy trail that leads .2 mile to Indian Lake is being rerouted to higher ground, and the road will be barred to vehicular access beyond the new trailhead.

In most of the Adirondacks, you have to walk a good distance to find an isolated and secluded lake bursting with wildlife and bordered with a colorful array of blooming plants and shrubs. The Moose River Plains is a major exception. Both Indian and Squaw lakes have loons and sometimes mergansers. Rarely do you meet other hikers visiting them in summer. You can count on one hand the number of other un-inhabited Adirondack lakes that are this lovely and this close to a road. The Moose River Recreational Area is an enormous expanse of recovering wilderness with a system of trails well designed around its access road so that you need to hike only short distances to reach any of its diverse lakes and ponds.

Near Beaver Lake

16

John Brown's Tract

Distance (full circuit): 9.4 miles
Vertical rise: minimal
Hiking time: 8 hours
Map: USGS 15' McKeever
Ha-de-ron-dah Wilderness Area

A hike in John Brown's Tract takes you farther west than any other route in this guide, beyond the mountain region that generally distinguishes the Adirondack Park. You will visit the rolling country that tempted early settlers. Their story is as fascinating as the walk through the deep quiet woods that now conceal almost all evidence of their presence.

The story of John Brown's Tract is a tragedy of greater proportion than any of the other failures that marked early attempts at Adirondack settlement, and it is one of the oldest tales in the mountains. It began in Rhode Island with the family and fortunes of John Brown, a businessman whose generosity to Rhode Island College caused that institution to be renamed Brown University. In 1796, one of his sons-in-law misspent a $210,000 fortune on the disputed title to 210,000 acres in Herkimer County. John Brown spent another $250,000 straightening out his son-in-law's folly and clearing title to the parcel, which was a part of the McComb purchase. Brown then divided the purchase into townships with the names of virtues he espoused: Industry, Enterprise,

Perserverance, Unanimity, Frugality, Sobriety, Economy, and Regularity.

John Brown only visited the area once, but he had a 25-mile-long road built from Remsen, north of Utica, for the settlers he enticed to his community of Middle Settlement in Township #1, Industry. No sign remains of Industry's log houses, barns, and clearings, but the hike outlined visits Middle Settlement Lake, and follows in part a trail along John Brown's Road.

The tragedies that befell a second son-in-law, Charles Frederich Herreshoff, were even more devastating. But, from the failures of Herreshoff's attempts to bring settlers to Township #7 sprang some of the Adirondack's most notable events. The community he founded later grew into the lovely resort of Old Forge. Otis Arnold acquired Herreshoff's mansion and turned it into the Adirondacks' first hotel. And that hotel was visited in 1856 by the first woman to make a camping trip across the Adirondacks. The isolation of that Adirondack wilderness is graphically illustrated by the story that that first female traveler, Lady Amelia M. Murray, lady-in-waiting to Queen Victoria, was the only woman other than their mother that six of Arnold's twelve daughters had ever seen.

You will want to read more of the history of the ill-fated settlements; the story of the failure of Herreshoff's iron mine, one of the first in the Adirondacks; and the adventures of the wild days when the trapper Nat Foster occupied Herreshoff's mansion and murdered an Indian. Either Donaldson's *The History of the Adirondacks* or Grady's *The Adirondacks, Fulton Chain-Big Moose Region,* would be a good introduction.

Your hiking introduction to John Brown's Tract is a long, level loop generally following the valleys between long ridge hills. The hike takes you past several lakes in the Ha-de-ron-dah Wilderness, each desirable as a camping or fishing destination. The route is designed to give you a feel for the wilderness that greeted those first settlers.

Trailhead parking is at a large turnout on the south side of NY 28, 3.5 miles southwest of Thendara. The trail begins opposite the turnout, and it is in better shape than any road the settlers ever saw.

The surrounding forests were burned in one of the worst of the 1903 forest fires, ignited by a spark from a wood-fired locomotive on the rail line near Thendara. In spite of that fire, the forest through which you will walk has almost regained wilderness stature.

The trail, marked in red, heads up a ridge, reaching state land in .2 mile. You can walk the .6-mile distance to Brown's Tract Road in fifteen minutes. You will return to this junction on the right-hand fork from Grass and Cedar ponds. For now, turn left on the yellow-marked Brown's Tract

Road. It is a lovely, smooth path, leading south-southwest around Bare Mountain. Only a few glacial erratics lie beneath the forest of enormous beech, birch, and maple. In twenty minutes, .9 mile from the junction, you should reach a second intersection. Here you will fork right on the blue trail, heading 1.9 miles to Middle Settlement Lake.

Narrower and showing much less use, this trail is a good stretch-your-legs, wilderness route. As you wind along a ridge only slightly elevated from the surroundings, you can see swamps opening beside Middle Settlement Creek. There is a particularly beautiful vista across a ferny meadow on your right as you cross a double-log bridge. I was most impressed with the openness of this forest's understory, and I stopped at least a half-dozen times to watch for black-throated blue warblers, vireos, and thrushes. You know you are nearing Middle Settlement Lake when suddenly, in the midst of the unbroken forest, one of the Adirondack's great big boulders appears. It is a part of the facing cliff that has split away. At the trail junction below the cliff you turn left on the yellow-marked route to walk the short distance to Middle Settlement Lake.

The trail winds across a wet inlet area between boulders and starts along the northern shore of this swampy little lake, whose shores are made muddier by the flooding of recent beaver work. No matter, for it makes a better home for the nesting loons you are sure to find. Within 200 yards of the inlet a red-marked trail forks right for a short detour up a steep pitch and around to the top of the cliff. The view is crowded by maples, but you do look out across the pond. Return to water level. The yellow trail continues west, past the clearing where a lean-to used to stand. To continue the loop, however, head back to the intersection below the cliff to take the yellow trail east. One overhanging section of cliff forms a small cave that appears to have sheltered hikers. You wonder if early settlers also found shelter here.

The yellow trail starts out along the left side of the draw, behind the huge split boulder and beneath the cliff. By this route it is just over 1 mile to Cedar Pond. After a twenty-minute-walk the trail crosses the end of the ridge and heads down. Where you can see a marsh through the trees is about the closest you will get to Cedar Pond on a trail. Just beyond

this spot you will meet a sign beside a creek that says, enigmatically, "trail." You are on the trail, but through the trees on your right you can see a small pond surrounded by a beautiful long meadow full of big, twisted stumps.

Ten more minutes should suffice to get you to the next intersection, which is within sight of the Cedar Pond lean-to, but a good way from the pond. You could shortcut your circuit of John Brown's Tract at this point and head back south on the red trail, but if you are still game for adventure, head north for 1.2 miles to Middle Branch Lake. The trail starts up a series of short ledges, goes over a height-of-land and down into a

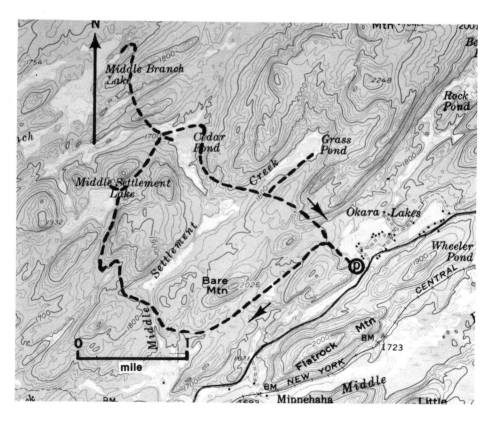

Grassy Pond

swale, and then cuts down more steeply and crosses a stream on the predictable split-log bridge. Only a thin layer of sand covers the valley bottom, revealing the glacial wash that is typical of the tract's long valleys. Beyond the stream you head up beside big ledges and round a cliff on your left. Across the second height-of-land you start to descend, and before long you reach still another intersection where you can see Middle Branch Lake through the trees. The right fork, still marked with yellow, heads to a DEC truck trail that circles back to Thendara. The left fork leads along a red-marked trail to a lean-to where you should stop for lunch. This is certainly the prettiest of the lakes you visit; its loons may swim by quite close and its shores are lined with Labrador tea.

The return from Middle Branch Lake to the junction near the Cedar Pond lean-to takes about forty-five minutes. Beyond the lean-to the trail shows much heavier use. The first stretch is very handsome, through a dense spruce bog with a beautiful ground cover of sorrel, bunchberry, creeping white winterberry, and beech fern. You keep to the long winding ridge of an esker with deep bogs on both sides.

The next unbroken chain of wilderness is measured by a series of minor events: two stream crossings; a stand of tall straight trees towering over a parklike settng where a variety of ferns carpets the forest floor a mottled rich green; a ledge covered with huge black cherry trees; more impressive fern-crested ledges; another small stream crossing; and finally, after nearly an hour of walking, the crossing of Middle Settlement Creek, which is the outlet of Grass Pond. Beyond, the trail makes a ninety-degree turn left, and the tree cover becomes smaller. The long level walk begins to lose its excitement just about the time you reach the Grass Pond trail junction, an hour and ten minutes from Cedar Pond lean-to. This section is definitely longer than the 1.5 miles stated on trail signs.

To visit Grass Pond, turn left and walk for .5 mile (fifteen minutes). A very old beaver dam holds almost no water. However, the pond is not merely grassy, for you can find sundew, lady's slippers, and the hoof prints of many deer along the shore.

When you return from the side trip to Grass Pond, the sign says you have a .75-mile walk to your car. This is actually the mileage to Brown's Tract Road. After a ten-minute walk along the red-marked trail, you reach a split-log bridge and a small triangular intersection. Continue 100 feet to a sign to reassure yourself that you should head right, over the bridge. The signs give mileages toward Thendara and back the way you came, but not for the direction you will take, which is a slightly circuitous route to the trailhead to avoid private land. The trail turns right and then left before reaching the intersection on Brown's Tract Road, where you are but .6 mile from the highway. It should take you almost thirty minutes to walk from the bridge to the trailhead.

17

Scenic Mountain Trail and Bald Mountain

Distance (total trip): 8.5 miles
Vertical rise: 1,300 feet
Hiking time: 7 hours
Maps: USGS 15' Old Forge, USGS 15' Big Moose
Fire Tower; closed Tuesday, Wednesday

The western foothills of the Adirondacks diminish to a series of long ridges whose major axes point slightly north of east. Few rise more than five or six hundred feet above the surrounding countryside, but glacial scraping has left many with steep cliffs flanking their long sides. The most visible and dramatic ridge is the row of hills along the north shore of the Fulton Chain Lakes, stretching from First through Fourth lakes.

Two trails on that escarpment connect a row of extraordinary vantages that stud the ridgeline like gems on a necklace. For the best walk in the Old Forge area, you should combine both trails into one long day's outing. The combination is possible because the Scenic Mountain Trail ends at the trailhead for the Bald Mountain route.

If you need a well-marked trail and have only a little time, you should just climb Bald Mountain on the western end of the chain. O'Kane's description of this trail in his 1928 classic *Trails and Summits of the Adirondacks* as ranking "first or nearly so in the amount of reward that it offers for a minimum of climbing" is still accurate. But if you are adept at following an unmarked and overgrown path and have the full day to hike, you certainly will want to walk the Scenic Mountain Trail along the eastern slopes. For this trail, and for the combined outing, it is best to have two cars, one at each trailhead.

The Fulton Chain, best known for its canoeing opportunities, dominates most of the views on this hike. Old Forge, at the west end of the Fulton Chain, was the major settlement in John Brown's Tract (see Hike 16), but unlike most of the tract, it failed to fade into the wilderness. In fact, it grew into a thriving resort community and now has many vacation possibilities. See Beetle's *Up Old Forge Way* for a delightful series of stories about this community. Several state and private campgrounds are nearby, and a visit to the Northeastern Forest Industries Exhibit Hall, .6 mile east of town, is most informative. In addition, you should not miss a lake cruise on the *Clearwater*, which makes a 28-mile tour of the Fulton Chain starting at Old Forge.

The new Bald Mountain trailhead, which is also the trailhead for the western end of the Scenic Mountain

Trail, is on Rondaxe Road just north of its intersection with NY 28, 4.6 miles east of Old Forge. If you are hiking the complete route, leave one car here and continue east another 3.1 miles to the County Lake Gift Store. That store is 1.5 miles west of Big Moose Road at Eagle Bay. The eastern trailhead, unmarked, is on the north side of the road 100 yards east of the store.

The Scenic Mountain Trail immediately heads northwest up the ridge. As you come upon a huge maple stump almost at the height-of-land, you will see a narrow footpath angling up the ridge to the west, left. The more obvious trail, which you take, continues straight. It leads to Bubb and Sis lakes, two pretty, shallow ponds. Bubb is a mere fifteen-minute walk from the highway. One of the area's typical long ridges frames its northern shore. The trail skirts its south shore and forks. The way right heads north around Bubb Lake to Moss Lake; the left fork leads 100 yards through a spruce thicket to Sis Lake. It takes no more than fifty minutes to visit both and return to the junction near the height-of-land.

Now bear right, west, onto the Scenic Mountain Trail. You'll spot a blue trail disk on a tree 30 feet beyond the junction; 20 feet farther, a blowdown blocks the path. The eastern end of the Scenic Mountain Trail was closed for a couple of years during the Indian occupation of Moss Lake in the late 1970s, and although the route is again open to the public, no attempt has been made to clear and officially reopen it.

You now begin climbing directly up ledges. Within five minutes you reach the beginning of the ridge and in another five come to the first open-

ing, which has a view north and east toward Black Bear Mountain. Now heading south of west along the razorback ridge, you continue climbing, but at a more gradual rate with the way often obscured by blowdowns. The water of Fourth Lake is visible through the trees. Fall, with its brilliant colors and sparser cover, might be the most desirable time for a trek along this ridge.

After walking forty minutes on the razorback ridge, you reach the first good view of Fourth Lake and the rolling hills stretching away to its south. Within ten minutes a second overlook with small views follows, just before the trail starts a short descent. The trail is almost impossible to follow here, so simply go down into the col between the ridge and the higher hill on the right. Blowdowns slow your way as you angle right, crossing the valley floor to pick up the trail again. In general, when the trail becomes obscured stay on the ridge, but here logic should direct you into the valley and then up the higher ridge that follows. Another opening follows, this one with a fireplace. You will then find the trail confusing as it goes from one open patch to another, but always staying close to the ridgeline.

You climb again to reach the most exciting series of openings along the Scenic Mountain Trail. The first, which you come to after an hour and twenty minutes on the ridge, has open rock edged with deep moss and spruce trees. If you have made the trip to Bubb and Sis lakes, this is two hours and twenty minutes from the start. You may want to stop here or at any of the next few overlooks for lunch. The view is east along Fourth Lake, past Gull Rock Point and several islands, to the right of which you can spot a broad mountain with a fire tower. That is Wakely (Hike 34), 18 miles away.

A second excellent opening follows in 100 yards, this one with an even broader view east, with Black Bear Mountain and Estelle Mountain, which is southeast of Raquette Lake, now visible. The third in this series of openings is perhaps the best of all, for it offers the sum of the previous panoramas plus a shot straight down, south, to Fourth Lake, which almost seems tucked below the intervening cliffs.

Although the route is not terribly obvious, you will have no trouble finding the next overlook about 100 yards farther along the ridge and an excuse to stop. Here you seem to hang directly over the lake. Beyond, the trail descends briefly before climbing again to the narrowest part of the razorback ridge at the top of a nearly vertical cliff. The crescendo of improving vistas continues, for not only is this perch placed dramatically and precariously on top of a nearly

400-foot vertical drop, but it permits points to the west to come into view. This spot marks the end of the long stretch of unbroken ridge line. If you pause often, as the changing perspective encourages you to do, your walk on just this section of ridge should take more than an hour.

The trail now descends and becomes obscure again in a small valley. As you climb the next knob, stay left, on the Fulton Chain side of the ridge, going around and below ledges that form a 12-foot-high cliff near the top. This is a very difficult spot to navigate since you go around and below the knob and then up it.

Handsome rock formations edge the descent into the next valley, and again it takes a good detective to find the difficult continuing route. Dense growth fills the valley and blurs the trail.

As you continue descending the ridge line, the forest suddenly becomes much taller and more handsome, but openings allow you some glimpses of Second and Third lakes.

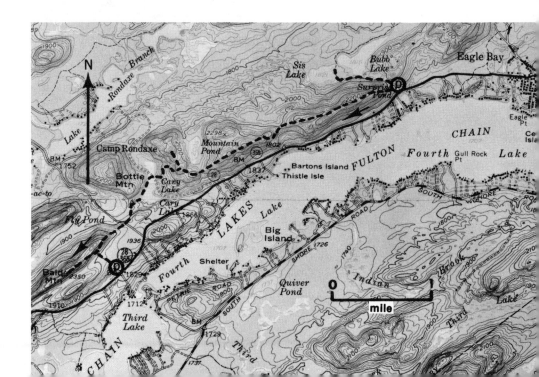

At the bottom of the next steep descent, you turn away from the Fulton Chain Lakes and intersect a freshly marked blue trail, which is the present official route of the Scenic Mountain Trail. The left, or south, branch goes down to an abandoned railroad right-of-way. For more views, take the right branch. Mountain Pond greets you almost as soon as you turn north. Beaver have recently raised the level of water in that pond, so dead spruce trees edge it and the walking is muddy and terrible.

Beyond the south end of the pond the trail heads up a ridge, climbing 100 feet into the saddle between two knolls. An extraordinarily tall and handsome spruce and hemlock grove greets you as you mount the ridge. Just as you cross the ridgeline a red-marked trail forks right up the knoll by a sign pointing to "scenic overlook." Of course you cannot resist another detour, so head up, staying right as footpaths branch off near the summit. You soon come to an overlook of Mountain Pond. From here, its deep emerald water looks infinitely more inviting than from the shore. Continue to a second overlook of Lake Rondaxe and the meadows that stretch east from it, with the cliffs of Slide Off Mountain facing the ridge behind. You will recognize that mountain as a carbon copy of the ridges you have been following. Beyond, a series of long hills stretches toward Big Moose Lake. You will be glad you took the side trip to this beautiful hilltop.

Returning to the main blue-marked trail, you drop precipitously along slippery needle-covered slopes in a hemlock grove, then zigzag right

View east from Bald Mountain

along a contour before dropping again, this time swinging left around the northern marshes of Carry Pond. High water here almost floods the trail just before it emerges on the roadway, where you turn right, back north, crossing the marsh on a causeway. On the far side of the causeway a state historical marker tells you that you are walking along the route of a standard gauge railroad that was constructed in 1899. Until 1933 the line carried passengers between Raquette Lake and Carter Station. The railroad had the first oil-burning locomotive in the Adirondacks, thus preventing the forest fires that were regularly ignited by the wood-burning monsters.

That sign at the end of the causeway is the only indication that here the blue trail turns left. It is .7 mile to the trailhead. The railroad continues north to Lake Rondaxe, but you walk south along the shore of Carry Lake. (The USGS map spells it Cary, but local signs and logic favor Carry.) This is a lovely stretch of trail with a needle-covered tread and views back to the mountain you just descended.

You cross the outlet on a log bridge and then climb another small rise, beyond which you can see Fly Pond. The trail heads south and up another ridge for .3 mile before reaching Rondaxe Road opposite the trailhead. The sign indicates it is 1.7 miles back to Mountain Pond, and with the additional detour to the overlook, you probably need one hour and fifteen minutes for that segment of the hike.

For the second part of this trek, where the view is equal to the sum of those along the Scenic Mountain Trail, you simply climb Bald Mountain. From the parking area the ascent is only 400 feet in less than 1 mile. If the climb were not too short to call a hike, or if you were not apt to meet hordes of other hikers, it could be one of the most satisfying treks in the Adirondacks. But, since you have certainly enjoyed a measure of solitude on the Scenic Mountain Trail, you should complete the day with this trip.

You do not really need directions for the trail. After a short level stretch, it begins to climb along the razorback ridge, angling up and over it, and reaching the first outcrop with a view in ten minutes. Gentle switchbacks bring you to the north side of the ridge, where you make a sharp left turn to cross a boggy swale on a bridge. Just beyond, the grade levels out, and you see the old trail that comes directly from NY 28 climbing the south edge of the ridge. Turn right to follow the ridge. The vista opens to include First and Second lakes and Moose Mountain. Stop and enjoy the amazingly narrow spine, the magnifi-cent view of Fourth Lake, and the incredible drop of the cliffs below to the south. Hollow footsteps on the exfoliated sheaves tell of ice-loosened slabs that may one day fall away like the ones you see against the forest below. The serpentine ridge continues west to the fire tower, to which the state has assigned the name Rondaxe Mountain Tower. It is open to the public, but you scarcely need to climb it for the view. The only significant improvement the short tower affords is a clearer look at two peaks on the distant northeastern horizon. The one on the right is Marcy, 56 miles away, and the one on the left is MacIntyre. You can be certain of their identity if you are looking to the left of Blue Mountain, which, only 25 miles distant, has an identifiable stubby profile. The best part of the view is unquestionably the panorama of the Fulton Chain spread out parallel to the knife edge of cliffs that constitutes Bald Mountain.

18

Cascade and Queer Lakes

Distance (one way): 9.7 miles
Vertical rise: some
Hiking time: 6½ hours
Map: USGS 15' Big Moose
Pigeon Lake Wilderness Area

Unusual names are not uncommon in the Adirondacks, but why would anyone name a place Queer Lake? No deep mystery surrounds this strange name; it probably only reflects the lake's eccentric shoreline. But, to appreciate just how queer the lake's shape is, you have to walk there, and the best way is on a route that also touches Cascade Lake and Chain and Windfall ponds.

These lakes lie north of Fourth Lake in the Fulton Chain and south of Big Moose Lake. Natives in the nearby hamlets of Eagle Bay and inlet will tell you just how the latter lake, Big Moose, and the surrounding country figured in the murder that Theodore Dreiser immortalized in his *An American Tragedy*. To reach the trailhead, drive to Eagle Bay on NY 28, 8.5 miles east of Old Forge and 25 miles west of Blue Mountain Lake. There, turn north onto Big Moose Road.

You will want to make this walk with friends so you can leave a car at each end of the loop. Start at the Cascade Lake trailhead, which is .9 mile north of Eagle Bay. There is a parking turnout on the east side of

the road around a bend past the trailhead. Arrange to leave a second car at an unmarked turnout 2.5 miles farther north, where a yellow-marked trail comes out from Queer Lake. The sign at the Cascade Lake trailhead clearly indicates that the dirt road heading east is the beginning of the 5.5-mile-long Cascade Lake Cross-Country Ski Loop. Your trip follows that roadway to the lake and then north along it a short distance, before continuing on to the other lakes.

The dirt road used to be the principal access to an old estate that later became a girls' camp. It is wide and improved with gravel, so you certainly do not need what few red trail markers there are to guide you. Trees along the roadside have been cut back for such a distance that the forest cover of tall, mature trees hardly forms a closed canopy. The road is so wide and straight you can see quite a distance ahead, sometimes as much as .2 mile, a most unusual phenomenon on Adirondack trails. The route takes you up a short hill and then down a long, gradual incline. An old road forks right as you cross a corduroyed section. Continue

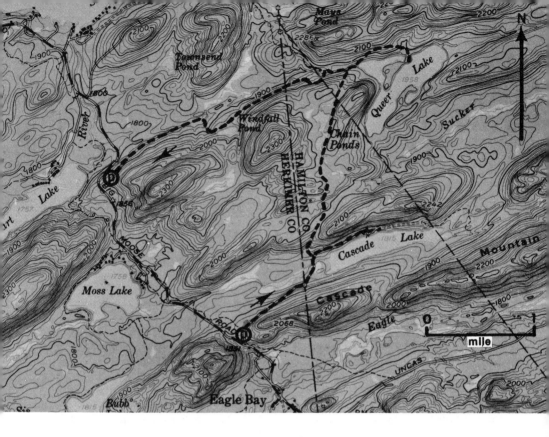

straight, through a spruce glen with marvelous bunchberry beneath, to a large field. Your trail is along its left border, which is edged in pine with a carpet of sarsaparilla and Canada mayflowers. Several good campsites can be found not far from the trail.

After crossing the outlet of Cascade Lake on a small bridge, the trail turns east for 100 yards to a junction that is almost exactly 1 mile from Big Moose Road. A sign points north, left, to a narrow footpath with red markers. Routes connected to it lead in 1.6 miles to Chain Ponds, in 2.6 miles to Queer Lake, and in 2.9 miles to Windfall Pond.

Unless you made a late start, continue straight for a trip along the north shore of Cascade Lake, a mile-long, thin body of water that is ideal

for camping and canoeing. The only drawback is its proximity to the trailhead; the lake is so popular it is sometimes crowded. The roadway is smooth enough for transporting a canoe the easy way, on a bicycle-wheeled contraption.

Many campsites are secreted along the several evergreen-covered promontories that edge the lake's shore. From the lake or its east shore, you can see the 200-foot-high cliffs that face the mountain to its north, but if you are going to finish the loop you will not have time for more than a .5-mile trek down the lake and return.

Back at the trail intersection, the narrow footpath climbs almost 200 feet to a spruce bog filled with lady's slippers, blueberries, and clintonia. Red trail markers define the route, which crosses the wet area and then rises gently to a mature forest with many yellow birch. Within twenty minutes you reach a height-of-land in a sort of natural rock garden where ferns seem to have found perfect niches among the boulders and tall straight trees.

Huge yellow birch, the first of the giants you see on the hike, appear beside the trail. The trail winds through the mature hardwood forests and then angles left in a sphagnum bog covered with tall spruce. Beyond the bog, you climb a small rise and then reach a trail junction. Here a sign tells you that it is 2 miles back to Cascade Lake. Both continuing trails are marked with blue disks; the left leads 1.6 miles to Windfall Pond and then out to Big Moose Road, and the right, the one you follow, continues .5 mile to Chain Ponds and 1.5 miles to Queer Lake. As you turn right you enter a small valley with an unusual ledge off to your left and an enormous birch growing from a boulder on your right.

The short walk to Chain Ponds is through a beautiful and majestic forest of hemlock and spruce, one of these deep evergreen pockets all too rarely encountered. A bog appears through an opening on your right just before you reach the outlet of Chain Ponds. Cross the outlet on a natural bridge of well-placed stones and stop for a moment to look up the lake and examine the old beaver dam that raised the water level to create a typical Adirondack stump forest around the shores.

The trail climbs a ridge on a carpet of sorrel and interrupted fern. Ledges twenty to thirty feet tall face the hillside on your right. Look for a balancing boulder on one cliff top. The walk along the shore is one of the day's high points. You pass a spruce-covered peninsula formed by the continuation of a rock shoulder that edges the left side of the draw that the trail now enters. The deep, dark valley formed by the beautiful cleft in the rocks is overhung on the right by moss-covered ledges. Caves and crevices are sources of cool air. Mystery and a feeling of suspense accompany you. As the draw narrows, the trail is squeezed between boulders and huge slabs that have fallen from the cliffs.

The draw is all too short, and within fifteen minutes the trail emerges and starts to drop sharply. Here the trail is narrow and rooted, and again you will be awed by the size of some yellow birch. In ten more minutes you reach a trail junction within sight of Queer Lake. An informal path angles back right along its shore. A yellow-marked trail heads west, left, 3.5 miles to Big Moose Road. This is the route you will follow after you have explored Queer Lake. For now, bear right, where a sign points to the Queer Lake lean-to, Mays Pond, and the West Mountain Trail.

You glimpse a small portion of Queer Lake as you cross the marsh at its western end on a slippery log bridge. You might notice an informal path that continues along the northern shore, but the trail, with its yellow markers, makes a sharp left turn uphill behind the lake. After a five-minute climb, you turn east and walk along the ridge, reaching another three-way junction within fifteen minutes. Here all the trails have yellow markers. The way left goes to Mays Pond and the route straight ahead leads to the lean-to in .5 mile. Continue right, on the narrow trail that shows little sign of use. It winds along the flat-topped ridge high above the lake, and then turns to descend, meeting on the way down still another trail. The yellow-marked route turns north, left, in 3 miles to Chub Lake, and the red-marked trail drops down to Queer Lake.

Your first approach to Queer Lake is at the beginning of a boggy isthmus linking the shore with the long narrow peninsula that almost divides the lake in two. Using a split-log bridge to cross the bog, you will walk along the north side of the peninsula under big spruce for 200 yards and then cross to a wind-swept promontory overlooking the larger portion of the lake. Here a lean-to has been placed to enjoy the best of both views and breezes. You may find a raft tied to trees below the lean-to.

An informal path continues from the lean-to to the end of the peninsula, leading to ledges from which there is good swimming in deep, clear water. This peninsula almost reaches the western shore of Queer Lake. When you are in one portion of the lake, the separation is so complete you have no hint of a lake on the opposite side. The shape is certainly peculiar!

When you start back, walk slowly along the boggy spit that takes you to the "mainland." Tall spruce protect an eerie shoreline edged with the naked spires of dead spruce, swamp laurel, and Labrador tea.

Return to the principal trail junction at the lake's western end and head right, west. Now is the time to enjoy the huge yellow birch. In the next hour of walking, you should spot dozens of these magnificent giants, some with diameters approaching four feet.

The trail begins through a valley, with low ground on the right and a steep hill on the left. Wet places make walking less than perfect, and roots poke out occasionally. A series of split-log bridges takes you across a wet meadow filled with lush ferns, clumps of oak fern, or *gymnocarpium.* A marker on a downed spruce beside a section of corduroyed trail where the valley narrows is the only warning you have that the trail turns to the left. The turn is poorly marked, but if you miss it, you will quickly see the buildings of a private inholding. The trail heads up the hill and across its face before continuing in the valley in order to avoid this private land.

Past the detour, you reach another intersection where a sign indicates you have traveled .7 mile from Queer Lake. There is no indication of the distance to Big Moose Road, but it is just about 2.5 miles; the walk out takes about an hour and ten minutes.

Stay straight ahead on the yellow trail to Windfall Pond, walking generally up the side of a hill for a half-hour on a ledge below long thin ridges. The footpath is narrow and appears infrequently used.

A spruce-covered plateau for camping lies between Windfall Pond and the trail. The lake is deep, its dark green waters reflecting the high hills that rim it. Its rock-edged shoreline invites swimming. The trail skirts the lake on the north as far as the outlet, staying most of the time 100 feet back from the water.

The "boat" at Windfall Pond is more peculiar than most. It is a rectangular wooden box, not obviously seaworthy. Visitors to the Adirondacks are often amazed at the boats secreted at almost every fishing pond

Paddling the boat at Queer Lake

in the mountains and wonder how they got there. Most have been dragged over the snow by far-sighted fishermen, and a few have been constructed on the spot, Huck Finn style. It's always tempting to bail one out for a better look at the remote ponds. Some are really in very good shape, and the fisherman's code permits you to borrow them if you return them to their proper place in good condition. Others sink as quickly as they are launched.

From the outlet it is 1.5 miles to Big Moose Road. The trail follows the stream, dropping through a rocky gorge in a narrow valley with ledges above and a tumble of boulders below. When you reach a meadow of ferns and Canada mayflowers, turn left. The sign says "Beaver Meadow," which is obvious, but it is curious. Do you suppose it was placed there when beaver had flooded the meadow, making people think that this was Windfall Pond? Yellow paint blazes and trail markers mark the trail as it circles the meadow. You cross a small stream on a split-log bridge, and beyond it, stop on a real bridge to watch the stream below flowing over smooth bedrock into a miniature chasm, complete with diminutive cliffs and a dark evergreen canopy. The trail pulls away from the stream up the valley's right side, following the stream for a short distance on a ledge and then dropping down to recross it on a log bridge.

Instantly the trail is wider. You have reached the point where "inbound" hikers stop, five minutes from the road. You turn away from the stream and a campsite that seems attractive to many (but think of all the beauty of the more remote spots you reached on this walk). In no time at all you are back at the unmarked trailhead and waiting car.

Stillwater Mountain

Distance (round trip): 2.4 miles
Vertical rise: 560 feet
Hiking time: 1 ¼ hours
Map: USGS 15' Number Four
Fire Tower; closed Thursday, Friday

The western Adirondacks have relatively few mountains to climb. This fire tower peak is almost too small to be called a mountain, and its short trail hardly offers a hike, but it is among the few mountains in this part of the Adirondack Park with a view. Finding the trailhead takes you on a journey of discovery to an area with which you ought to become acquainted.

The mountain is south of Stillwater Reservoir, an enormous impoundment for hydroelectric power. From a state boat launching site on the reservoir you can gain boat access to 117 miles of shoreline and forty-two islands. Canoe or motorboat destinations include many wilderness campsites and lean-tos. North of the reservoir lies a region of four dozen lakes, with the Pepperbox Wilderness on the west and the Five Ponds Wilderness on the east flanking a section of private land along part of the reservoir's northern shore. There are few trails in the region, so its forests and lakes are among New York's most inaccessible.

Even driving to the trailhead is a trek into the wilderness. Turn north from NY 28 onto Big Moose Road at the hamlet of Eagle Bay on the north shore of Fourth Lake in the Fulton Chain. In 6 miles bear left near Big Moose Lake toward Stillwater. You cross the newly restored Utica-to-Lake Placid Railroad 1.8 miles from the fork. Just beyond, in the hamlet of Big Moose, the road turns left and then right and adds Stillwater to its name. Most of the continuing road is hard-packed dirt. The surrounding land is owned by International Paper Company, which permits day use but no camping.

Traveling toward Stillwater is an adventure in itself. On an early summer day I counted a half-dozen deer, including one doe with a fawn, placidly grazing right beside the road. You pass a designated picnic area and a bay with views of the reservoir in the 9.7-mile drive from the fork at Big Moose to the trailhead, which is nothing more than a small parking turnout on the shoulder of the dirt road.

The trail heads uphill at a fairly gentle rate, generally below the telephone line leading to the tower. It follows a roadway and crosses an old

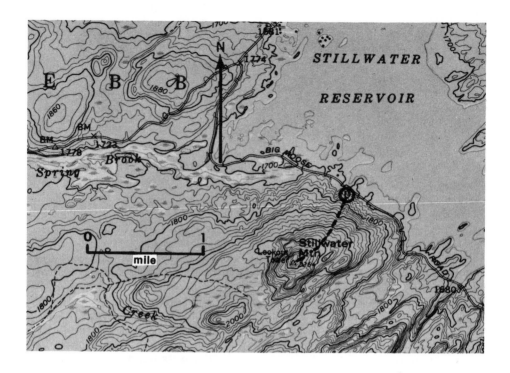

logging road about halfway up. It is amazing how thin the Adirondack soil is even on these moderate slopes. You walk on bedrock a short distance before passing a cabin. The tower is not much farther, and the whole walk hardly takes thirty minutes, even at a slow pace.

Trees on the summit crowd the view, hiding much of the reservoir, but you can look beyond it north to a series of low rolling hills. Farming country rolls away on the distant southwestern horizon. West Mountain lies due east, almost directly in line with Blue Mountain so only a portion of Blue is visible to the left of West. At 120 degrees magnetic you can spot Wakely Tower, over 27 miles away, with Snowy to its right.

North of east stretch the High Peaks, reduced at this distance to a range of small and not easily identified summits. Even on a clear day and with good binoculars it is hard to distinguish Santanoni, 48 miles away, from the MacIntyre Range, almost 8 miles beyond and slightly to Santanoni's left, the two appearing as one connected ridge. Clouds often top the High Peaks, and their cluster from this angle is maddeningly dense.

The trip down takes no more than twenty minutes. A summer walk through the rich hardwood forest on Stillwater's slopes makes it hard to imagine that the deepest snows and lowest temperatures in the state are often recorded nearby.

To extend your adventure here you can walk from the parking turnout to a stump-filled spit of the reservoir, or you can continue driving west toward the Stillwater settlement. Immediately beyond the trailhead you pass the fire observer's cabin. There is a spring at the roadside nearby.

In just over 2 miles a sign directs you to a turn right toward the boat launching facility and the ranger's headquarters, where you must regis-ter if you use the lake. You will even find a hotel and store in this outpost, whose location at the western edge of the Adirondacks places it almost as far from civilization as you can get in the Park.

Bay on Stillwater Reservoir, near the trailhead

High Falls on the Oswegatchie

Distance (round trip): 11 miles
Vertical rise: minimal
Hiking time: 6 hours
Maps: USGS 7½' Newton Falls; USGS 7½' Five Ponds
Five Pond Wilderness Area

The Oswegatchie is canoe country, and, understandably, this northwestern Adirondack river is very popular with canoeists. The long, flat waterway meanders so much that straightened out, is seems as if it might just stretch completely around the Blue Line of the Adirondack Park. The river's Indian name derives from the phrase for going around a hill. The region is also a favorite with backpackers and trout fishermen and has many, many more miles of trails and interesting destinations than are described here and in the Five Ponds trek (Hike 21).

The broad flood plain of the Oswegatchie has long had a reputation as a great hunting ground. In his *Trappers of New York*, Jeptha R. Simms tells an Oswegatchie tale that is as tall as the pine that dot its plains. Trapper Nat Foster and his younger brother Shubael were hunting along the river shortly before Nat's death, when his eyesight had begun to fail. They cornered a herd of deer against a ledge. Nat's brother shot several before Nat got one, but Nat quickly recovered. He said that if he could get a good piece of venison he

would be able to see, and after a meal of his favorite meat, he proceeded to shoot four more deer. Together that day the two men supposedly killed twenty deer.

The distances on the flat plains between ponds and along the eskers are so great that there are few good day hikes in the area. The trip to the High Falls is an exception. However, you may want to carry a pack in and camp, or use a canoe (see Jamieson's *Adirondack Canoe Waters: North Flow)*, for spending the night is the only way you can reasonably continue to Five Ponds and beyond. There are several good campsites within walking or canoeing distance of High Falls, and all are excellent bases for further explorations in the Five Ponds Wilderness.

This easy though long hike describes a journey to the lovely waterfall that breaks the otherwise placid river. The relatively open, level trail makes the 11-mile round trip seem shorter than it really is.

To reach Oswegatchie country, from Cranberry Lake, drive southwest on NY 3 and turn south on the road toward Wanakena. One mile from NY

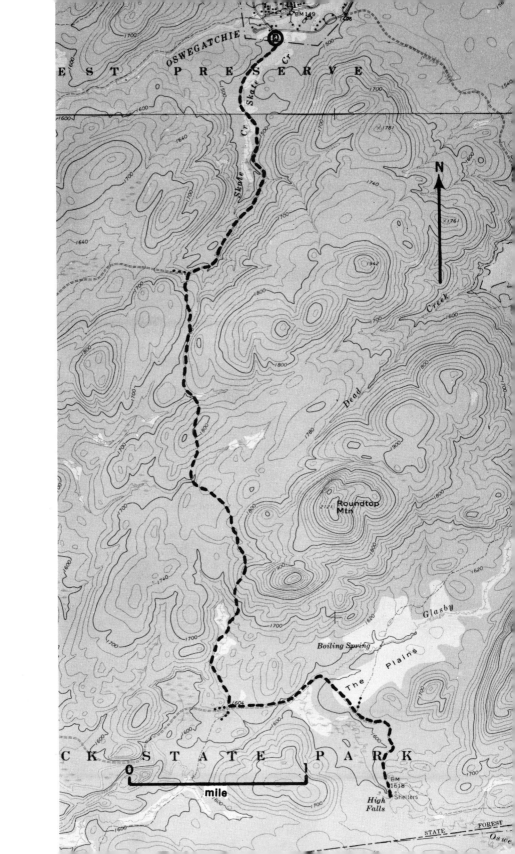

3, bear right, and then take a second right across a one-lane bridge over the Oswegatchie River. Just beyond, the road past the private dwelling is barred. Park before the barrier; the land is private, and a small fee is charged. No vehicular traffic is allowed on the continuing road, which serves as the fire truck route.

The edges of the hard-packed sand road are dense with masses of spring and summer blooming flowers, particularly the ones that need a bit of extra sunshine. The road follows a flow, and within fifteen minutes you cross the stream that feeds it. Shortly, you cross a second stream and then come to a pipe that carries water from a good, cold spring, spilling it across the trail. The sandy-bottomed watercourses that you cross are all flowing to the stream valley on your right. You cross two more small streams within a matter of minutes; by now you should be well aware of the area's drainage patterns. A myriad of small sluggish streams flow through the plains, the result of the sandy soil's poor water retention.

In theory you are walking on a red-marked trail, but the first markers you spot are just before a junction forty minutes and 1.5 miles from the trailhead. Here the red route, the fire truck trail, forks right. Your route is left along a narrow footpath marked with blue. A variety of ferns, many of them tolerant of dry conditions, covers the higher ground. There are also long wet stretches where sand has been placed in cribs to raise the footpath above the muck. Already a sense of quiet pervades your walk.

After walking for an hour you cross a bridge over a small stream. Almost imperceptibly, the forest has become taller. Beyond a pair of bridges over

intermittent streams you start to descend to the level of a grassy flow. A short walk along the flow leads to a bridge and a place to pause and enjoy the tamarack, spruce, and pine. There is a larger flow on your left now, and you finally spot the old, old beaver house that held the work parties who flooded this trail and created the pond that now fills part of the open meadow. If you are making the walk in late summer, you will want to stop also to enjoy the fields of bottle gentian and to pick a luscious dessert of blackberries. In another .2 mile, you intersect the truck road at right angles. The intersection is 4.6 miles from Wanakena and can be easily reached within two hours. The blue-marked trail straight ahead leads in under .5 mile to a bridge over the Oswegatchie, near which you will find several good campsites. The best is on the ledge north of the bridge. (The bridge is also the starting point for the Five Ponds hike.)

To reach High Falls, however, turn left and walk the red-marked truck trail for 1.6 miles. I cannot help thinking of it as a blue trail, for it is much more beautifully marked with the purple-blues of gentian, the soft green-blues of tamarack, and the expanse of blue sky that opens up above the broad natural plains beside the trail. The exquisitely lacey giant tamarack are most impressive. A ridge of tall pine and tamarack, a good camping spot, eventually gives way to a black water swamp. Just beyond, the trail angles to the southwest, and you can begin to see The Plains, which stretch northwest for almost 1 mile. The trail hugs the southern end of The Plains, and just

High Falls on the Oswegatchie

High Falls on the Oswegatchie **105**

beyond comes another intersection. Continue straight for .6 mile to High Falls, a short walk slowed in midsummer by enticing patches of raspberries.

Shortly you hear the falls. As you approach the pine-covered knoll beside them, several footpaths lead away from the main trail. The first goes to a perch looking up at the falls, and the second to a lean-to. Beyond that, the trail turns right to cross the river above the falls. It leads to a second lean-to south of the falls.

A funnel of smooth vertical ledges frames the 15-foot High Falls. You will enjoy the way the water breaks from the smooth stream above, frothing into a wild fury through a deeply channeled course and finally spilling into a deep, rectangular-walled pool where swirls of natural foam trace a pattern of symmetrical white curves on the dark brown water.

While the Oswegatchie abounds in wildlife, you are not likely to see deer in the quantity that Foster did. High Falls, like many other camping destinations in the Adirondacks, has become known for the bear who have learned that careless hikers' packs can be sources of food. If you do camp here, be sure and secure your pack high above the ground, suspending it by a rope from an overhanging tree limb. If you are looking for signs of wildlife, you are more apt to see the rather large footprints of the coyotes that have gradually moved into the Adirondacks from the west. I doubt you will see one of these animals, but they may just spend an evening serenading you, sounding almost like a pack of wolves.

The plains and marshes beside the river are noted also for their bird life. The Canada or gray jay and the northern three-toed woodpecker both make their way this far south. Be sure and carry your binoculars, for you will see many warblers and water birds.

21

Five Ponds, Wolf Pond and Sand Pond

Distance (round trip): 13.4 miles
Vertical rise: minimal
Hiking time: 10 hours
Maps: USGS 7½' Five Ponds, USGS 7½' Oswegatchie SE
Five Ponds Wilderness Area

On the hike to Five Ponds you have a chance to examine the effects of the most recent of the Adirondacks' major geological events. As the glaciers of ten to twelve thousand years ago began to melt, channels of water pushed through the ice pack, gradually funneling beneath it. These rivers picked up and moved sand, gravel, and boulders. As the melting slowed, the under-ice rivers deposited their burdens, leaving long, sinuous ridges of stones surmounted by finer and finer sand. The ridges, called eskers, vary from a few feet to over 150 feet in height, and stretch up to several miles in length. The longest eskers in New York developed in the flat lands of the northwestern Adirondack region.

Eskers are usually crowned with white pine, spruce, and hemlock, and in the Five Ponds Wilderness Area those trees exist in towering virgin stands. The tops of eskers vary in width from a few feet to a hundred feet. They can be gently rounded and wide enough to support a road, or they can be as narrow and sharp as a knife-edge, which is the case with one of the Five Ponds eskers.

This hike starts from a campsite on the Oswegatchie River and features a walk past all of the Five Ponds, and then southwest through magnificent forests that stretch in that direction toward Stillwater reservoir in a wilderness broken only by marshes and beaver flows. Best of all, this trek takes you far from other hikers to a world of solitude.

To reach the starting point, you have to walk the red truck trail and then the blue hiking trail to the bridge over the Oswegatchie as described in the High Falls trek (see Hike 20). If you head south from the campsite there early in the morning, you are apt to find the tall pine and tamarack etched in soft blues against the fog rising from marshes. These marshes line the two outlets of Five Ponds, and the trail generally follows the eastern of the two. After fifteen minutes you cross a small brook and then angle left away from the flow. Small sandy ridges accompany you on each side.

The trail begins to climb gently through a valley, and after forty-five minutes (1.2 miles from the bridge), it turns right to cross the stream. There are enough rocks to hop on, so a bridge is unnecessary. Stop and appreciate the great distances you can see through the open forest, and notice, too, the fantastic understory of blooming plants.

The hill on your right is the northern end of the Five Ponds esker, which you will want to study as you continue walking south beside the stream. The esker becomes steeper and steeper, attaining a forty-five degree angle. The large boulders typical of the lower margins of eskers make difficult footing along this section of trail.

A little under .5 mile beyond the stream crossing, about a fifteen-minute walk, you may be tempted to climb the esker. There are easier places to ascend, but here you can climb to beautiful pine that crown a dip in the ridgeline, just above Little Five Pond.

Return to the trail and continue south for .2 mile to a lean-to a few feet south of the trail on the shore of Big Shallow Lake. West of the lean-to an informal path heads up the esker, a climb of over 120 feet. From the top you can see a faint footpath that angles right, back toward the shore of Little Five Pond.

Your path, to the left, winds south along the top of the esker for about 200 yards through a magnificent hemlock grove, before crossing over the ridge and descending in a long southwest traverse to the outlet of Big Five. The path follows that outlet to the pond. The lovely stream exits from the pond over a natural cobblestone spillway of uniformly sized stones, sorted by the glacier. The pond itself is long and thin with swampy shores, much better to look at than walk beside.

Return to the lean-to and head north for 100 feet to the spot where the blue-marked trail crosses the outlet of Big Shallow, fording the stream on another bed of sorted stones. You climb a rise too small to show up on the survey maps, but as you walk south alongside it, you will recognize it as an esker. Just beyond the end of Big Shallow you cross a ridge dense with spruce, and Washbowl, a small cup of a lake rimmed with tamarack, comes into view on your left.

The ridgeline curves around the south end of Washbowl and shortly reaches the end of Little Shallow, another swampy-shored lake, although this one is filled with large stumps. Walk southwest along the shore to a second lean-to. There's a very cold fresh spring below the lean-to, almost at the water's edge.

The lean-to is 2.5 miles from the Oswegatchie as the trail goes, but if you climbed the esker a couple of times and poked about among the giant trees on its ridgeline, you have probably walked for well over three hours. Assuming that you can cover that 2.5 miles in much less time on the return, you might want to continue southwest toward Wolf and Sand ponds, which are an additional 2.2 miles and 4.2 miles along the trail.

Unusually lovely and strange places are few and far between in this vast, unvarying wilderness. You meet one shortly after you continue south, where a new beaver flow backs up a dark and murky pool. The recently constructed long chain footbridge is necessary to traverse the flooded spruce swamp. Otherwise, the 1.7-mile trek south to the side trail to Wolf Pond is rather uniform, if such a dull word could possibly be applied to trees of such significant proportions. The walking is easy, though, and you

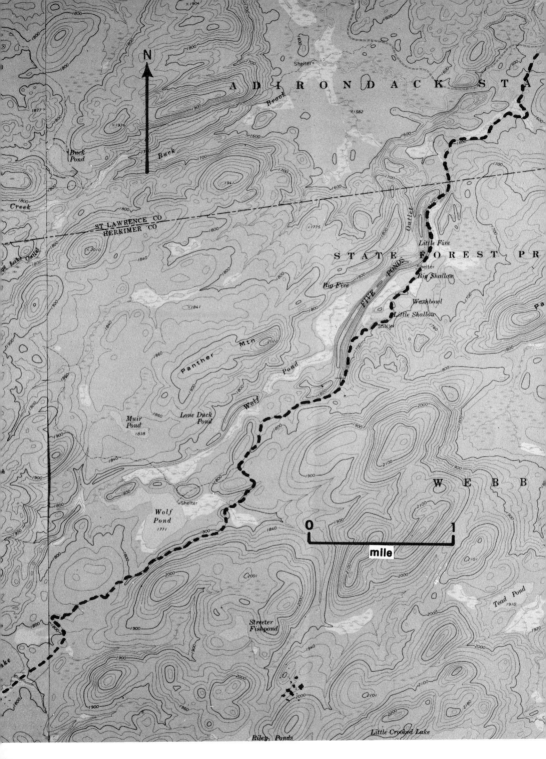

110 *Five Ponds, Wolf Pond and Sand Pond*

should reach a trail junction in forty minutes.

At the intersection the yellow-marked trail to the right leads .5 mile into the north shore of Wolf Pond. This detour would take you over a knoll that is covered with some of the best pine and spruce you have yet seen. Your route is left, though, where you begin, for the first time on your Oswegatchie trek, walking a trail that is hardly used. The narrowness of the footpath increases your sense of wilderness travel. This last 2.5 miles of the blue-marked trail to Sand Pond offers the region's best walking. You cross a knoll and descend through a narrow draw to a beautiful sliding rock falls that separates two flooded meadows.

You continue southwest up and along the side of a small hill, from which you have occasional glimpses of Wolf Pond through the trees. You then drop down to pond level. A short path back to the right allows you to detour to the water's edge, where there's a beautiful bog. Labrador tea and bog rosemary, bog wool and pitcher plants fill the sphagnum mats. You have another hour of walking before you reach Sand Lake, whose sandy shores are more inviting to hikers and swimmers than those of any of its predecessors.

When you reach Sand Lake you will have walked 6.7 miles, and you might wish you had carried a pack so you could stay put. There are several inviting campsites. As it is, on a day walk you probably will not have time to explore the esker that divides Sand from Rock Lake on the west.

Return the way you came.

Big Shallow

22

Saint Regis Mountain

Distance (round trip): 6 miles
Vertical rise: 1,235 feet
Hiking time: 3½-4 hours
Map: USGS 15' Saint Regis
Fire Tower; closed Tuesday, Wednesday

Saint Regis Mountain lies in the northwestern quadrant of the Adirondacks, overlooking the Saint Regis Primitive Canoe Area. Beautiful chains of ponds stretch south of the mountain. You may very well want to combine a climb up Saint Regis Mountain for an overview of the pond-studded wilderness with an extended canoe camping trip.

If you drive north from Tupper Lake on NY 30, passing Upper Saranac Lake, you will see the entrances to Fish Creek Ponds and Rollins Ponds state campsites. Both offer great waterfront camping and access. State maps of the Wilderness Canoe Trail are available from the DEC or campsite headquarters.

As you continue on NY 30 past Lake Clear, you can see the tower on Saint Regis in the northwest. At Lake Clear Junction, where NY 86 continues northeast, you turn north, staying on NY 30. When you reach the town of Paul Smiths, 7.3 miles beyond Lake Clear Junction, turn left off NY 30, and head west past Paul Smith's College for 2.5 miles. Turn left, south, onto a narrow road signposted for the Saint Regis tower,

3.5 miles away. Drive .5 mile to the parking area just outside the gate of the Merriweather Post Estate, one of the newest additions in this area to state lands. As of this writing (1980), it is still not open to the public.

Saint Regis is not difficult to climb. You should allow about four hours round trip, although you may meet forestry students from Paul Smith's College who regularly run up the mountain in under an hour, starting from the college grounds. The trail has been a laboratory for classes in trail work, and you will appreciate the results as you climb.

The trail, marked with red, makes a short climb into a maple and cherry woods, following the estate boundary. Huge erratics of Marcy anorthosite with large blue crystals of labradorite edge the trail as it begins a short descent and then climbs a small hill. You walk beside the estate line for nearly twenty-five minutes before turning right toward the mountain. Cross a small stream on a new log bridge, pick up the telephone line for the tower, and then head southwest through a mixed woods where the forest floor is wet. You cross some of

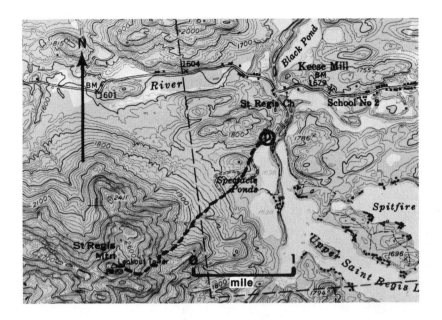

the wet places on corduroy, some on logs, and a bog on a bridge. The trail is relatively level there, hard-packed, and offers easy walking. After crossing another stream forty minutes and 1.5 miles from your start, you pass a picnic table and outhouse to the right of the trail, and to the left, the observer's cabin. The trail continues relatively level another .2 mile alongside the little brook and then turns away. You start to climb on stairs built into the side of the hill. The trail has been realigned and although it is very steep, it is well constructed with water bars for drainage and stairs to prevent erosion.

About twenty minutes from the picnic area the timber becomes much smaller, indicating where the 1876 fires swept the upper slopes of Saint Regis. The summit is bare to this day.

After a level stretch through paper birch and dwarf ginseng, a short climb bypasses an abandoned section of eroded trail. Steep ledges lie to the right. You circle them on newly cut and very steep sections. Gradually you gain glimpses of the lakes below. From an outcrop to the south of the trail you can see Whiteface across the Saint Regis lakes.

After thirty minutes of steep climbing, you emerge above treeline to see the tower ahead. A total climbing time of an hour and forty-five minutes reflects a fairly slow pace.

The summit is so exposed there is no need to climb the tower. The mountain seems to stand alone, with broad plains below stretching in almost every direction. Saint Regis is a solitary cone in a huge dish of ponds and lakes, edged with mountains on the horizon. Those to the northwest are low, the foothills of the Adirondacks, but from the north the sweep encompasses the rugged range that includes Whiteface,

McKenzie, and the High Peaks through Seward in the south. The High Peaks southeast across Lake Clear are often shrouded in clouds even on a clear day. Saint Regis Pond lies almost due south, with Little Clear Pond to its southeast and Saranac Lake stretching to the distant south. Long Pond is visible a little west of south, with Tupper Lake stretching out beyond toward the horizon. Fish, Lydia, and Little Fish ponds, on the Wilderness Canoe Trail, spread out at the foot of the mountain.

East of Saranac Lake, Ampersand Mountain stands in front of Seward and Santanoni, so overwhelmed by those higher peaks that identifying it can be difficult. MacIntyre and Marcy are obvious, with the cone of Colden between them. To the left, north of Marcy, peaks hiked on the Range Trail can be identified, from Cascade and the Sentinel Range north to McKenzie and Moose, which appear from this angle as one long mountain

range. Whiteface is just south of east.

The northeast is a patchwork of lakes and fields, some of them the potato fields for which the northern plains are famous. Both the Post estate and Paul Smith's College are visible on the shores of the lakes below you. Sand flats and glacial ridges stretch to the northeastern horizon. Two peaks with fire towers stand out a little east of north: Debar on the left, Loon Lake Mountain on the right. Both towers are closed. Even if you only carry the USGS Saint Regis quadrangle, you can probably name at least two dozen lakes and ponds in view. However, the pleasure of the climb will be enhanced if you also carry the Tupper Lake, Long Lake, Santanoni, Mount Marcy, Saranac Lake, and Lake Placid quadrangles, for most of the area they cover is visible from the summit.

Return the way you came. You will not have much trouble making the trip back in an hour.

View toward Whiteface and McKenzie mountains

23

Debar Mountain

Distance (round trip): 7 miles
Vertical rise: 1,600 feet
Hiking time: 6 hours
Maps: USGS 7½' Meacham Lake, USGS 7½' Debar Mountain

Debar Mountain is the Adirondack's northern sentinel, offering sweeping views across its dramatic northwestern slopes to the St. Lawrence Valley and neighboring Canada. Rock outcrops covering the mountain's small summit offer views that adequately compensate for those lost when the fire tower on Debar's peak was closed. Stunted spruce frame the cliffs that drop to steep wooded slopes and finally to the broad plain below, plunging over 1,600 feet in less than a mile.

The entire climb is through a magnificent forest that is as special as the views from the summit. The approach is from the southwest, gentle at first, then steadily uphill, and finally an 800-foot mad scramble up the last .5 mile, the steepest and most arduous climb of any on New York's fire trails.

The trail to Debar begins from the Meacham Lake State Campsite, a good place to camp before you climb. There, picnic and camping areas surround part of the 2-mile-long lake, whose cool waters washing sandy beaches will welcome you to a refreshing swim after your climb.

The Meacham Lake campsite is about 18 miles south of Malone on NY 30, far enough north so that signs are in both English and French to accommodate visitors from Canada. To reach it from the south also use NY 30. You will pass Paul Smith's College and continue north through level sand plains covered with spruce, pine, birch, tamarack, and poplar typical of forests in the northern Adirondacks. You will see a sign for McCollums 6.3 miles north of Paul Smith's College. It is the site of an old settlement; today the number of tombstones in the cemetery far exceeds the remaining buildings. An historic marker beside the road bears the legend that in October 1908 Debar Mountain and the surrounding land were burned in the wave of forest fires that struck the Adirondacks that year. The local fire consumed over 6,000 acres.

The sign for the southern access to the Meacham Lake campsite is 9.5 miles north of Paul Smith's College. A marked road angles right, east, paralleling the lake. A northern access is 2.3 miles farther along NY 30 near Clear Pond. The roads meet

View from Debar Mountain

northwest of Meacham Lake and continue as one .2 mile southwest to the main gate for the campsite. A day-use fee of $1.50 is charged. The campsite fee is $4.50 per night. Ask the gatekeeper for a campsite map and instructions, because the trailhead to Debar is not shown on the map and signs for it are missing.

Look for a dirt road just west of campsite #48. Take it and turn right at the first intersection in .1 mile. In .4 mile you reach a sand pit where you park. The trail commences along the gated dirt fire road heading east toward Debar. (If you start your walk from the campground, this trailhead is 1 mile from the main entrance. You do not have to carry water, except in very dry times, as you will find water .5 mile from the summit.

Walking the soft sand of the fire road is almost like walking on a beach, except that the road is shaded by a tall spruce forest. Beside the road, carpets of Canada mayflowers are punctuated by starflowers, golden thread, wild strawberries, false Solomon's seal, and acres of hay-scented fern. As the forest begins a transition to mature hardwoods, you will spot on a huge maple beside the trail, the first of the very few red markers that are supposed to de-

lineate the route. Beneath the hardwoods sarsaparilla and blackberries edge the road.

After you have been walking about twenty minutes, a glacial ridge appears on your right and a spruce bog opens on your left. The bog should be the first of the detours you take to enrich the trip. A true sphagnum bog, it contains most of the typical flowers: the predominant shrub is Labrador tea, which blooms here about the second week in June. Bunchberry in profusion, cinnamon and interrupted ferns, blueberries, and clintonia continue the great carpet of flowers beneath the tall trees.

Unless you spend some time enjoying the bog, it should take you less than a half-hour to walk the first mile to a bridge over Winnebago Brook. A barely perceptible woods road heads left from the fire road in the meadow near the brook. Continue on the more obvious road (you will find few markers but you really do not need them) for 200 yards to a marked fork. Here a sign directs you to turn left and continue on a wide woods road that begins the upward trip so gently you really do not sense you are climbing.

The first perceptible rise begins shortly in a forest of tall, straight hardwoods that cover a lovely woods floor where dryopteris ferns, mostly the evergreen wood fern, are interspersed with doll's eyes, lady's slippers, crinkleroot, and jack-in-the-pulpit.

As a few boulders appear beside the route and rocks pop through the roadway, you will realize how few stones there were in the glacial sand at the trail's beginning. For forty-five minutes you follow the road through a forest in which maples become more dominant. Huge boulders edge

the route, and a steep hill begins to appear on your right. You will cross several log bridges over a small stream before you reach a height-of-land 1.5 miles from the marked fork. The roadway descends slightly, and a steep valley becomes visible on your right. You will contour around to the head of that valley, which lies between Black Mountain and the peak of Debar Mountain.

As you begin to climb again, ledges are visible on your left, and you reach a lean-to with a fireplace. Beyond, the trees are shorter and noticeably more dense as the road climbs into a small meadow containing the remains of the fire observer's cabin. The state burned the cabin when it closed the tower, leaving a mess of stone and concrete. As you enter the meadow, the summit of Debar looms ahead of you. Cross the meadow and enter the woods to the left of the stone foundations. The trail is now just a narrow footpath.

The final .5 mile makes the first 3 seem dull. Suddenly the route seems to be straight up through a stunted forest. The white of paper birch contrasts with the dark tones of spruce. The mountainside is so steep that stone steps have been built into it. Within 100 yards a stream crosses the trail. It is a source of good, cold water. For a time it seems as if the trail is through the stream. Rock stairs lead past boulders glistening with outcrops of garnet. Deadfalls block the narrow trail, and the downed telephone wire leading to the fire tower could trip you up. You have to use your hands to pull yourself up some of the small ledges, but don't climb so intently that you fail to stop and look back when the forest opens up. A fine view of Meacham Lake and the mountains to its south and east appears through the trees. You can trace your route on the ridge you crossed during the lower part of the ascent, and you will be impressed by the steepness of the knob you are climbing.

The trail levels out in a deep ferny glen below a moss-covered ledge marking the last short climb. After you cross the last ledge and a short wet level, the sheer rock face of the tiny knob on which the tower sits seems to block your way. Walk right around the knob to climb it from the north. Fantastic views greet you as you emerge from the forest. Most exciting is the sweep along the mountain's steep-angled northwest face. Only a few more hills break the plain below as it fades into the distance across the St. Lawrence River into Canada. To the southwest you can see Meacham Lake, and in the west a series of small hills barely define the horizon. The view northeast is blocked by a row of small knobs that are a part of Debar itself. Do not attempt to climb the tower, which has been vandalized and is in a dangerously rickety condition. And be careful of broken glass.

There are no other rock outcrops with views, but if you walk around the summit your hollow footsteps will tell you you are walking across exfoliated sheaves, rock slabs that have been broken off by the expansion of ice in cracks in the rock. There is a very small camping spot northeast of the tower. If you climb in June you will also enjoy the bloom of huge clumps of painted trillium brightening the mountain dryopteris that covers the wooded parts of the summit with a lush soft background green.

Going down, you find that the mountain is so steep near the summit it requires almost as much time to descend as it did to climb up. Be careful on the stairs and rocks. When you reach the height-of-land between the cabin and the marked fork, pause for a moment to enjoy the magnificent forest around you. Notice how many of the yellow birch seem to be growing from boulders. One beside the trail is perched upon a stone with its roots crossed. It so resembles the caterpillar from *Alice in Wonderland* with his legs crossed upon a giant toad stool that I almost expected it to ask, "Who are you?"

Catamount Mountain

Distance (round trip): 3.6 miles
Vertical rise: 1,568 feet
Hiking time: 4 hours
Map: USGS 15' Lake Placid

If you like to scramble over ledges and boulders, inch along cracks and crevices on steep rock walls, and do a little nontechnical rock climbing, then Catamount is for you. This mountain, one of several with the same name, lies in the northeastern Adirondacks. The climb is great fun, but it will probably take no more than a half-day, allowing you time to explore some of the area's attractions on the way to the trailhead.

Driving north from Lake Placid on NY 86, your route is along the West Branch of the Ausable River, past High Falls Gorge, a private scenic attraction for which a fee is charged. Next north is the Wilmington Notch Public Campsite and Day Use Center, on a very handsome spot near the river. Here there is trout fishing and the best campsite for activities in this area. Beyond Whiteface Ski Center you can stop and walk beside the flume on the Ausable, a wild falls in a deep gorge within sight of the highway. You eventually reach a crossroads where NY 86 turns right toward Wilmington and NY 431 goes left for 2.8 miles to the entrance to the Whiteface Mountain Memorial

Highway, a toll road climbing nearly to the summit of Whiteface. That summit, at 4,867 feet, offers some of the Adirondack's best scenery, but you can get there by car, so for a trek on foot continue straight ahead on the unmarked county highway toward Catamount.

When you reach NY 17, head left, or north, for 1.7 miles, and turn left again, on to Forestdale Road, driving west toward Franklin Falls. In 1 mile you pass an intersection with the old highway. You are now headed southwest with the complex of Catamount on your right and the Wilmington Range on your left. Exactly 4.7 miles from NY 17 a small unmarked path heads to the right into an alder swamp. Easy to miss, it is the beginning of the trail up Catamount. If you are uncertain, continue for 1.25 miles to the Wilford LaHart Farm and turn around. The LaHart property borders the trail, and members of that family laid out the very handsome and well-designed route on Catamount. As you head back, you can enjoy the best view northeast to Catamount's ledges. Watch closely as you descend the small hill just beyond the edge of the posted property line. Now you should be certain the faint opening between the trees is the trailhead. Park off the road.

The narrow footpath follows an old road that is filling in with small balsams. The path is informal and not marked by the state. You should not let the overgrown condition of the first .25 mile deter you. The deadfalls and confusion last only a few minutes, for after .25 mile you come to an orange-painted pipe and cairn indicating the corner of the property. Turn left and follow the property line for .3 mile toward magnetic north. The straight line is marked with orange blazes and is easy to follow.

Hiking here through an old field, you are on one of the most beautiful and unusual stretches of trail you will encounter. Fires in the northern Adirondacks consumed acres of forest land. The burn on Catamount created a wonderful open-rock summit, but the fires in the valley exposed the sterile sandy soil, which is only now becoming reforested. Here the ground is covered in a pastel mosaic of soft limey greens, blues, and lavenders, the lacey growth of lichens turning the ground into a fairyland of tinted hoarfrost and sugar icings. Meadowsweet, hardhack, and blueberry shrubs make a colorful middle range. Pines and balsams grow in isolated clumps, with the pure white of birch bark for accents.

You can see the mountain ahead as you cross the field. Near the end where you start down a slight grade, a fairly obvious and well-worn footpath angles to the right and heads into the forest. There are few markings, only some rusted tin can lids and an

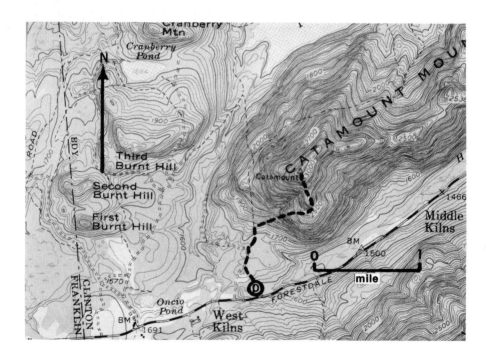

Climbing Catamount

occasional blue plastic ribbon. The path rises quickly into a lovely birch forest and then angles right and levels off as it crosses a small ridge. Within fifteen minutes you descend into a slight draw with an intermittent stream; in dry weather do not depend on it for water. After crossing the stream bed at right angles, you head up another incline and cross back to your left.

The footpath becomes less clear as it rounds several large boulders, still rising steeply on bedrock. A sharp angle left below an outcrop is indicated by a white blaze on a tree at a confusing turn where some hikers have obviously gone straight ahead. After rounding the ledge, the trail rises sharply, to emerge on the first of the bare rock patches of the summit. Cairns indicate the way across

Catamount Mountain **123**

each patch as the path weaves generally to the east between them and thickets of spruce and balsam.

Because you have to look carefully for the continuing route, it will probably take an hour to walk the 1.1 miles to the first outcrop, where there are views across the valley to the Wilmington Range.

The route turns north toward the summit as you walk across the outcrop. You are facing the sheer rock face of the southern summit, with the principal summit behind and to your left. It is an impressive sight, with the height and steepness of the peak exaggerated by the small size of the trees on the outcrop.

The path heads right to climb the lower summit from the east, first ducking into a thicket of large spruce and then emerging at the foot of the rock knob. It only takes a minute to rise above treeline on the knob, which is almost entirely bare except for patches of luscious blueberries. White arrows guide you across the bare rock in a scramble that leads to a southeast-facing chimney. Pull yourself through. Cairns direct you to turn right and then back left to follow a crevice up the steep, smooth face toward the first summit (approximately 2,750 feet elevation).

The principal summit is .3 mile away and 400 feet higher, almost due north across a small valley. The scramble over big boulders down into the col is not easy. Large spruce mark the low point, then the trail rises through a wooded slope to emerge again on open rock. Painted arrows and cairns guide you along a route, which zigzags through patches of woods and over sloping bare rock. It should take less than half an hour to reach the summit.

Your first impression is how small the first summit looks. Beyond it to the right is the sharp cone of Esther, with the summit of Whiteface behind. To the west are Franklin Falls and Union Falls ponds, expansions in the Saranac River; and in the northwest, Cranberry Pond and Silver Lake. Lyon Mountain is almost due north. The Champlain Valley stretches across the eastern landscape.

To spot the row of cairns for the descent, sight from the summit to the left of the lower summit, and retrace your steps.

25

Pokamoonshine

Distance (round trip): 2 miles
Vertical rise: 1,260 feet
Hiking time: 2 hours
Map: USGS 15' Au Sable Forks
Fire Tower; closed Thursday, Friday

The nearly thousand-foot-high cliff on Pokamoonshine Mountain seems to hang above the Adirondack Northway (I-87) south of Interchange 33. Rock-climbers look very tiny as they challenge the heights of the Adirondack's "most awe-inspiring cliff." This is the way Bradford Van Diver describes the mountain in *Rocks and Routes of the North Country.* Before you climb Pokamoonshine, you should consult Van Diver's book to learn about the mountain's geological history and the thick, dark bands of intrusions which etch the fault escarpment.

This is a mountain you will appreciate from below as much as from the summit. The best views of the cliff are from the Northway or from NY 9. Because the trail circles behind it to reach the summit, the major cliff is hidden from view; however, the tower on top does provide a spectacular panorama of Lake Champlain and the Green Mountains beyond in Vermont.

Fifty years ago when O'Kane wrote his book *Trails and Summits of the Adirondacks,* he remarked on the unusual display of ferns beside the trail. Today keen observers will be amazed at the variety of ferns that still edge the route. I counted twenty different species, ranging from maidenhair and silvery spleenwort to fragile fern and rusty woodsia. With ferns, views, and cliffs to enjoy, Pokamoonshine is a much more exciting climb than its short trail and low elevation would indicate.

The trailhead is in the Pok-O-Moonshine State Park (the state uses a spelling different from that of the USGS). Settling the spelling of Pokamoonshine seems as unlikely as determining its meaning. No one will probably ever know whether the mountain's peculiar name derives from the will-o'-the-wisp character of its cliffs and crags, or from the Algonquin words for broken and smooth, as proposed by Wm. M. Beauchamp in his 1907 treatise, *Aboriginal Place Names of New York.*

When you drive the 3 miles south to the park on NY 9 from Exit 33 on the Adirondack Northway, stop and observe the cliffs with their overhanging rocks and columnar structure. There is a $1.50 day-use fee at the park. the trail begins its steep climb within 100 yards of the southern end of the campground.

The narrow, rooted, and worn trail is marked with a very few old red disks, but so many hikers have preceded you that the way is obvious. Tremendous boulders and the ends of ledges rise above the trail. You angle right in a small draw, aiming at a sheer wall, and then turn left below an overhang. The route is fairly steep beneath the cliffs and moss-covered ledges. As the trail turns right along the ridge at about .3 mile, look for a side path that heads to a lovely overlook.

Beyond the overlook, the trail turns north, left, toward the mountain and, after a relatively level .2 mile in deep woods, it becomes steep again. This pitch is fairly short and leads to a level meadow and the site of the fire observer's cabin. An abandoned road heads west in front of the cabin, and there is a lean-to beside it within sight of the trail.

A footpath to the cabin's right leads to a spring on the side of the hill and continues steeply to a chimneylike opening with natural stairs between its walls. Follow it up to a level outcrop and overlook to the east. The path rejoins the red trail about 50 feet farther.

You might not have even noticed the official red trail, which headed away from the clearing about halfway between the cabin and the more obvious footpath. It leads, after rising 50 feet in elevation, to a lovely outlook through the valley to the northwest. Then it continues west to climb the summit ridge by a gentler and slightly longer route, meeting the footpath.

Beyond the junction the trail continues in the woods for 200 yards beside some irresistible blueberries and turns right to approach the tower from the west.

You can appreciate the view east without climbing the tower. From open ledges Lake Champlain stretches from north to south, wrapping around intervening hills, with the Green Mountains defining the eastern horizon. In the southwest and 1.4

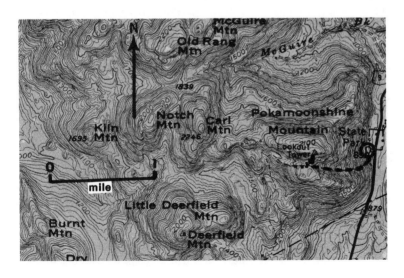

Cliffs on Pokamoonshine

miles away is the summit of Deerfield Mountain, which is almost as tall as Pokamoonshine. Beyond Deerfield is the Jay Range. The fire tower on Hurricane is visible to the left of Jay Range and serves as a guidepost for identifying Nippletop, Giant, and Rocky Peak ridge, which range to Hurricane's left.

Sighting to the north of Deerfield, you can identify the Sentinel Range, followed by Whiteface, which is due west. Continuing north, the Wilmington Range, the top of Catamount, and Loon Mountain with its fire tower line the horizon. Lyon Mountain, also topped by a tower, is toward magnetic north, 28 miles away.

Rattlesnake Mountain is east of Catamount on the shore of Lake Champlain. Sight toward Lake Champlain, just to the left of Rattlesnake's summit, and you will see Four Brother Island with Willsboro Point reaching north into the lake in the foreground. In the southeast the water of Lake Champlain is interrupted by the cone of Split Rock Mountain. These two mountains should serve to orient the rest of the vast eastern landscape.

Instead of bringing the USGS maps to help you identify the remaining mountains, lakes, bays and points on Lake Champlain, you might want to use the "Adirondack Region Atlas" printed by City Street Publishing Company of Poughkeepsie, New York. That map will be your best help for locating trailheads described in this guide, and it will replace, in this case, several USGS sheets. Most of the quadrangles for Plattsburgh, Willsboro, and Port Henry cover as much of the water of Lake Champlain as the land beside it.

Pharaoh Mountain

Distance (round trip): 6 miles
Vertical rise: 1,474 feet
Hiking time: 3½ hours
Map: USGS 7½' Pharaoh Mountain
Pharaoh Lake Wilderness Area

Few mountains have as much open rock and such beautiful exposures as Pharaoh Mountain, so when the surrounding area was designated Wilderness, forcing the closing of the fire tower atop its summit, the panorama was not adversely affected. The views encompassing the many ponds and cliff-faced hills of the Pharaoh Lake Wilderness Area are spectacular, and more distant views include a superb one of the eastern High Peaks 30 miles to the north-northwest.

You cannot help noticing Pharaoh Mountain as you drive north along the Adirondack Northway (I-87). From several places on the highway it is visible in the east beyond Schroon Lake, and its profile is most distinctive: the summit slopes south to a ledge, which in turn drops steeply south, ringed by exposed cliffs.

The entire Pharaoh Lake Wilderness is studded with hills and mountains topped by open rock, cliffs, and ledges. Most were laid bare by fires that swept the region at the turn of the century. Tall stands of hemlock mark the few areas the fire spared. The trail to Pharaoh Mountain passes through one extraordinary stand immediately south of Crane Pond and

then through a variety of second growth as it climbs the mountain's flanks, most of which were burned by those fires.

Several public campsites are near the trailhead. Two are accessible from Exit 28 off the Northway and either might serve as your base in the Pharaoh Lake Wilderness. The first is a small campsite on Paradox Lake, off NY 74 a short distance east of the exit. A much larger campsite is on the shore of Putnam Pond, at the edge of the Pharaoh Lake Wilderness. To reach it, drive east on NY 74 for 12.5 miles to Chilsom and turn south. The campsite is 3 miles south of NY 74.

A third state campsite, Eagle Point, is nearly at the southern end of the lake off this road and is more easily reached from Exit 26. For private accommodations, follow NY 9 south from Exit 28, paralleling the Northway and the western shore of Schroon Lake.

To approach the trailhead from the Northway's Exit 28, drive south on NY 9 for .6 mile and turn left, east, on Alder Meadow Road. After passing East Shore Road, on the right at 2 miles, the road continues as Crane Pond Road. It is a very pretty drive

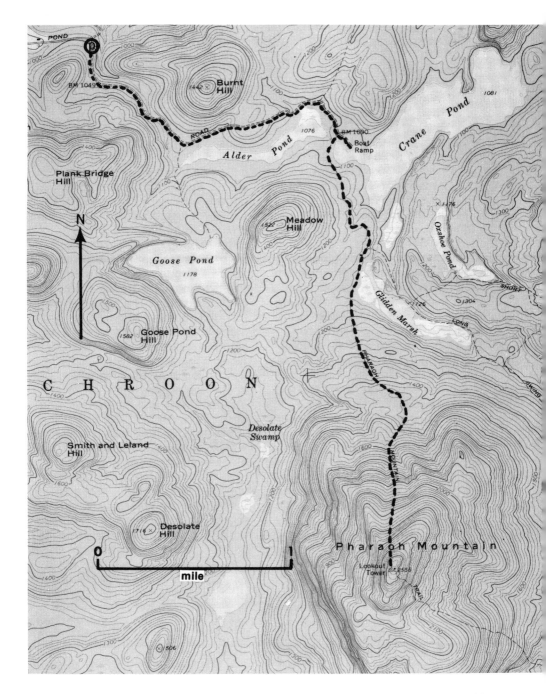

east, passing a lovely farm shortly before angling south at 4.5 miles. Park on the east side of the road at the turn. People do drive beyond, and motorized access is permitted. It you have a four-wheel-drive vehicle you may proceed with caution; if not, you probably should walk. Certainly adding 1.9 miles on a handsome dirt road to the trip is not too much for a day hike, though the total 9.8-mile hike now becomes a full day's outing.

Beyond the parking turnout, the road climbs a small valley beside Alder Creek in a deep hemlock forest. Enjoy the company of a few huge pines and the sounds of several small but handsome waterfalls. The road crosses Alder Creek on a small bridge (3-ton limit) and descends through a terrible washed-out stretch almost to the level of Alder Pond. Near the end of the road, .2 mile from the official parking area and registration booth, the road fords a flow created by beaver in Alder Pond. If the water is low, driving across the solid base is safe. If you are walking, fording may be wet and equally as difficult. The road ends in a parking area on a promontory covered with magnificent pines.

If you prefer wilderness camping, you will find numerous campsites and fire rings along the west shore of Crane Pond, a truly handsome body of water edged with white pine and huge boulders.

The Pharaoh Mountain Trail begins at the narrow spit of land separating Crane and Alder ponds. The route, marked with red disks, heads south across a bridge and immediately plunges into a deep woods. Hemlock and pine darken the needle-strewn trail. Even on a bright day, the route can be as dark as night, and the walking may be the best in the Adiron-

dacks. The forest is stately and mature, with pine exceeding three feet in diameter.

Within twenty minutes you reach a junction with another red trail. Turn right to continue south toward Pharaoh Mountain. The sign says the summit is 2.3 miles away. Within a few minutes you pass Glidden Marsh. Stop for a few minutes and walk toward the water to enjoy the reflections in the pond of surrounding tall pine and Pharaoh Mountain.

Boulders and erratics are strewn across the hillside as you continue, but the walking is easy. You pass a picnic table and a campsite and then cross a little stream on a moss-covered bridge. Foamflowers and white violets edge the trail. You soon notice a gentle rise in the trail, and the cover changes from evergreen to birch and maple. The route seems to fork, but you have just reached one of many intersections the trail makes with the telephone line that ran to the tower. The two intertwine most of the way up the mountain, the telephone line making the straightest, steepest route and the trail winding about more gently.

Stands of mature hemlock alternate with a hardwood cover of yellow birch and beech. Within an hour you are climbing fairly steeply, and already you will have arrived at sections where the trail has worn through the thin topsoil to bedrock. As the trees become obviously smaller, the dominant evergreen is spruce. After an hour and a half of walking you will notice the trees are quite small, and the trail is very steep and laced with tangled spruce roots. Ten minutes before reaching the top you will find a

View from Pharaoh Mountain

welcome spring on the side of the trail where water runs from beneath a rock shelf. The first opening gives you a view back to the High Peaks, with Giant clearly distinguishable. The fire tower is still standing beside a small cabin on the summit where grassy patches and blueberries cling to crevices between the smooth rock.

To enjoy the panorama, you should bring the USGS quadrangles for Schroon Lake, Elizabethtown, Mount Marcy, Lake George, and North Creek. First survey the pond-studded wilderness below you. The largest pond is Pharaoh Lake, which lies southeast below the mountain; Whortleberry Pond is to its right. Whortleberries are not an exotic fruit, just an archaic name for the blueberries that grow so profusely in the area.

Schroon Lake lies to the west, only a portion of its 10-mile length visible. Ranging south of west on the horizon are Gore, Eleventh, and Crane mountains. Continuing on toward south you can see the tops of the mountains that rim Lake George rising in the distance over Pharaoh Lake. The valleys of Lake George and Northwest Bay are obvious, as are Black, Elephant, Erebus, and Buck mountains on the east shore and the Tip of the Tongue on the west shore.

To the west, to the right of Gore, lies Moxon Ridge. Looking to the distant northwest you can see Blue Mountain and Vanderwhacker over the northern tip of Schroon Lake. To their right lie Blue Ridge and Hoffman mountains. Farther right, or north, is Boreas, and then come the High Peaks.

Skylight, Marcy, and Haystack have similar cone-shaped summits from this angle. They range up to 25 miles away. With familiarity you can name Basin, Saddleback, Gothics, Nippetop, McComb, and Dix, which follow next from left to right.

The valley of NY 73 as it cuts through the mountains beside the north forks of Bouquet and the Ausable is next, with Giant and Rock Peak Ridge standing isolated to the right. Northeast and close lies Treadway, whose rocky summit can be reached by a trail from Putnam Pond. The Green Mountains of Vermont stretch out in the distance to fill the eastern panorama.

If you do not mind carrying water from the spring, you will find several good places to camp overnight on the mountain, sleeping under the stars. Fireplaces and fire rings mark the best places.

The hour and a half it takes to return to Crane Pond seems remarkably easy, as does the whole day's outing.

27

Pharaoh Ponds Loop

Distance (around loop): 15 miles
Vertical rise: 1,000 feet
Hiking time: 8½-9 hours
Maps: USGS 7½' Graphite, USGS 7½' Pharaoh Mountain; or
  USGS 15' Paradox Lake
Pharaoh Lake Wilderness Area

Imagine visiting sixteen ponds in one day! The ponds are connected by a marvelous network of trails in the heart of the Pharaoh Lake Wilderness Area. The map for this area shows only fifteen ponds, but a brand new beaver dam now impounds the waters of a sixteenth, smack in the middle of one of the trails. Following the yellow trail markers there would have you marching straight into a watery forest, so the route also has you briefly bushwhacking around the newest pond.

There are numerous accesses to the Pharaoh Lake Wilderness Area, but the Crane Pond access, used in the preceding hike for Pharaoh Mountain (Hike 26), provides the shortest entrance to this loop.

Much has been written about the heavy use of the Pharaoh Lake area, but the greatest use is closest to the principal accesses: Crane Pond; the two trailheads on NY 74 in the north; Beaver Pond Road north of Brandt Lake, which is the southern access; and the Putnam Pond State Campground, an excellent base when you hike in the area. On this fantastic loop, you reach the heart of the

Wilderness and travel far from the popular areas. (Because this route is a loop, you may begin at other points; a logical alternate is from Putnam Pond, although the hike then is slightly longer.)

Starting from the Crane Pond parking lot, your first steps take you over the bridge across the outlet from Crane Pond, which flows into Alder Pond. The contrast between those two ponds is typical of what you experience throughout this hike. Crane Pond is fairly deep and has a high, dry shoreline dotted with paper birch; Alder Pond is a marsh with alders, reeds, and grasses crowding its wet shoreline.

The trail bears red markers for .7 mile, following the same route as the Pharaoh Mountain hike. The wide, needle-strewn trail through tall hemlock provides easy walking.

Within fifteen minutes, you reach the first junction, where the red-marked trail heads to the right toward Pharaoh Mountain. Take the left fork, marked with blue, straight into a small clearing and then back into deep forest on a narrow path. The signs here indicate that Crab Pond is

2 miles away, that Pharaoh Lake is 3.2 miles away, and that Putnam Pond is 8.3 miles away. There are inconsistencies on many of the signs in the Wilderness, and this one is no exception. Crab Pond is barely over 1 mile from the junction.

The route runs past huge boulders and glacial erratics, and into a deep hemlock valley where you cross a stream on a good hikers' bridge. It continues beside a small boggy marsh with corduroy stretches helping to keep the trail dry. Within ten minutes you cover the .4-mile distance to Glidden Marsh, a long, thin, shallow watercourse filled with lily pads and reflecting the tall pines surrounding it. A few steps past your first approach to the marsh you reach another trail intersection with confusing distance notations. A sign indicates correctly that the right fork, which climbs the hill northeast of the marsh, leads in 1.7 miles to Horseshoe Pond. You will use this route when you return much later in the day. It is not true, however, that any part of Pharaoh Lake is only 2.2 miles south, as posted, and it is obvious that 2.2 and .4 do not add up to the 3.2 miles the sign at the very first intersection indicated. Ignore the discrepancies and simply enjoy the diversity of ponds you meet.

At this junction, head south, now on the yellow trail, along the shore of Glidden Marsh. The trail, a narrow footpath showing little sign of use, winds through a mixed forest of birch, pine, and striped maple, a forest only fires could have created. It contrasts sharply with the huge hemlock of the first part of the trip. As you round a big boulder you have a fine view back the length of the marsh. Continue past the long, thick meadow of cattails, reeds, cedars, and spectacular

paper birch whose reflections glisten in the narrow watercourse flowing through the marsh.

After crossing the inlet stream on a slippery three-log bridge, turn away from the flow. The trail climbs into a very dense hemlock thicket, where you should spot one of the forest's giants, a spruce with a diameter exceeding 2½ feet. Again the forest changes, this time to mature hardwoods with tall straight birch and maple. An understory of horse nettles crowds the trail. You should learn to recognize these plants, for although their sting persists no more than a couple of hours, it is still uncomfortable.

You quickly reach an intersection where a red-marked trail heads back left, northeast, .4 mile to Crab Pond. Your route is straight ahead on the yellow trail, where the sign points optimistically to Pharaoh Lake just "1.5 miles" away. As the trail climbs the lower slopes of Pharaoh Mountain, a deep valley opens to your left. Beech die-back has caused a number of trees to fall across the trail, obscuring it slightly.

After walking perhaps an hour and ten minutes from Crane Pond, you should meet the new beaver flow. A new route may be marked around it, but the pond provides a good example of the impediments hikers meet in the Pharaoh Lake Wilderness. The valleys, scoured by glaciers, are all at roughly the same elevation, and all were glacial lakes in recent times. This makes it easy for beaver to enlarge or create new ponds, which they do every few years.

If the trail is not remarked, stay on the west side of the pond and ford the stream above the flow to pick up the trail again. You then continue high on the hillside in an area where dead beech have so opened the forest floor that underbrush is filling the trail. You continue beside the stream and a rather eerie little swamp filled with huge clumps of all the osmunda ferns: royal, cinnamon, and interrupted. Stumps covered with lichens and mosses are rotting in the algae-filled water. Beyond it, you begin a fairly steep descent of over 300 feet to Pharaoh Lake.

You first approach the lake near a small inlet stream and then head east along the sinuous shoreline, reaching a lean-to within twenty minutes. On the way, you cross a small hemlock-covered ridge dotted with paper birch. The east side of the ridge overlooks Split Rock Bay, which serves as a reflecting pool for a group of nature's more handsome sculptures, boulders worn smooth by the last glacier. As you round the bay you find a sign for a spring and a pipe spewing cold, clear water. Beyond it three split-log bridges cross the marsh at the head of the bay, and the trail leads to the hemlock- and pine-covered promontory where the lean-to is located.

The lean-to has one of the world's better settings: views of the pond and, overhanging it, Pharaoh Mountain, with its rock slides clearly visible. If you are lucky you may spot great blue heron nesting nearby. You surely should stop here for a rest and lunch. The lean-to is just under 4 miles from Crane Pond, and a candidate for a camping stop if you wish to break the hike into segments.

The yellow trail continues behind the lean-to up a small ridge covered with hemlock. The trail is so unused that little foot tread is visible. As you approach another of Pharaoh's swampy bays, look for a short waterfall on a small stream entering from the left. The trail continues just east

of south to still another bay, this one with a long view of the lake. You reach a major trail junction on the bay's shore less than twenty minutes from the lean-to. Here a sign directs you back along the shore of the bays to Wintergreen Point or Split Rock Bay, straight south along the lakeshore, or east toward Grizzle Ocean. The last route is the one you want. It is a narrow trail up a small hill. Within ten minutes you reach the end of Wolf Pond, a swampy-bordered, dying pond filled with water lilies and pond weeds and framed with high evergreens. Some of the tallest pines in this Wilderness grow on its far shore.

The trail continues along the flow, making a hairpin turn north to avoid swamps. In this vicinity you encounter several peculiar ridges, long thin sinuous chains. Because the trail stays high and dry on top of most, and runs up and down and across a few, you enjoy pleasant walking. The ridges, "roche moutonee," or sheep backs, were sculptured by glaciers. The residual hummocks of bedrock lying in the direction of the ice flow have smooth curved edges parallel to the movement of the ice. At the northern end of the hairpin turn you descend to the level of the swamps and then cross a part of them under a moss-covered ledge. As you climb the shoulder of a small hill, the marsh continues to accompany you on your right, now west.

You now begin to climb the hill east of the swamp, realizing that the hairpin detour took you nearly 1 mile, and ninety minutes, out of your way. First turn sharply left away from the swamp and follow a small stream on a trail that hardly appears to have been used. It passes through a tall and stately hardwood forest, very

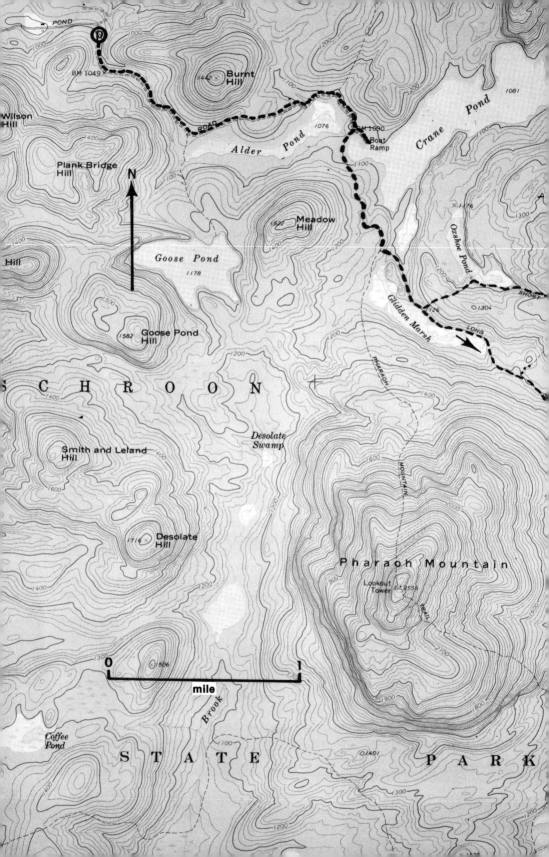

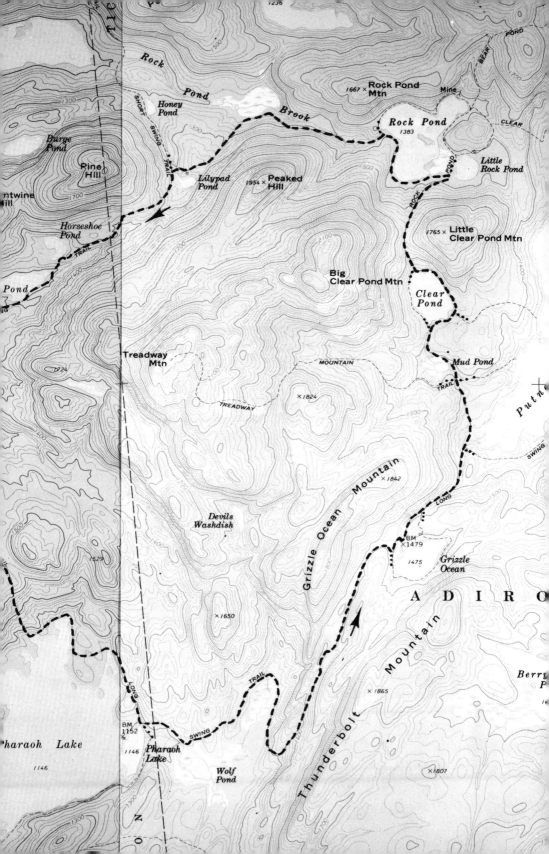

gradually gaining elevation. You are walking through the long thin valley between Grizzle Ocean Mountain and Thunderbolt Mountain. The stretch is probably the least exciting in the entire loop, a dull walk through what develops into an interminable draw. You need about an hour and a half to walk from the eastern bay of Pharaoh Lake to Grizzle Ocean. Perhaps you can enjoy spending part of the time speculating on the origin of Grizzle Ocean's name. It is certainly one of the Adirondacks' most inventive.

One Adirondack historian claims the name derives from the wild bragging of a fisherman named Tom Grizzle. His tales so astounded his listeners that they began to refer to his secret pond as Grizzle's Ocean.

Your first glimpse of Grizzle Ocean is at the edge of a narrow swampy finger of the pond where a forest of evergreen stumps gives a ragged look to the shoreline. A sign by a trail with blue markers (the state brochure shows them as red) notes, "trail around pond." Take that trail a short distance to the right, south, for a better look at the entire pond with its pine- and birch-covered shoreline, but with so many miles to go, you will probably want to go back to the sign and take the left trail for the shortest trek. A loop around the pond would add at least .5 mile to the planned route.

Bearing left keeps you on the yellow-marked trail, which almost immediately turns across a moss-filled swamp on a sinking and decrepit log bridge. It brings you into a forest of hemlock so dense it can seem as dark as night. You encounter another marked intersection in about .2 mile. Here the right fork leads to the east side of Grizzle Ocean and its lean-to, ".15 miles" away. The sign that says it is 6.6 miles to Crane Pond is incorrect.

Stay on the yellow trail, heading north. The trail shows a lot of use and can even be muddy. It descends steeply beside the outlet of Grizzle Ocean through a deep and handsome valley, crosses the stream, and continues beside it to a marked intersection, a distance of over .7 mile from your first approach to Grizzle Ocean. You could walk to Putnam Pond and the campsite there by following the right fork on a blue-marked trail. For the route past ponds less frequently visited, stay left on the yellow trail. Within a few hundred feet you glimpse a marshy end of Putnam Pond. Within fifteen minutes, approximately .3 mile, your trail intersects one that leads from a boat landing on the shore of Putnam Pond to the summit of Treadway Mountain.

The loop walk is full of lovely places, and one appears in the next 200 yards, where the trail follows the outlet of Mud Pond. Another marshy lake, it offers lovely views across to part of Treadway Mountain.

The trail continues beside a stream after leaving Mud Pond, this time the outlet of Clear Pond. Just south of Clear Pond a red trail forks left across the stream and heads around the west side of the pond. There you may choose either fork, for distance is no factor. However, the right fork, on the pond's east side, passes a lean-to, a perfect place to rest. It is perched on a small ledge above the pond, which has deep clear water and views of Big Clear Pond Mountain. Swimming is good from the ledge. A trail with yellow markers heads east behind the lean-to to another boat launching site on Putnam Pond. This access accounts for the signs of heavier use at Clear Pond.

The route north along Clear Pond has blue markers, and within ten minutes it intersects the red trail from the west side of the pond. The route north climbs through a deep valley with ledges on either side, facing the long round-topped ridges that characterize this Wilderness. The trail emerges on a saddle in a white birch thicket and then turns right to descend toward Rock Pond. As the trail turns, you can see Rock Pond down to the north through the trees, but the trail reaches it by a roundabout route, heading first almost to the shore of Little Rock Pond. Within thirty minutes from Clear Pond you reach another trail intersection. The intersection is 1.1 miles from the Clear Pond lean-to. The trail that continues north here eventually leading to NY 74, may be used to reach a lean-to on the northeast shore of Little Rock Pond. Leave the trail and walk east to inspect Little Rock Pond, with its lovely reflections.

For the loop, however, you turn left, west, at the intersection, on a red trail heading toward Lily Pad Pond. The stated distance of 5.5 miles to Crane Pond on the sign at the intersection is accurate.

After the trail passes the marshy end of Rock Pond, it follows closely the pond's southwest lobe. What a surprise the pond is, with rocks and boulders edging and emerging from it. Everywhere, smooth light gray ledges rise from the water. The trail is dry and little used, shaded with tall maple and white birch. The ledges are the best places on the entire loop from which to swim. After you cross a small inlet stream on the pond's southwest corner, you head north where the trail presents views northeast to ledges on Bear Pond Mountain. Small cliffs rise above you

on the west shore, and huge pine tower over the hemlock and birch that rim the pond. You walk on ledges thick with carpets of needles and bunchberry, and an opening with a view of the pond may entice you into a short break.

A sign near the outlet states that Lily Pad Pond is 1.1 miles away. By this time you may have solved the mystery of the lost miles. Someone has calculated the distances between ponds as if they were point sources, forgetting that the trails often follow the ponds' shorelines for quite a distance. The walk beside Rock Pond alone occupies twenty-five minutes.

The trail heads west near the outlet, and within ten minutes you should see an intermittent stream entering from the left, south. In wet times, it tumbles in a waterfall from the high ledges that face Peaked Hill. A short distance farther, less than a five-minute walk, you hear a waterfall on your right on the outlet of Rock Pond. This one should be explored, so leave the trail and walk below a small cliff from which the outlet emerges in a series of vertical drops, forming a cascade nearly 50 feet high. Be careful walking on the talus-strewn base of the cliff that leads to the edge of a small pool into which one chute of the waterfall plunges.

Return to the trail, and continue downhill to a marsh on your right. Another of the strange stump forests, it has recently been flooded and is full of birds. You should be able to spot Potter Mountain north across the swamp. The walking here is rough, for a new footpath has been worn to avoid the flooded marshes. You leave the marsh, heading southwest, beside a small stream along a trail choked with maple starts and viburnum, the new growth on the

forest floor filling the open spaces created by dead beech, a few of which lie across the trail. The relatively obscure trail from the outlet of Rock Pond to Lily Pad lean-to requires thirty-five or forty minutes of walking. You may want to stop at the lean-to for a brief rest. Just remember to keep at least two more hours of daylight to walk the remaining distance. Lily Pad Pond is minute, choked with lily pads, but nevertheless it is a beautiful camping place.

The red trail ends .1 mile from Lily Pad Pond, within sight of the pond's outlet. Here it intersects a blue trail. The right fork heads north toward NY 74. The sign points to Tubmill Pond, which you will not find on your map. It is another of the Wilderness's newcomers, a beaver pond filling the huge marsh east of Crane Pond. The area is shown as a marsh in the 1954 USGS 15-minute series, and as a real, but unnamed, flow on the newer 7½-minute series. Take the left fork, continuing southwest up a short steep pitch through low scrub on a trail that could become more overgrown in the future as the beech that cover it continue to fall.

The trail crosses a high pine-covered ledge with a crunchy lichen tread. Fires have opened the hillside, and a sign on the ledge points toward 2,248-foot-high Treadway Mountain and toward 2,551-foot-high Pharaoh Mountain. As the trail descends around a marsh you begin to notice steep ledges below on your left and a stream, which flows toward Crab Pond. If you are making the walk in summer you can enjoy a few blueber-

Crane Pond

ries on the ridge before descending to Horseshoe Pond.

Horseshoe is a half-hour walk from Lily Pad. A small rock promontory jutting into the pond from the west, gives it its horseshoe shape. The peninsula has been used for camping. The trail zigzags down a sharp, almost vertical, drop beside the rock wall over which the outlet flows. Immediately you see Crab Pond, for only a stone's throw separates the two ponds.

Crab Pond's picturesque shoreline hosts the trail for over .5 mile. Giant pines topping rounded boulders that seem to rise from the water provide delightful companions. But, before you walk beside its shores, you have to cross its inlet, and there is no bridge. In low water you may not believe this could ever be a problem. Suitable stepping stones can be found, even in high water, but you may have to walk away from the trail to do so.

All of the ponds are lovely, in their distinctive ways, but Crab is especially beautiful. Cliffs and ledges on its northern shore are accentuated with pine and white birch. You will spot at least one beaver house. This marvelously handsome section of trail is sometimes close to the pond and sometimes above it on a hemlock-covered knoll overlooking a new beaver flow. You will find a lovely rocky knoll for a brief rest about halfway along the shore, this one surmounted with red pine and white birch, lady's slippers and lichen, and within sight of the sheer rock face of Peaked Hill.

For a time the trail takes a course transverse to the ledges, so the route is up and over and down and up again. There is a short spur trail that continues southwest, but the signpost may be missing. In any event, you should continue around the western end of Crab, heading west toward Oxshoe. This route takes you through a mixed forest and past another unnamed swamp with a pine-covered knoll. Within twenty minutes you reach the southern end of Oxshoe Pond, where a lean-to caps a ledge covered with enormous white pine. There is a beautiful view up the pond's length across to wonderful ledges.

From here it should not take ten minutes to climb over a height-of-land west-southwest of the lean-to, and to drop over 100 feet, the last of it fairly steep, to Glidden Marsh. Here you take the right fork, the blue trail, north. You only have .4 mile to go on this trail before reaching the wide and easy .7-mile stretch that takes you to Crane Pond. It is surprising how muddy stretches and a little corduroy can trip you up at the end of a long walk. However, retracing the last .7 mile is so easy that you will almost feel refreshed as the trail emerges at Crane Pond with birches glistening and reflecting the setting sun.

You certainly can break this 15-mile day hike into a camping trip of at least three nights, using some of the lean-tos noted; but the easy, relatively gentle route makes a fantastic one-day hike.

Severance Hill

Distance (round trip): 2 miles
Vertical rise: 880 feet
Hiking time: 1¼ hours
Map: USGS 15' Schroon Lake

The walk up Severance Hill is so short and gentle that you can easily make it your first climb in the Adirondacks even after a long day's drive. If you are planning several days of hiking in the eastern Adirondacks, this small mountain is an ideal place to become acquainted with the region's hills.

The summit of Severance Hill offers several rocky open perches with commanding views of Schroon Lake and the Pharaoh Lake Wilderness to the east. The 880-foot climb to the 1,693-foot summit is scarcely more than 1 mile long and takes forty-five minutes at most. The summit is a perfect place for a picnic, perhaps over an early evening campfire to watch the rays of the setting sun play across the normally dark summit of Pharaoh Mountain. From here you can understand why that mountain was first known by Indians as Ondewa, or the Black One.

From Severance, Schroon Lake stretches out to the south between low hills. The origin of that lake's name is still shrouded in mystery. Donaldson in the *History of the Adirondacks* wrote that early French settlers at Crown Point "named it in honor of Madame Scarron, young and beautiful wife of the famous wild and comic writer Paul Scarron.....I am not alone in wishing the story might be true—that this humble but fascinating goose-girl, who became wife of a physically misshapen poet, and later, as Madame de Maintenon, the wife of a morally misshapen king, had given the imprint of her memory to a lovely lake in the American wilderness."

Severance itself bears the name of settlers who reached the area in the early 1820s. Walking the hills in the Adirondacks you cannot help but be fascinated by the origins of the names, and the histories of the families who once lived in what is now the Forest Preserve. Most of the early nineteenth-century settlers were loggers and lumbermen. The few farmers eked out a meager subsistence in the cold north. Many early families in the Schroon Lake area were attracted by work in the iron mines north of Paradox Lake.

The beginning of the trail up Severance is perhaps unique in the Adirondacks. The Adirondack North-

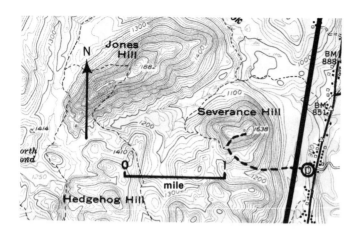

way (I-87) cut direct access from Schroon Lake to the range of hills west of the lake and NY 9, so a hikers' underpass was constructed beneath the highway. Take the Northway's Exit 28 at NY 74, north of Schroon Lake village, and head south on NY 9 toward town. Driving less than .6 mile south you pass Crane Pond Road on the left. Immediately beyond that road turn left into a parking area.

Before starting make sure you have water, for the summit is very dry. The trail, denoted by yellow markers, begins at the western edge of the parking area. Your first steps take you through a narrow culvert under the Northway and then through a flat area on a broad trail covered with pine needles and shaded by a low forest of pine, maple, birch, spruce, balsam, and popple. After five minutes you start to head gradually up into a tall cedar forest. The broad, smooth trail soon becomes steeper. A small stream gurgles in the valley to your right, and you may notice an old roadway entering from that side. Continue straight, and within twenty minutes the trail briefly levels out.

Here the forest is open enough for you to see the top of Severance Hill ahead. You may still hear traffic noises from the highway below as you enter a patch of wet woods that throbs with bird songs. I spotted a scarlet tanager and a black-throated blue warbler, both at the side of the trail.

Beyond a hikers' bridge you come out of the cedar swamp thicket to begin climbing again, this time into a forest of magnificent tall trees with huge pine and hemlock shading ground cedars and other lycopodia on the forest floor. You may want to stop and study the pines spared by early loggers. Most of the largest have double or triple trunks, which were spurned by loggers, but a few significant single trunks can be found. The route seems straight up through evergreens and immense paper birch. You cross a second level, angling south, then zigzag back to the north and begin to climb again. The trees, now mostly beech and considerably smaller, open out to rock ledges from which the views begin.

The first lovely promontory you reach looks across to Pharaoh Mountain and down the full length of Schroon Lake. Patches of wild columbine grow beneath the scrub oak that cover the summit. You will find several stone fireplaces on the open rock. Walk north to a second opening that overlooks Paradox Lake and the mountains to its north. High water brings Paradox Lake two outlets; hence the name, to explain that peculiar phenomenon.

The summit in early spring seems to be a choice place for watching migrating warblers. Within a half-hour I identified the Blackburnian, the blackpoll, the yellowthroat, and an ovenbird.

Because the walk is so short, consider combining it with a visit to the Natural Stone Bridge and Caves at Pottersville, west of the south end of Schroon Lake. The caves are a privately owned tourist attraction, and an entrance fee is charged. Plenty of signs direct you from NY 9 at Exit 26 off the Northway, west 1.7 miles to the caves and adjacent lunch and picnic facilities. More than enough signs point out the scenic wonders along the self-guided tour through the site. The path winds past caves cut out in the Grenville bedrock and beside huge potholes scoured out in the stream bed by giant grindstones. Trout Brook, whose waters created the caves, disappears into clefts in the rock, reappearing again in the gorge below to provide reflecting pools for the handsomely sculptured rock walls.

The Pottersville caves are a great place to begin learning the geology of the Adirondacks, and the owners can tell you much about the area's more common minerals. Their gift shop has a range of literature on geologic subjects to enhance all your walks through the mountains.

View from Severance Hill, with Pharaoh Mountain in the distance

Crane Mountain

Distance (around loop): 4.8 miles
Vertical rise: 1,300 feet
Hiking time: 4 hours
Map: USGS 15' North Creek

Crane Mountain is my favorite Adirondack peak. I have introduced many people to its trails, and because they share my enthusiasm, they, too, return almost yearly to enjoy this perfect hike.

Crane is a massive mountain, isolated from surrounding peaks and commanding great views in all directions. Its steep slopes offer a challenging climb, and its bare rocks provide unrestricted overlooks.

If you are coming from the north or west to climb Crane which lies in the middle of the southeastern Adirondacks, you will find the easiest approach is from NY 8. Turn south at Johnsburg onto South Johnsburg Road and drive to Thurman. There, take Garnet Lake Road, which is marked with a sign for Crane Mountain.

There is no easy route from the south and east. You could take the Adirondack Northway (I-87) to Exit 25 and head southwest on NY 8 through Chestertown to Johnsburg. Or, you could pull out a road map and improvise a route through Luzerne or Warrensburg. The major roads trend north-south, so winding east toward Thurman by way of Stony Creek or Thurman Station inevitably involves a

circuitous route on a number of back roads. You never know what you will discover along them, so allow a little extra traveling time if you choose a complicated approach.

Shortly after turning onto Garnet Lake Road you are treated to a lovely view of Crane. Drive west from Thurman 1.2 miles to a fork and bear right, continuing west on a newly widened dirt road whose condition depends on the amount of recent rainfall, despite constant care. After 1.5 miles the road turns sharply left toward the Ski Hi Lodge, but you continue straight for just under .5 mile to the marked trailhead.

Were you to continue on Garnet Lake Road to circle Crane Mountain by car, you would have a dozen places to view its sheer rock faces and its companion peak to the north, Huckleberry Mountain, which appears to have been split off Crane by some giant cleaver. The name Huckleberry should be your clue to plan your trip in midsummer, for some of the best blueberrying in the Adirondacks is on Crane and Huckleberry mountains.

The trees near the trailhead are reminders that Crane, like so many Adirondack mountains, was ravaged by fierce fires. Aspen, maple, and birch saplings are sprinkled with white pine, all pioneering trees. Both ends of your loop meet at this trailhead. By the northern route, on which you start this hike, it is 1.9 miles to the summit. You return on the western spur, a trail that bypasses private land and leads quickly to Putman Farm Road and another trail up the mountain. By this route, which takes you past Crane Mountain Pond, it is 2.9 miles from the summit to the trailhead. You may, of course, walk the loop in the opposite direction.

Following the red disks of the northern, or right-hand trail, you soon enter a forest with a deep canopy cover of white and yellow birch interspersed with beech and maple. Within ten minutes, the grade becomes quite steep. You are about

to climb 700 vertical feet in .4 mile.

As the grade steepens, the trees become smaller, with pine emerging dominant. Many rock outcrops appear, and very early on you come to openings with views back to the southwest.

After a forty-minute walk and a climb of about 600 feet, the trail approaches ledges of anorthosite gneiss, where you find good views to the west. Within another five minutes you reach a second large rock outcrop, where the continuing trail is poorly marked. Walk about halfway out on the open rock before heading up across it. You should see a marker a little east or north on a dead pine. Within another three minutes you reach a trail junction. The left fork is a spur trail leading .4 mile west to Crane Mountain Pond.

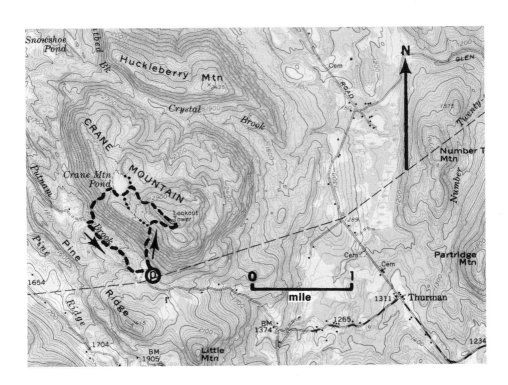

Across the outlet of Crane Pond

Turn right for the .8-mile continuing climb to the summit. Your route is toward the east, moderately uphill at first, but steep enough in one place to require use of a new 6-foot ladder. The trail enters a balsam and spruce thicket and heads almost southeast below the cliffs that face the summit, trending northwest to southeast. Less than fifteen minutes from the junction, you will have covered most of the distance to the summit, leaving only a bit more than a 100-foot scramble up the cliff. The trail turns sharply left, climbing on almost bare rock. A 15-foot ladder is wired to the hillside to assist your ascent. If the ladder appears shaky, there are also good handholds to the ladder's right. As you reach the uppermost rock ledge, head left about 100 yards to the actual summit.

You will find views from almost every point along the summit ridge. The first view east stretches all the way to the southern end of the Green Mountains, with the mountains on the east shore of Lake George clearly identifiable in between. To the south Moose and Baldhead almost conceal the summit of Hadley. Walking west along the ridge you can enjoy the view across the valley defined by Garnet Lake Road. Garnet Lake is southwest, and the string of sharp hills on its western shore lead to the rocky cone of Mount Blue.

Views to the west and north improve as you continue west. The best are from a large outcrop at the end of a short spur path branching south, left, .2 mile from the summit. So many hikers have walked this part that you should have no difficulty finding the unmarked turn. The outcrop overlooks Crane Mountain Pond. Across the pond, in the northeast, lies massive Eleventh Mountain. Use it to orient the distant horizon. Over it and 24 miles away lies Snowy, the knob and cliff face of its summit always easy to identify. To its left is Speculator Mountain; Pillsbury is a little north of east, between Speculator and Snowy on the horizon. North of Snowy and 7 miles farther is the summit of Blue Mountain. To the right of Eleventh Mountain is the steep and unmistakable cone of Height of Land Mountain, and next, toward magnetic north, is Gore.

In the small angle between Gore and due north, the High Peaks are visible. It was easier to name individual peaks before the new tree growth began to crowd the vista, but Santanoni on the west and Nippletop

on the east offer the easiest profiles to identify. Dix and Giant are to the right of Nippletop, Marcy, Haystack, Basin, and Gothics are prominent between Santanoni and Nippletop. If you want to be certain about the peaks you see, you will need the USGS quadrangles for the area and good binoculars.

Continue descending the main trail toward Crane Pond. When you reach a muddy stretch at pond level, turn left to continue the loop. The intersection is not well marked. (If you are adventurous, turn right on the unmarked path, which dwindles out as it approaches a small knob north of the pond. You can easily wind between rock outcrops to a point on the southern side of the knob that has a special view across Crane Mountain Pond to the outlet, with the summits of several distant mountains unexpectedly rising over treetops in the south.) Heading generally west around the southern edge of the pond, you pass the intersection with the spur trail, several places campers have used, and a smooth rock that leads to a good swimming spot.

There is no mystery about the name Crane, for old-timers tell stories of crane nesting in the vicinity of the pond. However, the mountain's namesake pond, which lies nestled on a shelf west of the summit, has provoked comment. There are rumors that it has no outlet and that it has two outlets. There is some truth to both. Midsummer droughts can so reduce water draining into the pond that no water flows from it along the principal outlet to the southwest, which you will soon cross. A swamp on the north of the pond drains into Crystal Brook, and in high water times water sometimes also flows into the brook, seeping from the swamp as if from a hidden outlet of the lake.

It is 1 mile from the summit to the outlet of the pond, which you cross to begin the steep descent toward Putnam Farm. Again, if you are adventurous, you can easily make your way north-northwest along the top of Crane's western summit ridge toward several other outcrops with good vantages south and west.

Crane, like all the mountains west of the Hudson, was scoured by the glacier, leaving a gentler slope on the northwest but scraping smooth the cliffs on the southeastern flanks. And, like many neighboring mountains, Crane was ravaged by forest fires so intense that the thin organic topsoils that had accumulated since the last glacier were also consumed. The pattern of open rock interwoven with pockets of shallow mineral soils is typical. From the pockets spread the pioneering lichens and mosses that slowly create soil to support scrub balsam, spruce, and birch. In June, pink lady's slippers thrive beneath the evergreens. And along the sunny edges, blueberries produce abundant crops.

Stay on the trail beyond the outlet crossing for the smooth, rounded slopes are deceptively steep. This trail is steeper than the route up, dropping nearly 900 feet in little more than .5 mile. It heads east-southeast, generally following the outlet and crossing it after about a 200-foot drop in elevation from the pond. This is the only place you may have problems on the descent. Stay close to the stream and do not venture out on the escarpment.

After .4 mile the trail heads south, away from the stream, to intersect Putnam Farm Road. Just before reaching the road, about .8 mile from the pond, the trail crosses a stream on a natural stone bridge. The tiny stream disappears into a cave of Precambrian marble, and re-emerges about 50 feet away, only to disappear permanently in a still larger cave. The cap of granitic gneiss that constitutes the bulk of Crane Mountain overlays a belt of marble. There is a second layer of marble and easily eroded rock at the level of the pond; it has been worn away to create the bench that contains the pond and gives Crane its distinctive stepped profile.

Beyond the cave, turn left to follow the old road toward your car. Both the roadway and a bypass, .2 mile from the parking area, are marked. The bypass circles private land to reach the trailhead.

You can make the circuit described in four hours, but I have never spent less than six hours on the mountain. There is so much to see and enjoy that you may want to plan an even longer trip.

30

Siamese Ponds

Distance (round trip): 13.2 miles
Vertical rise: 600 feet
Hiking time: 7 hours
Map: USGS 15' Thirteenth Lake
Siamese Ponds Wilderness Area

The Siamese Ponds are a favorite southern Adirondack camping destination. They lie at the heart of the Siamese Ponds Wilderness Area, a region so remote that the trails to them are the only break in some fifty square miles of surrounding forest.

The Siamese Ponds access trails are among the few marked, state-maintained trails in the Wilderness Area. Most other destinations in this forest are reached by either informal paths or bushwhacks (see *Discover the Adirondacks, I* for details of over ninety nearby trips).

Hikers carrying a pack for overnight camping need four hours for the roughly 6.6-mile trek into the ponds, but day hikers can make the 13.2-mile round trip in seven hours. That is just walking time, though. You should add at least three more hours for exploring, swimming, and picnicking.

This hike follows the East Branch of the Sacandaga access trail, which begins on NY 8 between Wells and Wevertown. If you are traveling from the south or west, turn east on NY 8

at the intersection of NY 8 and NY 30 north of Wells, and drive 13.5 miles northeast. That section of Highway follows the East Branch of the Sacandaga River and is one of the prettiest drives in the mountains. Coming from the east or north, the trailhead is 4 miles southwest of Bakers Mills on NY 8, south of Wevertown. The trailhead is designated by a state historical marker, and the trail is marked with both the blue hiking and yellow ski-touring disks used on state-maintained trails.

You begin by climbing 200 feet up the shoulder of Eleventh Mountain in .5 mile and then dropping 400 feet to the valley of the East Branch of the Sacandaga in a little over 1 mile. The short pitch on the latter rise always seems formidable to tired hikers on their return.

The trail reaches the confluence of Diamond Brook and the Sacandaga in a most attractive beaver meadow. From the flow you can see the cliffs on Diamond Mountain on the north, those on Square Falls Mountain in the southwest, and the highest of all, those ranging across Eleventh Mountain back to the southeast.

The trail continues east-northeast beside the river for a little over 2 miles to a junction. Occasionally, where the valley is very narrow, you walk close to the water, but most of the time the route is back from the river on slightly higher ground. The trail you are following was once a principal route north, used by loggers and tan-barkers to transport logs and hemlock bark from the interior to mills along the river at Oregon and Griffin or east to settlements in the Town of Johnsburg. The trail was thus designed for practicability, not for the scenery.

You see few signs of the early settlers; only their names survive. Big and Little Hopkins mountains to the west were named for two brothers who joined the settlement near the Curtis Clearing. That clearing was named for Norman and William Curtis, who settled in the area after 1865 and whose sisters, Eliza and Electra, married the Hopkins brothers. Later, John Sawyer harvested timber

in the area now called Burnt Shanty Clearing, which is halfway between the Diamond Brook crossing and the intersection.

At the trail junction the right fork heads due north toward Thirteenth Lake. You want the left fork, which continues near the river for .5 mile to a lean-to by an enormous modern hikers' bridge, a few feet upstream from the ford used by outfitters who transported hunters and their camping gear into the wilderness via horse and wagon.

The trail to the ponds heads west, circling the southern edge of the flows that edge Siamese Brook, and then swinging north around Siamese Mountain. After the trail crosses Siamese Brook, it begins to climb toward the west-southwest, rising 300 feet to a plateau before dropping to the shore of the eastern pond. You will probably notice the climb only if you are carrying a heavy pack.

Several campsites edge the trail and the eastern lake's western shore. Another choice camping spot can be found on the spit of land separating the ponds. Occasionally, you will find

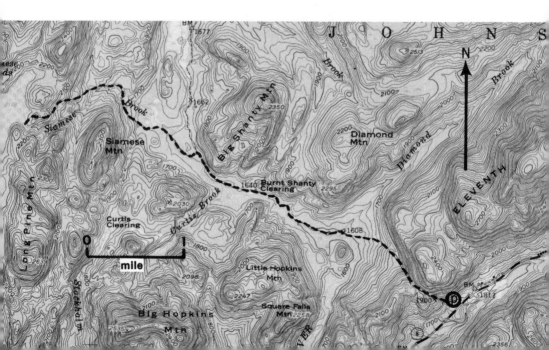

Diamond Brook Flow on the East Branch Sacandaga Trail

a rowboat on the eastern lake suitable for the trip across to the western lake. Many campers bring inflatable boats to Siamese Ponds, a wise move for those who wish to fish or simply to get away from other campers.

As you explore the ponds, you may find it hard to believe that the area was once heavily logged, and that not too many years ago a guest cabin for hunters was maintained on the eastern lake shore. If you are spending the night, you may have to share the lakes with other campers, but it is usually possible to find a camping spot in a hidden cove or bay, away from everyone else.

31

Chimney Mountain

Distance (round trip): 2.5 miles
Vertical rise: 900 feet
Hiking time: 4 hours
Map: USGS 15' Thirteenth Lake
Siamese Ponds Wilderness Area

Chimney Mountain serves as an excellent introduction to the story of the rock mass that underlies the Adirondack landscape. Nowhere is that geological tale more vividly depicted. Hiking Chimney Mountain takes you back millions of years to the birth of these mountains and allows you to confront directly the results of many of the forces that shaped today's Adirondacks. This adventure to columns, caves, and crevices is as exciting as any climb up a "big" mountain.

The story of the Adirondacks begins about 1.4 billion years ago with the Grenville Sea, a shallow body of water. Slowly, throughout the Precambrian period, sediment accumulated in this sea, which remained at a fairly constant shallow depth because the sea bottom gradually subsided under the increasing weight of the deposits. Sediments finally filled the trough, or geosyncline, to a depth of over 40,000 feet. Layers of sand, clay, and calcium carbonates from land on the west were sandwiched between layers of volcanic ash and lava from a ring of islands to the east.

About 1.1 billion years ago, cataclysmic forces buckled these sedimentary rock layers, thrusting up a chain of young mountains, many of which reached elevations of over 20,000 feet. The Grenville Orogeny, as this mountain-building period is called, created extremely high pressures, transforming the compressed sedimentary rock into gneisses, marble quartzite, and other metamorphic rock, and warping and distorting the stratified layers.

Igneous matter then penetrated the mass. The heat deep within the mountains' core was so intense it caused some of the rock to melt, ultimately producing granite, gabbro, syenite, and anorthosite. These igneous masses metamorphosed and intruded the overlying layers.

The cores of those young mountains are today's Adirondacks, but only the rocks themselves can be recognized as belonging to that distant time. The landscape has completely changed. Erosion has worn down the peaks and filled the valleys with sediments. The period of erosion was so prolonged that it exposed the anorthosite intrusions that are now seen in the High Peaks.

Later upheavals created the long faults whose valleys are today dotted with lakes and whose sides form the steep cliff faces of the ridge mountains. The glaciers, which last receded only 10,000 years ago, then removed most of the overlying soil and bared anew the mountain tops, scraping them into the forms of today.

Where exposed, the softer Grenville deposits—the rocks that were formed first in this series of events—eroded away. Today, Grenville rocks are generally only found deep in valleys where overlying rock has only been cut away in recent geologic time. Chimney Mountain is an exception. Here is a *mountain* formed of Grenville deposits. It is theorized that the harder layers of igneous rock that protected the mountain was worn away as recently as the last ice age.

Finally, a force, small in comparison with previous geologic events, caused a triangular block on the western face of Chimney Mountain to tip and fall away, leaving a deep rift valley near the summit. It looks as if a giant cleaver had hacked apart the mountain, exposing on both sides of the fracture identical lines in the geologic record. A tumble of boulders and rock fills the valley, creating caves and crevices that extend several hundred feet. The most dramatic remains of all is the column standing above the rim of the eastern face of the valley, the towering "chimney" for which the mountain is named.

The rift valley is 600 feet long, ranging in width up to 250 feet and in depth to 200 feet. The Chimney itself rises 35 feet above the eastern rim, which falls beneath the Chimney, presenting a vertical drop of over 80 feet. Most of the caves that fill the valley and line the western rim should

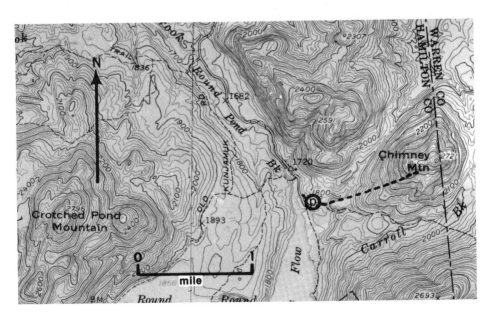

be explored only by those with spelunking experience and equipment. A detailed map of the caves and paths through the valley is given in my *Discover the Adirondacks, I.* For a marvelous introduction to the geology of the Adirondacks, you should also look at Van Diver's *Rocks and Routes of the North Country.*

To reach Chimney Mountain, you drive south on NY 30 from Indian Lake village for .6 mile to Big Brook Road, on the left. Approaching from the south on NY 30, you drive along Indian Lake, one of the Adirondack's longest lake-filled fault valleys. From this direction Big Brook Road is a sharp right turn at the bottom of the hill below the marked scenic overlook. You will be disappointed if you stop there for a look east to Chimney, because the mountain is tucked behind intervening hills, but the view is great, nonetheless.

Driving southeast on Big Brook Road, you cross the Abanakee Causeway. At 1.5 miles, turn right, or south, continuing on Big Brook Road. There is a second, unmarked, right turn about 2.2 miles farther. Continue 2.5 miles from that fork to the end of the road at Kings Flow, by a former Scout camp. Before its closing, hikers were permitted to park for a fee and cross the campgrounds to the trail on state land. You should still park in the designated area.

Walk east through the field beside the large barn that occupies the camp's northeast corner. Immediately east of that building a footpath leads into the forest. This is the route up Chimney Mountain. Easy to follow, it curves from due east to northeast as it approaches the crest of the mountain. The 900-foot, 1.25-mile climb takes under an hour.

At 1.1 miles you reach the first overlook with views back across Kings Flow. The overlook is just south of the rift valley. Immediately beyond the overlook, the path forks. The way left leads to the west rim; the way right, to the Chimney.

Bear right and continue climbing until you enter a walled corridor beneath ledges that extend from 8 to 15 feet above the path. Just as you enter this draw, note the small path heading down into the rift on your left, for you return here after inspecting the Chimney and absorbing the view. For starters, climb now to the top of the ledges on your right, from their northern end. From here the views of the mountains north of NY 28 are spectacular, with Vanderwhacker's cone silhouetted against the High Peaks.

Return to the end of the draw and make the 8-foot climb over the ledge to the left. It leads to an outcrop that overlooks both the valley below and the Chimney above. Be careful near the cliff edge. If you walk around the Chimney on its eastern side, by first descending from your outcrop directly to the Chimney's base, you find a window in the boulders that artfully frames the view of the western rim.

When you return to the draw to find the path into the rift, be careful. Although it is not quite as steep as others, it is still a precipitous drop to the rift floor. Diverse paths lead through the valley, and you will want to poke about as much as time and ability allow. In summer blasts of cold air emerge from the deeper crevices, and sometimes bursts of fog alert you to their presence. The walk-

The Chimney

ing is very rough, and it is easy to jam a foot in a crack between rocks.

The north wall of the rift valley is a jumble of broken rock and talus rising about 12 feet. You can climb its western corner and find several large holes and a cave with ice in early July. If you walk across the valley floor on any of many footpaths to the southwest corner, you will pass several large openings. Shine a flashlight in them. One cave has a distinctive round opening about 4 feet in diameter facing north at the edge of a huge free-standing boulder. It drops 6 feet to a ledge from which you can almost always see ice and icicles in the late summer.

After you have explored the valley, continue southwest, walking behind the rock that shields that ledge-cave, to find the unmarked path up the west wall. (Remember, all of this is really bushwhacking, improvising your own route, for no path in the valley is marked. It is a small area so you are not apt to lose your way, but do watch your footing at every step.)

As you climb out of the valley toward the west wall, a narrow spine of rock, look for a clearly defined, but still unmarked footpath. Turn right, uphill, on it to find the highest

overlook along the wall. Here, the view of the Chimney is spectacular, with the lines showing variations in the Grenville deposits clearly defined.

There is also a great view to the southwest. Beyond Kings Flow, Round Pond is visible, flanked on the north by Crotched Pond Mountain and on the south by Kunjamuk Mountain. Farther south, the split cone of Humphrey Mountain rises over the end of Kings Flow. Only the tops of Snowy and Squaw mountains on the west side of Indian Lake show above the intervening range.

The path leads south along the west rim for a quick descent to the fork above the first lookout. Several paths diverge from it, some leading back along the west face of that rim to deep and usually ice-filled crevices. You continue angling to the east to rejoin the path to Kings Flow.

Only the main footpath up the mountain is formally marked, so you should have a map and compass for this trip. You will also want a flashlight. Do not attempt to go in any of the caves without proper equipment, and knowledgeable and experienced leaders. I cannot stress enough that the majority of the caves are for experts only.

32

Pillsbury Mountain

Distance (round trip): 9 miles
Vertical rise: 1,887 feet
Hiking time: 5½ hours
Maps: USGS 15' West Canada Lakes, USGS 15' Indian Lake
Fire Tower; closed Wednesday, Thursday

The hike to the Pillsbury Mountain fire tower is long and challenging. However, the view from the summit is considered by many to be the most exciting of any of the Adirondacks' fire towers. The intimate look it permits of the Adirondacks' most remote, inaccessible, and hidden lakes and forest region, the Canada Lake Wilderness Area, makes Pillsbury a must on anyone's list.

There are four gateways to the West Canada Wilderness: a long trail from the north that begins after a tedious drive along a dirt road into the Moose River Plains; the Northville-Placid Trail from the northeast starting at the Cedar River Flow; the Northville-Placid Trail from the south starting at Piseco; and a route, principally on logging roads through disturbed lands, from the east. The trail to Pillsbury Mountain begins from this eastern access to the Wilderness.

Inaccessibility has always enhanced the romantic aura surrounding the West Canadas, but the exploits of one of the region's former inhabitants, the trapper French Louie, have added spice to that image.

French Louie's trap lines were strung between the region's lakes, circling the interior wilds. He knew every fishing hole in the wilderness and harvested hundreds of deer, bear, martin, beaver, mink, and otter skins. Each year, using part of the route you will follow on your trek to Pillsbury Mountain, he walked from his home on West Lake or from his shanty on Whitney Lake to Newton Corners, now Speculator, pulling a sled piled high with skins. These he exchanged for money, which in turn was exchanged for the whiskey that fueled some of the north woods' most notorious drinking bouts. Stories of his excesses and antics survive in tales contemporaries related to Harvey L. Dunham. His book, *French Louie, Early Life in the North Woods*, is your best introduction to the West Canada Wilderness, as well as a most amusing account of nineteenth-century life in the backwoods.

The road north from Speculator to Indian Lake originally passed through Perkins Clearing before heading west into the wilderness. One mile or so west of Perkins Clearing, the road reached Sled Harbor where the condi-

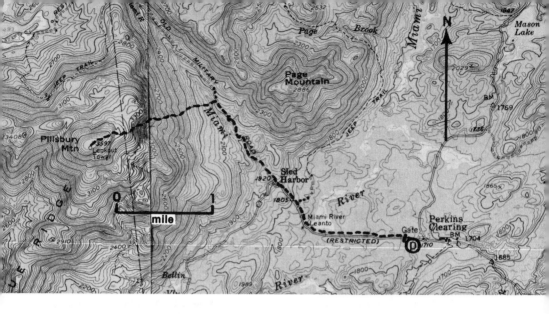

tion of the roads originally demanded that wagonloads be shifted to sleds or sledges before continuing to distant lumber camps. Then the road, following precisely the route of the military road laid out in the War of 1812 to transport men and munitions from Albany to Sackett's Harbor, headed northwest through the Miami River valley between Pillsbury and Page mountains. Branches of the road reached Pillsbury Lake and the Cedar Lakes.

A trail now follows part of that road before heading southwest to the Pillsbury Mountain fire tower. The road sections are currently being used for logging operations by International Paper Company. The road, and hence part of Pillsbury's trail, passes through land that is a checkerboard of state forest and heavily timbered paper company holdings. A proposed land swap would consolidate the various parcels and provide future wilderness protection for this eastern flank of the West Canadas. For the present, however,

the 3 miles you hike toward Pillsbury, following the old roads, is not particularly exciting, in spite of its long and varied history.

No signs guide you to the tower until you come within 1.5 miles of the summit. Even the route to trailhead parking near Perkins Clearing is not correctly shown on the current USGS sheet. The southern part of the loop road connecting Perkins Clearing to NY 30 is shown on the USGS sheet, but it is not usable today. From either the south or north, the approach is by a dirt road that heads southsouthwest from NY 30 just north of Mason Lake. The turnoff is 16 miles south of Indian Lake village and NY 28 and 8 miles north of Speculator. The road follows the west side of Mason Lake, passing many campsites near the lake's shore. Drive 3.3 miles to an intersection, where a state historic marker says that the road was the first New York State trail marked for recreational use. The date given is in the 1920s. Turn right, west, and in .3 mile you reach a pair of small parking turnouts on opposite sides of the road, beyond which a barrier stops all but DEC or logging traffic. There is a trail register near the barrier.

The trail, designated by not more than one or two old markers on telephone poles alongside the dirt road, runs through logged forests. Within fifteen minutes you pass a spruce bog, filled in early July with blue flag. The hill ahead is part of Pillsbury. The walking is so easy you cover the 1 mile distance to the Miami River within twenty minutes. You cross on a substantial log bridge. Beyond the river there is a lean-to on a knoll on the left. In five minutes you reach a junction, where a road bears right, north, along the Miami River, but you stay left, or more precisely, straight ahead. A canopy of tall trees shades the roadway most of the time.

The road angles south up a small hill, rounding a gravel pit. One hundred yards past the pit a smaller roadway makes a ninety-degree turn to the right. Turn right at this intersection, which is marked with a sign simply reading "trail." By now you have walked nearly 2 miles, climbing only 200 feet.

Within 200 yards there is another barrier across the road. You begin to hear the Miami River, and shortly the road swings close to the river, following it through a lovely valley. It should take less than an hour to reach a little cabin made of birch logs. It is typical of the hunting cabins scattered about on land leased from the paper company. Just beyond, a marked trailhead indicates the road ahead leads to the Cedar Lakes, Pillsbury Lake, and the West Canadas. The distances given are not accurate, and the elevation given for Pillsbury Mountain is not accurate,

either. However, the start up Pillsbury, to the left, is correctly and clearly marked.

The trail begins as a very narrow and little-used footpath leading downhill to the Miami River. You may want to fill your canteen here, although there is a small spring near the summit. A single split-log bridge crosses the tiny stream, which is here overwhelmed by the appelation "river." On the far side you climb immediately, and within fifteen minutes you are rising at an incredible rate. The steep pitch leaves you puffing, and the grade only gets steeper.

The handsome woods surrounding the Miami River soon give way to solid beech groves, stands where the die-back is just beginning to change the forest cover. At first the trail does relatively little traversing across the hillside. It just heads straight up. Within thirty minutes you notice a lot of blowdowns, the beech of course, but also good-sized birch and striped maples, making the mountainside a scene of desolation. You zigzag under telephone lines for the tower, climbing steadily. A few erratics perch on the hillside. In some sections, the treetops have been lopped off, creating a weird and eerie scene of destruction. Through the trees you can make out Page Mountain and the outline of the Miami River valley north toward Lewey Lake. You may want to pause beside the stump of a huge yellow birch that once grew from a boulder beside the trail. Beyond the boulder the trail levels in a fern meadow remarkable for the lack of forest cover. Grasses, sorrel, and viburnum grow beneath the few spruce. On the next rise the trail is worn to bedrock with seepage, so the footing is slippery.

Changes in the forest cover are

Pillsbury fire tower

your clues to how far you have climbed within an hour of crossing the Miami River. Spruce, birch, and balsam predominate, and bunchberry and blueberries fill the spaces between ledges. Sections of corduroy pave damp patches of sphagnum that fill niches in the bedrock. Trees less than twenty feet tall shade patches of golden thread and scrub evergreens.

Approximately an hour and twenty minutes from the Miami River you might notice a trail leading back off to your left. This is an old route to the summit. Five minutes later the trail forks. The way right leads 150 yards to a spring. The left fork starts to climb again, steeply over ledges. Suddenly the cover opens, providing a spectacular view northeast past Indian Lake to the High Peaks. You must stop here for a picture.

A little more climbing brings you to the summit, which you cross on a narrow rock ridge, spotting the tower after some two hours and fifty minutes of hiking. The narrow trail to the summit from the river is not much more than 1.5 miles long, but the 1,700 feet it rises will restrict you to a slow pace.

The tower is manned and open to the public. Many points on the horizon should be obvious. Due north lies Wakely, and to its left, west-northwest of the tower, Manbury and Little Moose mountains rise above portions of the Cedar Lakes. Both mountains have open rock slides. To the right of Wakely, Blue Mountain presents its rocky southern slopes. In the foreground to the northeast, Blue Ridge and Cellar mountains lead to cone-shaped Lewey Mountain. Panther is the peak to the right of Lewey, and next, Snowy's unmistakable profile rises above the valley of Indian Lake.

To the right of Snowy, over the north end of Indian Lake, stretches one of the most exciting views in the Adirondacks. The eastern High Peaks, 50 miles distant in the northeast, are clearly visible above the lowland valleys of Indian Lake and the Boreas River. Only a couple of intervening mountains interrupt the string of summits.

Rock faces, scars, and slides present clearly recognizable patterns on the distant peaks. To the left of Indian Lake the mountain with two big open rock patches flanking its bare summit is Gothics. Between it and Snowy, but hardly obvious, lie Mount Marcy and Haystack. To the right of the foot of Indian Lake lies Vanderwhacker, and to its right on the horizon the outline of a range of mountains traces the shape of a bracket pointing skyward. The apex of the bracket is Hough, with McComb and Dix flanking it, each baring rock slides that appear nearly identical at this distance.

Closer to Pillsbury the mountains east of Indian Lake are readily identified. These include Bullhead, Puffer, and Gore with its rock cut. Crane Mountain lies due east on the horizon, almost in line with Dug Mountain. Whitaker Lake is visible southwest of Dug's summit, and the Kunjamuk Valley is outlined beyond it. A little east of south, Speculator Mountain rises behind Lake Pleasant. Much of Sacandaga Lake is also visible. Southeast from the lakes lies the valley of Piseco Lake, and you should be able to recognize the mountains on its western shore.

In the west you can see the valley of the West Canada Creek stretching to the horizon. Nearer the tower you can spot a corner of Pillsbury Lake, and beyond it, Noisey Ridge, with more bare rock patches. Hills behind the West Canada Lakes also have rock slides and cliffs. Perhaps the most striking aspect of the view from Pillsbury is the number of hillsides with open rock ledges. Because many of the smaller lakes are concealed between rugged hills, relatively little water is visible.

The trip back is easy and uneventful.

33

Snowy Mountain

Distance (round trip): 7.5 miles
Vertical rise: 2,100 feet
Hiking time: 6 hours
Map: USGS 15' Indian Lake
West Canada Lake Wilderness Area

Some trails require and deserve rich and detailed descriptions. Others need only be located, for the route is obvious once you have arrived. The trail to Snowy Mountain is of the latter kind. The mountain is, after all, the Mount Marcy of the southern Adirondacks—it is the tallest and the most popular, with an overly worn trail to prove it. However, while this guide omits the trail up Mount Marcy on the grounds that it is often "as busy as a walk down 42nd Street," Snowy cannot be overlooked. Its views are too spectacular, and its striking profile too important as a reference from every other mountain in the southern and eastern Adirondacks. You have only to see its angular summit or its cliffs reflecting white in the sun and you know you must climb it. And even though you can no longer climb Snowy's closed fire tower, you will be able to pick out a vast number of the Adirondack's mountain tops from Snowy's cliff top vantages.

So, choose a brilliant day, in midweek if possible, and be rewarded with a solitary walk to this magnificent peak. Though long, and pre-

cipitously steep near the summit, the trail is easy enough to follow. NY 30 is the access route; when it was recently improved, a parking turnout for the trailhead was constructed on the east shoulder. The turnout is 17 miles north of Speculator and 7 miles south of Indian Lake village.

The trail, marked with blue trail disks, begins directly opposite the turnout. Rising 2,100 feet in just 3.7 miles, the trail is among the most challenging in the southern Adirondacks, so allow plenty of time.

The first 2.5 miles is over rolling terrain, and the climb is gentle, as you only gain 800 feet in that distance. The trail is fairly well maintained, with some wet places, but the markers are sparse. The foot tread is so obvious markers are unnecessary, though.

The trail heads northwest at first, through a mature forest of aspen; white and yellow birch; striped, red, and sugar maple; and beech interspersed with balsam, spruce, and hemlock. Within 1.1 miles you approach Beaver Brook, which accompanies the trail at varying distances for another 1.5 miles. The trail

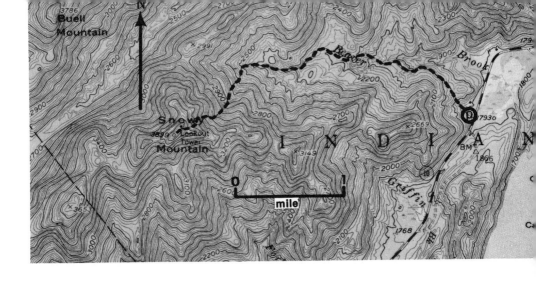

crosses it several times. It is a source of drinking water, and informal campsites near it beckon backpackers. After the second crossing, at 1.9 miles, the trail is quite close to the brook or one of its tributaries for .6 mile.

It is in the last 1.2 miles or so that you encounter steep pitches, with the last .5 mile so steep you have to use your hands. Only old blazes and cairns indicate this section of trail at present, but there is little chance of becoming confused. Approximately 3.2 miles from the trailhead the trail branches. The way left leads to a brook for drinking water and a rest. Continue on the right branch, where the real climbing begins.

The summit of Snowy is so steep that little realignment of the trail would even be possible, in spite of considerable erosion. The trail is worn to bedrock, deeply cut through the soil in places, but fairly stable. In wet weather, danger exists both for the trail and hikers, however, for then you are forced off the slippery rock to the sides. Pulling at trees and roots for support further erodes the trail sides. Old and unused telephone lines

leading to the abandoned fire tower also litter the trail, providing other hazards.

In the last .5 mile, the forest changes dramatically from tall to scrub trees, mostly balsam, mountain ash, white birch, and striped maple. Long before you reach the summit you can enjoy views of the mountains on the east side of Indian Lake. The trail climbs through a draw between two cliffs and emerges on the top of the eastern cliff beside the fire observer's abandoned cabin. Nearby there is a spring and the best ledges from which to enjoy a view of Indian Lake.

You should be able to pick out Crotched Pond and Kunjamuk mountains a little south of east, across Indian Lake. Behind them range Bullhead, Puffer, and Humphrey, the latter a distinctive, regular cone. On the horizon between Crotched Pond and Kunjamuk mountains, the slash of the Barton garnet mine clearly identifies Gore Mountain. Farther to the south, right, is the broad summit of Eleventh Mountain, and beyond, to the right, is Crane Mountain, whose summit is 24 miles distant. You may be confused by the jumble of hills farther south; the view of them was better from the tower.

Walk west from the cabin to an open rock ledge on the west side of the summit. Narrow footpaths winding across the scrub covering the summit lead you to it. The rock surmounts a cliff, so wooded that it is scarcely noticeable from western vantages; however, the opening provides my favorite vista from Snowy. The dense row of hills, in which Snowy is almost central, is cut with a deep cleft valley trending northeast to southwest. The heavily wooded and remote valley is really not obvious from many other points, but it is one of the Adirondack's deeper ones. Two brooks rise in the valley, Squaw, which flows northeast into Indian Lake, and Little Squaw, which flows southwest into the Cedar River Flow. The valley is bordered on the east by Squaw, Snowy, and Lewey mountains and on the west by a steep little knob called Onion Hill on the USGS map, and by Buck, Buell, and Panther mountains, ranging to the north. The latter's summit is only 34 feet lower than Snowy's. Panther's peak is toward magnetic north from Snowy, and to its right is Burgess Mountain.

Beyond Lewey Mountain is a chain of mountains. Cellar is to its left, south, with Blue Ridge Mountain between them. Farther to the right of Cellar you can spot Pillsbury Mountain, which lies, as does Snowy, on the edge of the West Canada Wilderness.

Farther to the south you can see Lewey Lake, and the long finger of Indian Lake that fills the valley through which the Jessup River once flowed. To the east of south, Dug Mountain is obvious.

Returning to Panther, look to its

Indian Lake from Snowy

south for Buell Mountain. Immediately south of Buell, in the distance, is Wakely, which also has a fire tower (see Hike 34). To its right on the horizon you should be able to spot West Mountain, exactly 20 miles distant.

You need a really clear day and good binoculars to pick out the High Peaks. While views from the north summit both east and west are marvelous, the tower certainly did enhance the most distant views.

To name the High Peaks, start again with Panther. To its right and 12 miles away lies the top of Blue Mountain. Moving around to the right, on the distant horizon, you should be able to identify the Seward Range, in which Seymour presents the most obvious shape, a steep cone. Santanoni is next, a huge mountain on the horizon. It is reported that the top of Whiteface can be seen above the right side of Santanoni, but it is 51 miles away and requires a perfectly clear day. I have never been certain that I could see it.

Moving to the east, right, MacIntyre is obvious, as is the cleft of Indian Pass that precedes it. The sharp valley to the right of MacIntyre is Avalanche Pass, and to its right range Colden, March, and Haystack, 36 miles away. The jagged summits that follow are the Gothics and Sawteeth, the Nippletop. Vanderwhacker is the isolated mountain in the mid-distance; it lies between the Hudson Valley and the High Peaks, in line with the eastern range of the High Peaks and the end of Indian Lake.

Even with this outline and the appropriate USGS maps, you may at first have trouble recognizing the profiles of distant mountains. In your climbs you will find that the change in perspective from one crest to another completely alters the distant profiles, so it may take several trips before the mountains become familiar. Snowy is a marvelous place to begin to make their acquaintance.

Wakely Mountain

Distance (round trip): 6.4 miles
Vertical rise: 1,636 feet
Hiking time: 3 hours
Maps: USGS 15' West Canada Lakes, USGS 15' Blue Mountain,
  USGS 15' Indian Lake
Fire Tower; closed Mondays, Tuesdays

In 1978 only 200 visitors made the climb to Wakely, while 5,200 made the trek up Blue Mountain, just 11 miles away. Perhaps the long drive to the trailhead on Cedar River Road deters some people, but that trek is part of the fun of discovering Wakely. Wakely's fire tower is still manned, at present by a friendly young ranger.

The Cedar River Flow, a long lake, begins .3 mile beyond the Wakely trailhead, and it is a popular camping spot as well as a gateway to the Moose River Plains (Hike 15). Consider camping there when you climb Wakely.

Hikers who become acquainted with the Adirondacks by approaches from the south and east are often unaware of Wakely's existence, because from that direction it is hidden by the range of mountains west of Indian Lake. However, if you hike the low hills in the northern and western Adirondacks, you soon discover how commanding a position Wakely holds. The panorama from its summit includes the only overview of the Moose River Plains, which reach

to the southwestern horizon.

The fact that Little Moose and Manbury mountains block the view to the southwest and to Cedar and West Canada lakes, is more than compensated by the view to the east over the Cedar River Flow and valley, which leads up to the western profiles of Panther and Snowy mountains. Best of all, the Cedar River Valley opens out to permit a view north-northeast to the High Peaks.

To reach the trailhead, drive west from Indian Lake village on NY 30-NY 28. You cross the Cedar River in just under 2 miles. Cedar River Road is a left, west, turn at the point the highway turns north .2 mile beyond the bridge.

William D. Wakeley, a British-born hotelkeeper, pushed this road through to Cedar River Falls, where in the 1870s he built a dam, a sawmill, and a hotel. His Cedar Falls Hotel was "so remote that each night bonfires were required during his first season to keep the wolves from his tethered oxen. The impressive hotel had a three-story main building, with two-

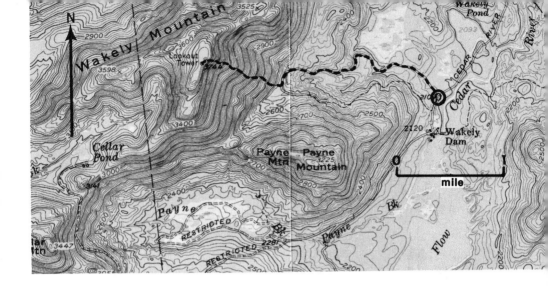

story wings, and sported a bar." According to his advertisements in Wallace's *Guide to the Adirondacks* of 1878, his hotel was located in the finest sporting grounds of the Adirondacks, and his table abounded with game and fish. The hotel burned in 1878 and was rebuilt on a smaller scale, only to burn again in 1884. Wakeley apparently spelled his name with a second e although the USGS map spells the flow and mountain named for him without it.

Throughout the late 1800s Wakeley ran a stage from North Creek to Blue Mountain, with connecting coaches to the Cedar Falls Hotel. At that time, the main road from Indian Lake followed the Cedar River Road south to a dirt road that is now the route of the Northville-Placid Trail between McCanes and Lake Durant.

Cedar River Road changes from macadam to dirt within 3 miles from NY 30, and it is so rough you need at least forty-five minutes to drive the 12 miles to the Cedar River Flow. On the way west the road intersects the Northville-Placid Trail at McCanes.

From McCanes south the trail follows the road for the 7.1 miles to the flow. Near McCanes the handsome view southwest across nearby fields is of Burgess and Panther mountains.

With the exception of a short stretch within 1 mile of NY 28-NY 30, the Cedar River is just out of sight. The guideposts along the road are a series of short hills to the west; Round Top is first in the north; Sugarloaf with its dramatic rock face is next, and Water Barrel is just north of Wakely Pond. Sugarloaf's resemblance to an old-fashioned cone of sugar is so striking that the mountain actually looks like a miniature of its Brazilian counterpart. Your best view of it is looking north from the road, 2 miles north of Wakely Dam.

You will cross the outlet of Wakely Pond 5.5 miles south of the Northville-Placid Trailhead. Pause a moment on the causeway to view Wakely and its tower, and then continue a little over .6 mile to a dirt road on the right. This tote road is marked as the trailhead for Wakely Mountain. Do not try to drive on it. It leads to logging

operations on private land and may be improved in the future, but its current condition is marginal.

The roadway is marked with red trail disks and heads west through a scrub forest of popple interspersed with spruce thickets. The road fords a small stream at .2 mile and continues with the stream close on the left, or south. As you walk you have occasional glimpses of Wakely. Some of the surroundings appear to be fields returning to the forest, and you will spot the remains of several buildings. The trees beside the road are uniformly small and dense, with several unusual patches of cherry saplings. The road begins to climb gradually past a swamp, and as it makes a long curve to the left, another road enters from the right at an acute angle. All this occurs within the first mile and twenty minutes.

After crossing a bridge you pick up another stream on your left, this time the beautiful brook that feeds the swamp. You continue beside it and its merry, tumbling course, and the only indication that the tiny stream could be anything but innocuous are the deep cuts and huge stones in the road, washed out by a raging overflow. As you continue gently uphill you can see the tower ahead.

You cross a brook on a washed-out bridge, and within ten more minutes reach a sign pointing right, 1.2 miles to the tower. Here you leave the tote road and begin climbing a foot trail. The rest of the way is steep, for you still have 1,200 feet to gain before reaching summit. Plastic bottles on a tree at the intersection indicate that you should probably carry water to the summit. A spring near the summit

View from Wakely

is often inadequate even for the ranger, and the stream beside the tote road is good drinking water.

Red markers guide your way on the narrow footpath, a dry, hard-packed, little-used trail up the heavily logged hillside. A few old stumps indicate the size of the forests that once covered the mountain, but the walk is one of the longest through a scrub forest in the Adirondacks. International Paper Company owns most of the land over which the trail passes.

A mixture of beech, maple, and yellow birch gradually gives way to spruce, and finally balsam. A cherry railing helps to keep you on track when, forty-five minutes past the intersection, you find the trail becomes very steep, rocky, and a bit washed out. More railings guide you along the zigzag path through a largely evergreen forest to the summit and the tower.

You should reach the tower after walking an hour and forty-five minutes from Cedar River Road. You have to climb the tower for the view, for the summit is mostly tree-covered. The tower is ninety-two feet tall, the tallest in the Adirondacks. The fire observer is off on Monday and Tuesday, but on other days he will be able to help you orient landmarks.

Blue Mountain lies beyond the helicopter pad north of the tower. If you are lucky enough to have climbed on a really clear day, you should spot Whiteface in the distant north to its right. The eastern High Peaks range farther to the right, and you can name Santanoni, MacIntyre, Colden, Marcy, Haystack, Gothics, Giant, and Big Slide.

The view east is not as distant, for the range of mountains west of Indian Lake valley block the horizon. From north to south they are Panther,

Snowy with its tower, Lewey, Cellar, and Blue Ridge. Directly south lies Pillsbury Mountain, also topped by a tower.

The view west and northwest encompasses many lakes, with Fourth Lake, the largest of the Fulton Chain, beyond Lake Kora: Sagamore Lake north of Kora; and Raquette Lake to its north. West Mountain is visible across Raquette. The wooded summit of the Blue Ridge, the second group so named and visible from Wakely, shuts out a view of Blue Mountain Lake, but the tower on Blue is clearly visible. Rondaxe tower on Bald Mountain is visible on the rocky ledge overlooking Fourth Lake, and Goodnow tower can be seen in front of the High Peaks.

For the first part of your descent, you will find you are walking almost as slowly as you climbed, for the way is really steep. Still, a half-hour should see you past the worst, almost down to the tote road intersection. You should be able to make the return trip to your car in an hour and fifteen minutes.

Rock, Cascade and Stephens Pond

Distance (one way): 7.5 miles
Vertical rise: 370 feet
Hiking time: 4 hours
Map: USGS 15' Blue Mountain
Blue Ridge Wilderness Area

Lake Durant Campsite is an ideal location from which to discover the heart of the Adirondacks near Blue Mountain. If the weather is not clear enough for a mountain hike, you will enjoy the variety a visit to three remote ponds provides. A handsome loop connects Rock, Cascade, and Stephens ponds, all in the wilderness just south of Lake Durant. The eastern end of the loop terminates at the Lake Durant Campsite. The western end is at the opposite end of the lake. If you do not have two cars, one to leave at each end of the loop, you can make a full circuit by walking back along the highway between the two trailheads, adding 2.2 miles to the trip.

The entrance to the Lake Durant Campsite is on NY 30, 8.5 miles north of Indian Lake village and 2.5 miles southeast of Blue Mountain Lake and the junction of NY 30 and NY 28. On part of the loop you follow the Northville-Placid Trail, New York's famous trail that winds along both footpaths and roads, from Northville in the south, through wilderness areas and villages, to Lake Placid in the north, a distance of 119 miles. A park-

ing area for the Northville-Placid Trail is immediately west of the entrance to Lake Durant Campsite, and day hikers may wish to begin there to avoid the campsite's day-use parking fee.

Otherwise drive or walk west beside Lake Durant for 2 miles to Durant Road and bear left .2 mile to the trailhead. The trail begins by following a dirt road alongside a cemetery. The road goes to a picnic spot on the shore of Lake Durant, passing a big glacial erratic and an outhouse. The trail turns south opposite the outhouse. The intersection is not well marked, although there are some informal red blazes to indicate the trail, which immediately crosses a small stream on a footbridge. Now you see the first of the official red trail markers.

It is only .8 mile to the long bridge separating Rock Pond from Lake Durant. From the bridge Blue Mountain appears to loom over the water. Across the bridge the trail becomes a narrow footpath heading up and over a ridge. The route is so little used you really need the red markers here. As you cross the ridge you see a second hill across a small valley. A short, steep descent into that valley takes you to a small stream. Cross it and turn right to parallel it, climbing through the valley along the prettiest section of the day's hike. Tall, straight hardwoods make a forest so open you can see the hills on both sides.

At the head of the valley the trail turns left for the short climb southwest over the end of the ridge. A long, almost level stretch through a hemlock thicket follows before you reach a trail junction. The right fork is unmarked, but the left is designated as being .9 mile from Cascade Pond. The sign says it is 1.8 miles back to Rock Pond and 2.3 miles to Blue Mountain. The mileages on signs you see on this trip do not quite add up, but the walking time to this point is about 1 hour and fifteen minutes.

Bear left. The trail turns southeast to follow an obvious old road walled in with tall, straight hemlock and spruce. As you first approach Cascade Pond a path forks right to an evergreen-covered promontory with a good camping spot. The trail continues to a lean-to at the foot of the pond and there crosses the outlet on a collapsed bridge. Struggle across on the log remains. Recent beaver work has flooded the stream below the bridge, creating a new trout pond.

Southeast of Cascade Pond the trail is good and broad, offering a lovely twenty-minute walk through a forest with many white birch and lots of spring flowers. Then, for the next fifteen minutes, you descend slightly to an intersection 1 mile from the Cascade Pond lean-to, and .6 mile from the Stephens Pond lean-to to the right via the blue-marked Northville-

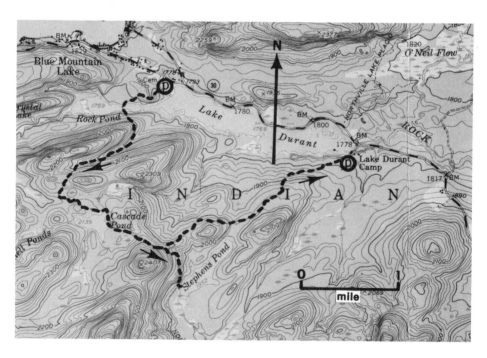

View across Lake Durant to Blue Mountain

Placid Trail. The left fork, also marked blue, heads 2.5 miles northeast to the Lake Durant Campsite.

Bear right to Stephens Pond. The walk is very pretty, heading east and then southeast down a long hill to the lean-to. You often find nesting loons and sometimes good fishing in the pond, though reputedly not as good as at Cascade Pond. Much of the shoreline is swampy, but there are several good campsites near the southwestern corner.

As you head back to the intersection and then on toward Lake Durant, you will be impressed by the width of the Northville-Placid Trail. The route northeast from the intersection runs moderately downhill a short distance and then slopes more gently the rest of the way to the campsite. Here the forest is less exciting, and the trail is fairly heavily used. It is typical of that trail's passage through the Adirondacks; in comparison, nearby routes are often much more fun.

Rock, Cascade and Stephens Ponds **175**

Blue Mountain

Distance (round trip): 4 miles
Vertical rise: 1,560 feet
Hiking time: 3½ hours
Map: USGS 15' Blue Mountain
Fire Tower; closed Thursday, Friday

A combination of extraordinary views and easy accessibility attract thousands of hikers yearly to the 3,759-foot summit of Blue Mountain. The 2-mile climb of 1,750 feet requires less than two hours and is not overly strenuous. The walk down usually takes only an hour and a half, so even with a picnic on top, exploring Blue Mountain is a half-day outing, allowing you plenty of time to visit the nearby Adirondack Museum at Blue Mountain Lake. The Museum is 1.1 miles north of the intersection of NY 28N and NY 30 and the trailhead is .4 miles north of the museum on NY 30.

If you make the climb in the early morning you can enjoy the play of sunlight across the Eckford Chain of lakes that stretch west from Blue Mountain to the distant horizon. If you visit the museum first and then climb the mountain, the western sun will best illuminate the distant crest of the eastern High Peaks. Either way, the museum is a good introduction to the Adirondacks. Hikers will find the museum's large relief map of the region especially appealing. Lights can be switched on to indicate many of the more famous mountains.

The Blue Mountain region was almost the first area in the Adirondacks to be developed as a resort. The first hotel was started on the lake's shores in 1874 by John Holland. The principal developer of this part of the Adirondack interior, however, was William West Durant, the son of the Union Pacific railroad baron who was also responsible for getting the first tracks to North Creek. The younger Durant invested his time and enthusiasm for the North Woods in acquiring huge tracts of land, including all of Township 34, in which the Eckford Chain of lakes lies. Blue Mountain Lake is the northernmost in that chain; Eagle and Utowana stretch to the southwest and are connected, via the Marion River and its famous carry, to Raquette Lake. Durant built for himself the magnificent Camp Pine Knot on Raquette Lake as well as several homes in the style the noted Adirondack writer Donaldson calls "Camp Beautiful" on nearby lakes, among them Uncas on the lake that now bears that name.

Durant also encouraged the development of Blue Mountain Lake.

But while Raquette Lake was "dominated by the camp beautiful idea, Blue Mountain succumbed, structurally, to the hotel horrible." The lake's original hotel took its name from the mountain that rises to the lake's east, and Blue Mountain became the dominant feature of the landscape in name as well as fact.

The mountain looms over the surrounding countryside, almost always appearing in shades of blue, a dark, imposing hulk, scarred on its southern face with rock slides and presenting a distinctive silhouette as a reference from almost every direction.

Driving north on NY 30 to Blue Mountain, watch for the signpost just north of Lake Durant that marks the divide between the St. Lawrence and Hudson River watersheds.

There is a new trailhead, at the height of land north of the museum, replacing the traditional beginning which crossed private lands. This new route, slightly longer than the original, saves about 200 feet of climbing. It commences from the same point as the trail to Tirrell Pond. The trailhead situation represents a rather typical Adirondack problem. While 40% of the Adirondack Parks is State land, only 10% of the land accessible to public roads is owned by the State. This creates many difficult situations throughout the park where access to public land is blocked. And, as in this case, private landowners have denied the public access over some traditional routes.

The Environmental Bond Act moneys are dedicated to the purchase of lands for the Forest Preserve and access sites are high on the list for purchase. When purchases are not desirable or possible, as in this case, the DEC has recently been active in securing easements and rights-of-way across private lands. Negotiations with private landowners, including Finch-Pruyn Lumber Company, made possible access over this new route.

Its beginning is more leisurely, rising 600 feet in 1.1 miles to intersect the old trail as it becomes quite steep, about forty-five minutes into the walk. That first section is all on private land and the new trail meets the old at the Forest Preserve boundary where a steep pitch begins beneath white birch towering over the balsam and spruce that fill out the forest.

After an hour, water from an intermittent stream may join the trail. The route is now very steep, so steep that sky seems to emerge deceptively through the evergreens, prematurely alerting you to the summit. After another twenty minutes, the trees are noticeably shorter, and soon the trail levels and becomes quite narrow as it passes through a boggy swale just below the summit. Some ten minutes later, you spot the tower and quickly reach the top.

The best views are from the tower. The sweep of ponds and lakes fading into the distant west is amazing. Blue Mountain's isolation from surrounding hills means the views are especially good. The closest summit that exceeds it in height is more than 12 miles away. Most spectacular is the vista northeast across Tirrell Pond to the outcrops of Tirrell Mountain. Beyond them rise Dun Brook Mountain on the right and Fishing Brook Range on the left, with many of the High Peaks recognizable on that distant horizon.

To the east you have the lovely view across Blue Mountain Lake and its sisters in the Eckford Chain. "Sisters" is appropriate, for originally all three lakes were named by the surveyor Emmons for the daughters of Henry

Eckford: Janet, Marion, and Catherine. Eckford first visited the lakes while participating in the 1811 State waterway survey.

You need the USGS Santanoni, Mount Marcy, and Lake Placid maps and a good pair of binoculars to help identify individual mountains. From right to left beyond the north side of Dun Brook Mountain are Dix, Colvin, Marcy, Colden, the MacIntyre Mountains, and Santanoni. The most distant identifiable peak is Whiteface, which appears behind Sawtooth, with Seward, Kempshall, and Ampersand filling out the row of significant summits to the north.

You would need quite a map folder to show all the peaks within Blue Mountain's viewing range. South of Dun Brook Mountain you can pick out Vanderwhacker, and if conditions are right, Pharaoh Mountain on the far eastern edge of the Adirondacks. In the south, Wakely is obvious, but Snowy is harder to spot because you see only a small portion of it behind

Panther. Immediately south lies Lake Durant, with Stephens Pond visible behind it. Completing the panorama back to Eagle and Utowana lakes are the Metcalf Mountains and the Blue Ridge.

Looking northwest across South Pond with its several islands, the double summit of Owls Head, with Mount Sabattis to its north and a little closer, completes the view back to the north and Kempshell. Once you have picked out the major peaks, you can more easily name the numerous bodies of water.

The northeast face of the summit is bare, so it offers good views without climbing the tower. There is a picnic table north of the tower, and several other places along the ridge are ideal for a picnic, offering a panorama of the sweep of mountains beyond Tirrell Mountain and Tirrell Pond. In 1853, Irish immigrants were brought to the shores of Tirrell Pond from Ticonderoga by a Catholic priest, Father Olivetti. The rigors of the

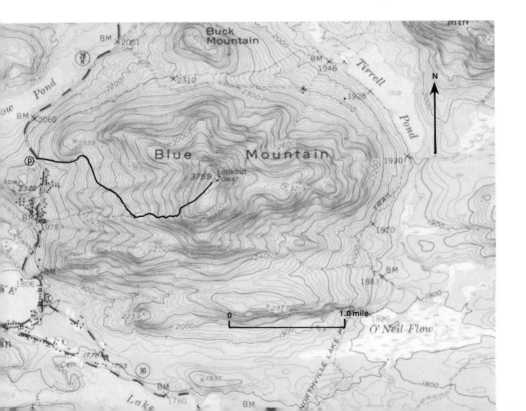

View west from Blue Mountain

woods proved too much for them, and they quickly moved on, abandoning the sixteen log cabins they had erected, but leaving the name of their foreman, Pat Tirrell.

To the north of the summit rises a radio relay tower, but there are no good views from the exposed rock that covers the summit in that direction. The slides you see while driving north on NY 30 are all well below the summit on the south face and fairly difficult to reach.

Almost exactly 100 years ago, the summit of Blue Mountain was the center of surveying efforts to produce an accurate map of the Adirondacks.

Much of the top was cleared to gain a view of distant peaks, but scrub spruce have re-established themselves in the thin soil, effectively blocking most of the views. One of the more amazing happenings in the preparation of the survey was the way in which observations were synchronized: each night at nine a charge of gun powder was set off to alert observers on distant summits and coordinate their efforts.

Return by the same route. For the first half-hour of your descent, watch your footing, for the trail is steep and rugged.

37

Owls Head Mountain

Distance (round trip): 7.2 miles
Hiking time: 3½ hours
Vertical rise: 1,060 feet
Map: USGS 15' Blue Mountain

From NY 30 along the eastern shore of Long Lake you can spot the double peak that inspired the name of Owls Head Mountain. Owls Head overlooks the southern end of that 14-mile-long lake, which is really just a widened section of the Raquette River. South of the lake on the river is Buttermilk Falls, one of the Adirondacks' choicest spots. Since the climb up the mountain should take no more than five hours, plan a morning visit to the falls before you reach the trailhead and an afternoon trek from the mountain trail to Lake Eaton for a swim (that 1-mile detour is included in the hike total above). With all these opportunities you are sure to remember the day as one of your great ones in the Adirondacks.

If you are coming from the south, certainly visit the falls first. Drive north on NY 30 from Blue Mountain Lake for nearly 8 miles, where the highway angles right and another road turns sharply left. A state sign designates the road as the access to the Forked Lake Campsite, a good base for explorations near Long Lake. The sign that indicates the road also leads to Buttermilk Falls is visible

only if you are driving south from Long Lake village, 3.5 miles to the north.

In 2.1 miles there is a small unmarked parking turnout, which is not even 100 yards from the falls. No camping is allowed in the vicinity, but there are picnic tables and fireplaces. The light in the early morning, shining through the pines, is especially good for photographing the falls, whose roar is evident even at the parking turnout. The falls are so handsome you may want to return for a picnic after you climb Owls Head.

To reach the trailhead, now drive back north to NY 30 and follow it for 3.5 miles to Long Lake village. Continue on it .6 mile past the bridge over Long Lake to Endion Road, which is unmarked, and turn left, southwest onto it. (Adirondackers learn they should not expect marked roads or trails, for signs have a way of disappearing.) The macadam surface of Endion Road ends in 1.2 miles, and you come to the marked trailhead and a small parking turnout .4 mile beyond.

The trail, marked with red disks, is narrow at first, paralleling an old road that is now a state-marked snowmobile trail. Within ten minutes the trail intersects the road, and the routes continue together. Corduroy along the road and huge stumps beside it indicate the route was originally used for logging. You climb gently for another ten minutes and then level out in a wet woods with a spruce bog on the left. As you head up Owls Head, you will cross the telephone line for the abandoned fire tower several times; it follows the straightest course up the mountain, while the trail winds about, keeping to easier grades.

After twenty-five minutes of walking, you reach an intersection where a sign indicates the way left to Owls Head is 2.1 miles long. The right fork leads to Lake Eaton. Bearing left, within two minutes or so, you come to a second intersection, where another trail right leads in .5 mile to Lake Eaton. Stay left and continue on the red-marked trail through a good deep forest of yellow birch, spruce, hemlock, and maple. In no time at all you reach a third intersection. This time go straight, on the right-hand fork. The way left leads to Forked Lake Campsite. The trail is now generally level, a great, dry route, hard-packed and smooth through a mixed forest of mature trees and smaller saplings.

Thirty-five minutes into your walk, the trail enters a little draw with a small stream, a possible water source. Follow the stream on its right bank; perhaps you will spot signs of both bear and deer. You walk for another twenty minutes before you notice you are really beginning to climb. Fifteen minutes later you encounter the first rock-strewn section of trail as the old logging road joins an intermittent stream bed. A deep valley begins to appear on your right and a small one on the left. The trail becomes noticeably steeper with a water-washed, rubbly base. Stay left of the watercourse, in a shallow draw, for the trail disappears in a section of deadfalls. A few huge maples and beech have fallen across it, and higher up there has been a significant blowdown of striped maples.

View from Owls Head   *photo: William J. Burke*

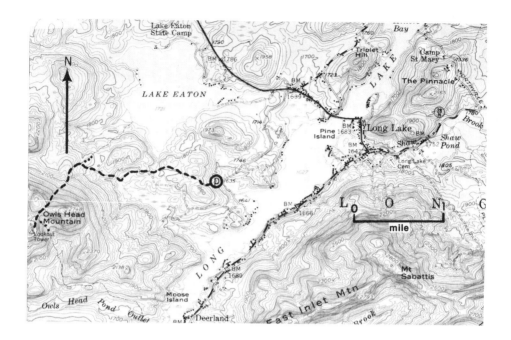

As you emerge from the draw you will see high ground on your left. You cross a height-of-land and descend nearly 100 feet in elevation to a valley that lies below the summit of Owls Head with the abandoned tower. The remains of the ranger's cabin occupies a portion of the meadow of hay-scented fern that fills the valley.

Immediately beyond the cabin site you climb again, now on a much narrower and steeper trail. The footpath zigzags across the steep face of the summit knoll. A few of the rock stairs and ledges constructed by the tower's first ranger survive, although all the railings are gone. The route is just steep enough for you to need an occasional handhold.

As the trail swings west just below the summit, you catch glimpses through the trees of the watery panorama that stretches to the southwest, including Raquette and Forked lakes. You should be able to climb the small summit knob in twenty minutes or less, in spite of the route's steepness.

The fire tower is still standing, minus its lower staircases, but the tower is not necessary to take in the spectacular view to the east. A cliff faces the mountain's eastern side, keeping the vista open through more than 180 degrees of the compass. To the southeast you can see Blue Mountain across South Pond. Owls Head Pond is the dark emerald gem a little west of south just below. Due south, Snowy and the mountains adjacent to Indian Lake stand out on the horizon.

Not much of Long Lake is visible from the 2,780-foot summit, for the lake is narrow and tucked between mountains that range to the northeast. A little south of east, East Inlet and Sabattis mountains rise above one of the few parts of the lake that can be seen. Over it in the northeast you can spot Kempshall Mountain, with Santanoni in the distance beyond. Just to the right of Santanoni you should be able to discern Marcy and the eastern High Peaks fading into the distance.

The northern spur of Owls Head bisects the range of the High Peaks in the northeast. to the left of the spur lies Seymour, then the Seward Range.

These views from the cliffs are the best the summit has to offer, for there are no really good vantages from which to survey the sweep of lakes that lie to the southwest. The drop below the tower summit is several hundred feet, a distance that provides a marvelous updraft for soaring hawks and a windswept perch to keep the bugs away.

When you descend, even if the day is not warm enough for swimming, consider visiting Eaton Lake. Within three minutes from the marked junction, you intersect a snowmobile trail from Endion Road (you use a shortcut to this route on the return). It hardly takes ten minutes to reach the lake, so the .5-mile distance stated on the sign must be a bit exaggerated.

The road approaches the lake and then turns west to round it. Walk to the first opening you see, a lovely grass-covered spot below tall spruce. The lake's sandy shores invite you to swim. The opening is a landing site and access to the trail for boaters from the Lake Eaton Campsite, an excellent state-run campground that could also serve as a base for hiking in the Long Lake area. The campsite is off a right fork from NY 30, 1.4 miles northwest of Endion Road.

On your return to the Owls Head trail, bear left on the more obvious fork. (If you were climbing to the summit from Lake Eaton, you would probably miss the right fork completely.) You will intersect the trail that takes you back to Endion Road in less than ten minutes. Without the detour to Lake Eaton, the descent should take little more than an hour and a half.

Nehasane Preserve

Distance (round trip): 9.4 miles
Vertical rise: 460 feet
Hiking time: 5 hours
Maps: USGS 15' Tupper Lake, USGS 7½' Wolf Mountain,
  USGS 15' Big Moose

Since 1894 land that the state has acquired for the Forest Preserve of the Adirondack Park has come from many sources. A few parcels have been outright gifts and some have been purchased by conservation groups, but the vast majority have been bought with state funds. In the early years of the Forest Preserve, most of Adirondacks have been heavily logged so that huge tracts with depleted value were often offered for sale to the state or taken by the state to cover back taxes. Over the years, though, the most exciting purchases have been the huge tracts of land, encompassing thousands of acres, amassed by private clubs or wealthy individuals during the second half of the nineteenth century. The latest to be acquired by the state is Nehasane Preserve, once the private park of Dr. William Seward Webb.

This major addition places within the public domain the largest wholly state-owned lake in the Adirondacks and a huge preserve that offers great opportunities for hiking, camping, canoeing, and fishing. The walk described here only introduces you to the area; I am certain that once you

have visited Nehasane you will want to return for a longer stay to explore other parts of the preserve.

Nehasane originally encompassed over 140,000 acres and even with the sale years ago of 50,000 acres in what is now the Five Ponds Wilderness Area, Nehasane was still larger than either Litchfield or Whitney parks. The lands around Lake Lila have not been logged for over fifty years, so this newest addition is a true wilderness gem.

Dr. Webb was the builder of the Adirondack & St. Lawrence Railroad. It stretched across the Adirondacks, connecting Utica on the south with Malone on the north. That railroad, which has recently been reactivated as far north as Lake Placid, once carried Webb's guests by private railcar from New York City to his personal station just north of the lodge.

At Nehasane, you can enjoy the woods as the railroad baron might have, for parking restrictions limit the total number of hikers and campers in the area to approximately the number of guests Webb could entertain at one time at his huge, twenty-bedroom lodge and a cluster of guest

Interior of Nehasane lodge

houses on the shore of Lake Lila.

Before you start, you should note two things. First, the three USGS Maps listed show you the principal routes described, but not all of the new acquisition. For that you also want the Five Ponds and Raquette Lake quadrangles, both available in the 15-minute series. Second, the land around Lake Lila has been classified Primitive, while the rest of the estate has been given Wilderness protection. This means that no motorboats are allowed on the lake and only DEC vehicles are permitted on the road that is the principal access trail to the area. Further, special rules govern use of the estate. Parking is permitted only at the designated area, not along the access road. Where the road passes through private lands still held by Webb's heirs, you must stay on the road. No trailers are permitted, and you may not camp within .25 mile of the parking area. All campsites must be at least 150 feet from the shores of Lake Lila. Later, all camping will be restricted to designated sites only.

To reach Nehasane, turn west from NY 30 on County Route 10 a little over 6 miles north of Long Lake Village. A second road, similarly designated, also heads west from NY 30 farther north, approximately 11 miles south of Tupper Lake village. The roads intersect near Little Tupper Lake and continue west past

Whitney Headquarters toward Sabbatis. County Route 10 is good macadam and fairly attractive, for it follows part of Little Tupper Lake's shores after crossing its inlet.

In 7.5 miles a sign points left to "Access Road to Lake Lila 5.8 miles." This dirt road leads southwest across private land, part of which is currently being logged. It is closed during part of the winter and is apt to be muddy in very early spring. If you are planning a trip then, check with the DEC ranger in Long Lake to see if it is usable. The road ends in the designated parking area, which accommodates twenty-five cars. If it is filled you will have to return to County Route 10 to park, and then walk in.

The roadway continues southwest to Lake Lila, but it is barred to vehicles. You start your walk here, but first remember to sign in at the registration booth. If you plan any canoeing, notice the path heading south from the trailhead. The shortest portage to Lake Lila, it takes you in .3 mile to a northeastern arm of the lake.

Your hike is an easy 3.2-mile walk

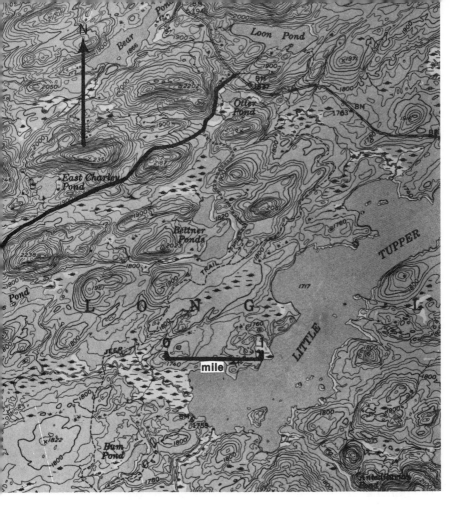

along the roadway to the lodge site. Part of the time you see the lake through a screen of hemlock, spruce, and yellow birch. To vary the tempo, look for a large boulder on the right side of the road with a red marking "Sta. 230" a bit more than 1 mile from the parking lot. Beyond it the trail starts to descend to lake level, but instead, climb the ledges on the shoulder of Harrington Mountain. As you walk along them, parallel to the roadway, enjoy the excellent views of the lake. Return to the roadway by following the ledge tops as they descend toward Lake Lila.

The road first approaches the lake at 1.5 miles. Note that distance if you want to return and use a hand-wheeled carrier for portaging a boat or canoe. The road's hard gravel surface is ideal for these contraptions.

You cross Harrington Brook about 2 miles from the trailhead. This very pretty little brook drops over a series of large boulders in its final rush to reach the lake. About 400 yards beyond the brook an old logging road forks north, right. It is typical of the many logging roads that lace the estate, allowing you to explore the preserve's recesses.

At the first main intersection, just before the lodge, a road forks right, north, to the old railroad station. The lodge site faces east, commanding a fine view of 3-mile-long Lake Lila, named for Webb's wife, who was the daughter of William Vanderbilt. The estate's inclusion in the Forest Preserve means that all the buildings will soon be removed. All that will remain of the main lodge will be the chimney and fireplace, which is dramatically framed in stones nearly a yard square.

Many of the lake's sandy beaches are suitable for swimming. The fishing is as good as in any of the Adirondacks' rapidly acidifying lakes. There is an excellent stock of lake trout as well as land-locked salmon and brook trout. Be sure to bring binoculars, for the lake's remoteness makes it a good spot for viewing the bald eagles and osprey that nest in the area. There are many loons as well as other shore and water birds.

For the best view of the estate, continue south along the gravel road. At the intersection just beyond the lodge, bear right. This roadway heads west, crosses the railroad tracks, and then swings north into the draw between Webb and Frederica mountains.

Climb into the draw to the height-of-land, about 1 mile from the lodge. A pile of stones beside a skidway should alert you to an unmarked path (scheduled for trail designation) on the right that climbs east for under .5 mile to a rustic bark lean-to. It should take you only forty-five minutes from the lodge site to reach the lean-to, which is on the crest of open ledges that face the south side of Frederica Mountain. Older maps designate that mountain with the name Smith, after the region's first settler, a trapper who arrived about 1830.

The view is outstanding from the southeast through the southwest, encompassing all of Lake Lila and the Beaver River Valley through to Nehasane Lake. You should spot the fire tower on Mount Electra a little south of magnetic west.

Notice the open ledges on many of the surrounding mountains. All are the result of fires that swept the area in 1903 and 1908, after the period of heaviest logging. Those fires created another unusual feature on the Nehasane estate, one that has few counterparts in the normally heavily wooded Adirondacks. Many huge, open fields dot the preserve, and you will want to return another day to visit the larger ones. They stretch north of Frederica Mountain beyond Rainer Brook and are most easily reached from the old railroad track.

Ampersand Mountain

Distance (round trip): 6.2 miles
Vertical rise: 1,790 feet
Hiking time: 3¾ hours
Maps: USGS 15' Santanoni, USGS 15' Saranac Lake
High Peaks Wilderness Area

Ampersand stands almost isolated from other mountains in the center of one of the Adirondacks' great expanses of mountains and water. To the north and west, ponds and lakes stretch to the horizon; to the east, the High Peaks range north to Whiteface; and to the south beyond Ampersand Lake, Seward, Seymour, and Santanoni form an impressive chain. Ampersand is a mountain to enjoy as you would a great painting or savor leisurely as you would sip a rare vintage wine. Walking up it is as beautiful and special as the views from the summit.

The summit is entirely bare, and its clearing is the work of man: in 1873, when Colvin was making his mountain survey, he had paths cut to expose triangulation lines to other mountain tops. Erosion did the rest. The removal of the fire tower does not limit in any way the full panorama you can enjoy from Ampersand's bald crest.

Trailhead parking is on the north side of NY 3, east of Tupper Lake and precisely 7 miles east of the intersection of NY 30 and NY 3. The turnout is just over 8 miles southwest of Saranac village. The trailhead itself

is on the south side. NY 3 has become a very busy highway, so cross carefully. The sounds of the highway may pursue you most of the way to the summit.

The trail enters the woods on an old roadway blocked by a barrier. The barrier seems to provide an immediate separation from the civilized world, for crossing it you enter a deep, quiet woods. Large and stately hemlock mingle with maple and yellow birch to shade the rich understory of oak fern, long beech fern, golden thread, sarsaparilla, and almost the complete array of the spring-blooming flowers typical of eastern forests. Moss-covered rocks edge the rolling trail with its soft root-free tread.

Within a few minutes you cross a sandy-bottomed stream flowing from the right. A stretch of old corduroy leads you to a fantastic hemlock grove with a view of the mountain through the trees. No trail markers guide your way, and none are needed. A long section of corduroy elevates you above the muck of a thriving deep spruce swamp. Huge spruce tower over an understory of ferns and bunchberry growing in the sphagnum

bog. You may find yourself walking more slowly than usual, in spite of the easy trail, for the woods are worthy of an observer's pace.

You cross several intermittent streams and, after a half-hour's walk, come to a washed-out bridge, no impediment to crossing the larger stream here. Within forty minutes you begin to climb. Another section of corduroy may lead you to conclude you are on one of the more carefully built Adirondack trails. At fifty minutes, after climbing a steep pitch, you should enter a minute clearing, the site of the fire observer's cabin, 1.7 miles from the highway.

From here an abandoned trail heads straight ahead across Dutton Brook and up the mountain. The trail was maintained by the fire observer, Walter Channing Rice, who earned the nickname the "Hermit of Ampersand." Wooden steps and railings, log and earthen risers, and stone stairs once provided an easy way to mount the nearly 1,500 feet remaining.

Today, the trail makes a ninety-degree turn to the right and then swings left close to the brook. Shortly the way becomes very steep; sections here have been called the worst in the Adirondacks. Strangely, they do not detract from the walk. Some trail work is certainly necessary, though the uniform abruptness of the mountain precludes much effective rerouting. The trail is now a narrow footpath, rooted and rutty, with slippery muck in a few precipitous sections. The steep pitch is compounded by blowdowns, some old, some quite new. At times the trail is a scene of destruction, at others it takes on the romantic aura of wilderness that pervades some early Adirondack photo-

View from Ampersand

graphs. The trail reminds me of early pictures of mountain gorges, with a jumble of trees lying across huge boulders. It only needs a few women in long skirts, their escorts encumbered with wicker packs to complete the illusion.

The trail enters a narrow gorge with a moss-covered wall on the right, ferns dotting the ledges. You will probably have to pause for breath, leaving plenty of time to enjoy the scene. Beyond the top of the gorge, a view opens through the trees, glimpses of island-studded waters hinting at what is to come.

The forest cover shrinks and becomes predominantly spruce as you approach the summit, but the narrow, washed-out trail continues. In several places blowdowns have forced hikers to develop new footpaths. None of the detours are more than 100 feet long, but the nearly vertical slopes make you pause and question the proper route. In most cases your choice will not matter, for you have to scramble in any case. By this time you have stared at enough eye-level mud-covered ledges so that the thousands of hikers' footsteps that preceded you have destroyed any notions that this could be a pristine wilderness.

Just about the time you despair, in a terrible, steep section where the average slope must exceed forty-five degrees, you emerge in a level valley filled with exquisite paper birch and ferns. Even huff-and-puff hikers should take no more than an hour to reach this spot from the cabin site, a distance of .8 mile. The 1,000-foot climb is excuse enough for the slow pace.

A few spruce and balsam dot the glen, which is edged on the left by the cliffs that ring Ampersand's

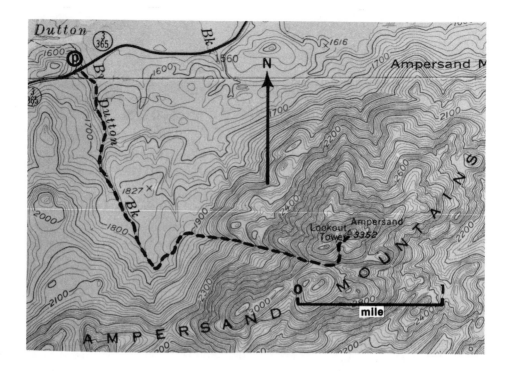

summit and on the right by an unbelievably large boulder. "Boulder" is hardly adequate; the rock might better be called a miniature mountain. Moss clings to its nearly vertical sides, ferns fill its crevices and fissures, and spruce perched on the top have managed to grow to mature size. If you are planning a full day on the summit, wait until your return to photograph the birch glen, for then afternoon sun highlights the trees against the grey cliff walls.

The trail continues through the glen, rising to pass under an overhanging velvet moss-covered rock. If you are curious, look just before the overhang for a footpath heading to the right around a massive pile of boulders. Follow it and explore a cave concealed in the rocks, a razor-thin shard of rock is wedged above it between overhanging boulders. Cold air emerges from this and several other openings, hinting at deeper crevices. Take time to clamber around the rock, looking for little caves and openings.

Continuing, you walk under another overhanging rock, dip into a small cleft, and emerge from the woods facing a sheer, smooth rock wall. A gentle alternate path swings right, but your exuberance should carry you up and over the ledge, following yellow arrows painted on the rock.

You arrive at the summit on the westernmost of three knobs, each of which offers different exposures. The truly great emerging views reward you for your climb of two hours and fifteen minutes. Turn around first to look back the way you have come, past a series of ledges to a cone that is a part of the flank of Ampersand and then to Stony Creek Mountain. To the south, at the foot of the mountain, Ampersand Lake is nestled in the center of a giant handful of mountains.

Everyone who writes of Ampersand Lake reminds you of the brief role it played in the life of a distinguished group of Boston scholars that included Ralph Waldo Emerson, James Russell Lowell, and Louis Agassiz. The story of their choice of Ampersand for an Adirondack camp, the "philosopher's camp," is beautifully told in Donaldson's *A History of the Adirondacks.* Donaldson also discusses the origin of Ampersand's name as deriving from a corruption of Amber-sand Lake, which in turn was inspired by the "bright yellow sandy shores and islands which make it truly Amber-sand Lake."

You should have with you at least the following USGS maps, all in the 15-minute series, to assist in identifying distant mountains: Saint Regis, Lake Placid, Mount Marcy, and Long Lake. Directly south across Ampersand Lake, the Seward Mountains climb impressively skyward, rising 1,000 feet higher than your perch, but nowhere commanding a finer view. To the right of Seward lies Kempshall, its long and rounded summit in the distance beside Long Lake. Between the two, on the horizon, lies Blue Mountain, its profile a narrower one than is usually seen from other vantages. To the west of Long Lake lies a mountain that appears so large from this perspective its lack of name is peculiar.

In the distance, immediately left of Stony Creek Mountain, lies Mount Morris, topped by a fire tower; Buck is the long mountain to its left and farther away.

Looking back again beyond Ampersand Lake, a narrow cleft separates Seward and Seymour mountains. In front of them, extending from the lake, a valley stretches southeast toward the Duck Hole. On the far side of the valley, Santanoni stands next to Seymour to the east, with Henderson beyond it. Continuing to your left, Mounta Adams is the small peak in the distance next in line.

East, between Ampersand and its pond, lies Van Dorrien Mountain, and if you follow beyond its summit you see the Sawtooth Mountains, whose peaks dip down to border the northern edge of the valley leading to the Duck Hole. On the horizon beyond Sawtooth range Nye Mountain in the north, Street Mountain next south or right, and then, overshadowing everything and blocking farther views east, the MacIntyre Mountains.

Walk east along Ampersand's summit to the middle knob, from which the views north are best. Immediately below the mountain is Middle Saranac. Upper Saranac begins on its left and curves around it to the north, with Boot Bay Mountain in between. Lake Clear is due north, with Saint Regis and its tower to its left. You can see only a little of Tupper Lake in the west, with Raquette Pond to its north. Mount Arab, also a fire tower mountain, can be spotted west of Tupper.

The best eastern views are from the farthest perch, beyond the knob that once held the tower. As you walk across the summit, you will enjoy the magnificent feeling that the mountain drops away, with cliffs facing all exposures.

Lower Saranac Lake is just east of north, with Kiwassa and Oseetah lakes ranging east. Over Lake Oseetah lies McKenzie Mountain, with Whiteface and its distinctive white slide behind it. Slide, Hurricane, and Cascade complete the eastern skyline back to Nye. With binoculars and a clear day, you can spot three more fire tower mountains in the north, from left to right, Debar (Hike 32), Loon, and Lyon.

The huge dark crystals of labradorite imbedded in the anorthosite exposed on the peak are fascinating to geologists, but to ordinary mountain climbers, the mountain is a gem by itself. You see so much: water expanses to the north and west, impressive peaks to the south and east, and all so separate from your perch, as if placed to form a perfect panorama. None of the higher peaks with their barer summits are as open and expansive as this.

As you start back across the summit to return, look for the plaque erected to the memory of Ampersand's hermit, facing the ledge below the tower knob.

McKenzie Mountain

Distance (round trip): 10.2 miles
Vertical rise: 1,286 feet
Hiking time: 6 hours
Map: USGS 15' Saranac Lake
McKenzie Wilderness Area

McKenzie is an isolated peak rising north of the High Peaks between Saranac Lake and Lake Placid. Its wooded summits do not permit a single complete panorama, but overlooks on the east and west sides of the northern summit cover a surprising portion of the compass. Moose Mountain, a slightly taller peak, lies in the northeast blocking views and creating the impression that the two are part of one long mountain range. From the overlook west of McKenzie's summit, the panorama extends from Moose Mountain through the north with low hills, fields, and ponds; the west with Saint Regis Mountain; and the southwest across the Saranac lakes to Ampersand and Scarface mountains. The views from the second overlook, on the east, encompass Whiteface, the Sentinel Range across Lake Placid, and the High Peaks. That view includes the MacIntyre Mountains and ends with the eastern flanks of Scarface.

The beginning of the trail to McKenzie is being rerouted at the time (spring, 1984) that the revisions of this guide are being prepared. Problems with the crossing of private land have necessitated a new trailhead and a replacement for the first .9 miles of trail.

The projected trailhead will be located at the site of an old Department of Transportation sand pit, 1.6 miles east of the Department of Environmental Conservation Office in Raybrook. That office is on NY 86, 3.7 miles southeast of NY 3 at Saranac Lake. You may wish to stop there to double-check the status of the new trail and its precise relocation. The most direct probable route is west northwest over a shoulder of Little Burn Mountain, but as this still entails crossing a portion of private land, the new route will probably be as much as .3 mile longer than the 1.6 miles projected and included in the summary above, information marked tentative by the DEC. To completely avoid private land, the route would have to climb as much as 500 feet up the side of Little Burn. If negotiations permit the new route to cross private land, it will likely contour around the hillside, making the route easier, but still making it longer than the direct 1.6 miles stated. Trail markers will undoubtedly make the route simple, but checking with DEC will help you judge any additional time needed.

Red trail markers will continue to denote the route, which is maintained by the Albany Chapter of ADK. The new beginning will require at least a forty minute walk to reach the old, intersecting it where it first entered deep woods, beginning a gentle rise along the valley of Little Ray Brook. Little waterfalls and rapids mark the stream, which tumbles through a very handsome gorge, covered with tall hemlock and a sprinkling of huge yellow birch and cedar.

In just over an hour, at 2.2 miles, you reach a fork. Yellow disks mark a left turn to Haystack. Stay straight ahead up a hillside, continuing through the valley in a long level stretch. At 2.5 miles you cross one stream; 100 yards farther, a second; and just short of 3.1 miles, a third. Here you meet a bad stretch of trail, rocky and washed, with exposed roots.

A snowmobile trail from Whiteface Inn to McKenzie Pond crosses your route .2 mile farther. Continue ahead on a gentle rise for ten more minutes. At 3.6 miles, the trail appears to hit a sheer wall. You start climbing, straight up and then angling across bare rock and mucky slides in a slow zigzag pattern. To scramble up the ledges and then traverse the long slope to the northwest as far as the first overlook will take you over thirty minutes, but you will have climbed 800 feet in .5 mile.

Walk to the right of the trail at the overlook and then turn left below more ledges, descending a few feet

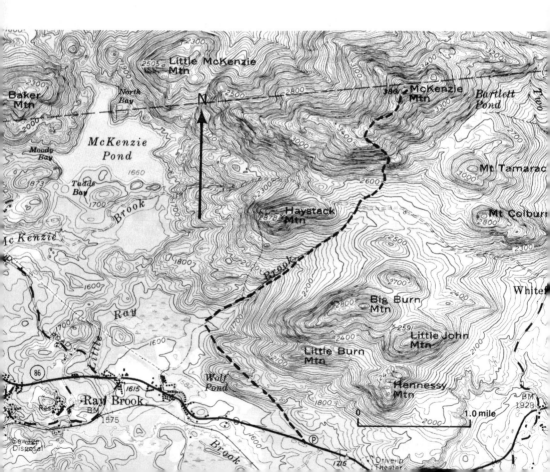

Climbing McKenzie

into a deep, ferny glen. This walk along the wooded summit ridge is McKenzie's most attractive feature. Stands of sorrel and mountain dryoperis fill every niche below the open balsam cover. The top of McKenzie has one of the state's most handsome stands of mountain woodfern, a lacey gem that is among our most ornamental ferns. This dryoperis is common from the sub-arctic through Canada and into northern New York State, but it is rarely seen and even then only at high elevations south of the northern-most Adirondacks. The species constitutes most of the tall fern cover on McKenzie's ridge. It can be recognized by its broadly triangular form (and by the fact that the lower subleaflets are obliquely triangular).

The trail winds northeast through the fern woods, climbing two short rises before reaching a path that leads a few feet left to an overlook atop a cliff. The northern summit is visible on the right, still over .4 mile away.

The trail ducks back into deep woods, climbing a few feet in .1 mile to the southern summit, which has a limited view southeast to Scarface. Then the trail slides down a steep pitch into a col, reaching the bottom in .1 mile and crossing a second beautiful wooded glen. You encounter two steep pitches on the climb to the north summit.

About 100 feet past the last rock scramble, a path turns left for the western overlook. In the foreground the view of McKenzie Pond is neatly framed by Little McKenzie, Baker, and Haystack mountains. You will probably want the Saint Regis and Santanoni USGS maps to help you identify the distant mountains.

The second overlook is scarcely 100 feet to the north. That intriguing sharp cone to the right of Whiteface is Moss Cliff Mountain. The Lake Placid and Mount Marcy USGS maps will help you identify the rest. From both outlooks you will marvel at the way the mountain drops steeply away from the summit ridge.

Your return trip should take you just a bit less time than the ascent.

Pitchoff Mountain

Distance (one way): 5.2 miles
Vertical rise: 1,440 feet
Hiking time: 5 hours
Maps: USGS 15' Mount Marcy, USGS 15' Lake Placid
Sentinel Range Wilderness Area

Pitchoff Mountain lies immediately north of the High Peaks Wilderness Area between Lake Placid and Keene and offers some great views south to the High Peaks and north to the Sentinel Range. Pitchoff is not a simple mountain; it is actually a series of small summits, which are connected by a range trail as varied and exciting as you could wish. That trail begins and ends on NY 73 in the Cascade valley; the two trailheads are 2.6 miles apart. The best way to enjoy Pitchoff is to walk the full length of the trail, leaving a car at each end; you will have nearly 300 feet fewer to climb if you begin at the western end.

The western trailhead, on NY 73, is 4.4 miles east of Heart Lake Road, directly opposite the trail to Cascade and Porter mountains. Because NY 73 has recently undergone reconstruction, look for the trail at the top of the new retaining berm. The eastern trailhead is a little over 4 miles west of Keene; this end of the trail starts on a bridge over an unnamed tributary of Cascade Brook. The tributary rises in a spring on the side of Pitchoff near the end of the trail. Unfortunately, it is the only water you en-

counter on the trip. You will need water long before you reach the spring, so be sure to carry plenty.

The upper, western, trailhead is less than .5 mile west of Upper Cascade Lake. One of the rewards of this climb is the rapidity with which you gain the first views of the Cascade lakes and the sheer cliff faces of the Cascade Range bordering them on the southeast.

The trail is marked by red disks and begins with a steep pitch through a forest cover that indicates the area burned perhaps seventy-five years ago: small spruce and balsam are filling the spaces between striped and red maples, and white birch. The short pitch north for .2 mile is followed by a level trek northeast along a ridge parallel to the road. You drop down into a spruce thicket and then climb gently over rock outcrops to reach the first overlook, a boulder, .8 mile from the highway and less than a twenty-five-minute walk from your start.

Standing out on the boulder here, the sheer drop makes you feel as though you could easily jump into Upper Cascade Lake. From this spot you can see the spit of land that separates it from Lower Cascade Lake. This overlook also offers the most dramatic view of the cliff behind them. Even though you've barely begun your hike, take time now to enjoy this view.

The trail clings to the side of the hill around the boulder, climbing a small pitch, then a modest rise, and then another pitch above steep ledges to the right. Birch, balsam, bracken, and dry, scrubby growth mark the way. A second outcrop appears within five minutes, offering another beautiful excuse to pause.

As you descend from this outcrop, a wall of rock rises ahead of you across a small, damp woods with large red baneberries. The trail heads almost straight up, and it is slippery with loose dirt. You angle left, below a ledge, and then climb, steeply again, on an almost polished marble base.

About an hour into your hike (if you have stopped to enjoy the views) and 1 mile from the start, you reach an intersection. The trail used to go straight up the rock ahead, a difficult scramble. Take the new, slightly longer but less difficult, route on the left, and then backtrack to enjoy all the sights of the steeper route. The new trail, a narrow footpath, hugs the outcrop, heading almost west, then north, and after descending a little, finally northeast again. You pass under an overhanging rock that looks like the entrance to a cave. Here the trail climbs again. A smooth, vertical rock rises above you as you traverse the wooded back side of the ridge. In fifteen minutes you intersect the older route.

Turn right across the ridge on the old trail for a detour to one of the day's best promontories. Stepping on

parts of a giant jigsaw puzzle made of huge, angular, flat slabs of interlocking rock, some with deep crevices between, walk west to three huge reddish boulders. Glacial erratics, they are precariously perched on a beaklike rock. To the south, the views west from the shoulder of Cascade include Basin, Haystack, and Marcy, Colden, and Avalanche Pass. The MacIntyre Mountains are to the right of the pass, with Santanoni, the Sawtooth Range and Ampersand filling the horizon around through the west.

A half-hour will suffice for the detour, unless it is blueberry season, when you will just have to stop every other step for another handful. Your trip will have covered about 1.7 miles when you duck back into the woods and pick up the trail again. It continues northeast between scrubby patches and open rock, circling left around a bare outcrop and then angling right on open rock. Intervening clumps of balsam have a good, rich, spicy smell. You walk through a birch glen with a fern meadow beneath and then rise through mountain maples and taller spruce. As you climb between two boulders, you reach a wooded height-of-land, the highest point on the range walk. You have to leave the trail, walking to the left, for even limited views, which begin to include the Sentinel Range to the north. In spite of a leisurely pace, it has probably taken you less than two hours to walk the over-2.2-mile route to the summit.

Continue northeast along the ridge, descending a little through a fern glen and then ascending .2 mile to a rock ledge with a spectacular over-

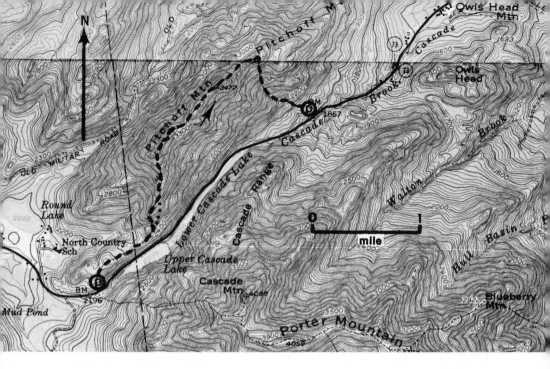

look to the north. What a drop to the valley below! There is a big slash on Slide Mountain to the north. Pitchoff's ridge is so narrow that you can see most of its length, a series of knobs and summits that appear as high as your perch.

Blueberries, ledges, balsam, and gorgeous views continue before the trail drops into a wooded glen. Within a half-hour of the wooded summit you reach a narrow spine of open rock. The trail turns left at 2.9 miles to climb the highest rock along the spine. Now you can enjoy the view back, past the spectacular ridges you have traversed, to the summit of Cascade. The knobs ahead are equally impressive. The view north is across the deep valley to Black Mountain and North and South Notch mountains, which are about as tall as Pitchoff.

Again you descend, but the roller-coaster trail immediately climbs to follow a cairn-marked route across open rock at 3.3 miles. In the northeast another summit in the chain appears and to its right, across Cascade valley, range Hurricane Mountain and, on a clear day, the Green Mountains of Vermont rising above Lake Champlain. Farther right, just to the left of Cascade, Giant and its distinctive slides are clearly visible.

Northern views continue as you walk across ledges that hang steeply above the valley on the north. Prostrate spruce and tall blueberries cling to the thin soil on the summit. At 3.6 miles, you should glimpse a small, steep knob in the valley that separates you from the last summit. Walk about 15 feet to the left, off the trail, to enjoy the view of the last summit across the peculiar knob.

Next, yellow arrows painted on the rock guide you into a steep gully below and north of the ledge. Be careful; it is slippery! After dropping to the col, turn sharply left, below the outcrop, then climb through a cleft, head down a slide, and cut sharply up a ridge for a view northeast to the last summit in the range. It takes fifteen minutes to cover the distance from the col, just over .2 mile.

You are climbing on bare rock now, guided by more yellow arrows. Do not forget to look back; those views are great, too. You approach the last summit from its northern side: the south and west are too steep. You reach it just short of 4 miles from your start and after three hours and fifteen minutes of walking. Stop, rest, and enjoy the curious rock formation below you to the south; it is easy to see why it was named the Sleeping Elephant. You have a slightly different perspective on the eastern views you enjoyed from the previous summit; this last knob is only a little more than 300 feet below the highest one. You will marvel at the steep drop to the south and east to Cascade Valley, with Owls Head Mountain a little north of east across it.

Your route down is as steep as the way up. To find the continuing trail, walk a short way northeast, following arrows and cairns on the open rock. A few of the signs are concealed by the spruce and balsam that fill the crevices. The trail make a sharp, hairpin turn to the right, dropping below the ledge and doubling back southwest beneath ledges into a draw below the summit. Rocks and rubble fill the steep and difficult trail. It is really a scramble to descend through the birch-covered slope. Erratics cover the hillside and boulders fill the trail. It is so steep that you probably need an hour to cover the final 1.25 miles to the highway.

About halfway down, you cross an intermittent stream, and within a few feet you can hear the spring emerging from below a boulder about 50 feet east of the trail. Pause for a cool drink and a refreshing rest.

Below this point, the slope is noticeably gentler. Your route is close by a small stream on the right, across it, and then across the main stream. Following a fairly steep section, you cross and recross the stream. Finally the route levels out, just before emerging from the woods on the bridge by NY 73, where you have left your second car.

You will agree that this is not a long or difficult trail, but there is a fair amount of climbing between the summits. Be sure you have allowed at least an hour a mile for the trek and extra time for picking blueberries and enjoying the changing views.

Blue Ledge on the Hudson

Distance (round trip): 5 miles
Vertical rise: 230 feet
Hiking time: 3 hours
Map: USGS 15' Newcomb

The Hudson, New York's mightiest river, has more beautiful vistas than the fabled and historic rivers of Europe. But from its birth at Lake Tear of the Clouds high in the Adirondacks, to its passage through the Hudson Highlands, and then to its mouth below the skyscrapers of New York City, no more inviting place exists than the narrows of Blue Ledge in the heart of the Adirondacks. The towering cliffs that give the gorge its name rise above one of the river's wildest stretches of rapids. The boiling white foam contrasts with the deep blue shadows of the rock. On a sand beach opposite the ledges you can picnic and in spring watch the noisy antics of a pair of nesting ravens. Their nest is usually secreted in a dark niche high on the cliffs, and the black young birds would be totally concealed if they did not reveal themselves with gaping brilliant red mouths, screeching for food.

The 5-mile round-trip walk to Blue Ledge can be made in less than three hours, but you should allow twice as long to appreciate the gorge's uniqueness. The walk begins after a long drive on the handsome but rugged North Woods Club Road in a high, open forest typical of this part of the Forest Preserve. The easiest access to the dirt road is from NY 28N, driving north from its intersection in North Creek with NY 28. By this route you pass a lovely view of Moxham's slide 3.5 miles above North Creek and go through the hamlet of Minerva at about 7 miles. At 9.4 miles turn left, west on North Woods Club Road. The road bridges Deer Creek, heads west, and then swings south through the valley between Kellogg and Venison mountains.

The road descends a steep side hill to a one-lane bridge over the Boreas River 3.8 miles from NY 28N. There is a picnic area at the bridge from which several informal fishermen's paths head along the river.

Beyond the bridge you cross railroad tracks that serve the titanium mine at Tahawus. In the early nineteenth century iron was the raison d'etre for the mine's existence. It was the failure to build a good road or railroad that prevented the mine's development then, and impurities, namely titanium, made the mine a marginal operation. In 1871, Dr.

Thomas Clark Durant completed the Adirondack Railroad, which was first chartered in 1839, from Saratoga to North Creek; however, it was not until the early years of World War II that the road was extended all the way to Tahawus to ship out the titanium, which turned out to have greater value than the Adirondacks' fabled iron.

From here the dirt road can be rugged; you have to drive so slowly you can easily spot some of the lovely clumps of wildflowers that edge the road. The trailhead is exactly 3 miles from the bridge over the Boreas. Park at the marked turnout at the east edge of Huntley Pond.

The first part of the trail south crosses a boggy area covered with huge yellow birch and hemlock. Blue trail markers denote the route, which heads up and away from the pond along a dry and narrow footpath. The easy gradual climb through mixed forest is followed by a gentle descent into a little valley through a sort of natural gate formed by two huge boulders and two huge yellow birch. The valley is filled with many spring-blooming plants, which form a multi-colored carpet of wild oats, dog-tooth violets, and spring beauties.

After crossing a small stream you continue generally southwest to an area of low scrub and brush beside an old shanty, all signs of logging. The place is about 1.2 miles in, and here the footpath intersects an old roadway with a stonework base. The trail continues on the roadway toward the Hudson, passing to the south of a long beaver flow with extensive signs of both old and new beaver work. The high open canopy of huge trees (through which the old road passes) creates a parklike setting. The Hudson was used to flood logs to

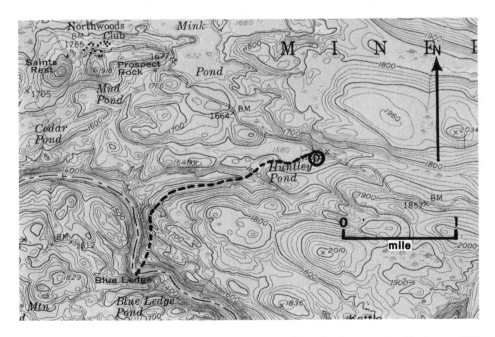

206 *Blue Ledge on the Hudson*

sawmills throughout the last seventy years of the nineteenth century and into the twentieth century, and this road was undoubtedly a principal route for dragging logs to the river.

Just about the time you first hear the Hudson, the trail reaches a section with posted signs designating North Woods Club property. You cross the property line and head straight up a narrow pathway that traverses a knoll bearing old blazes on the trees as well as the blue markers. The low shoulder of a hill separates you from the Hudson. As the roar of the river grows louder, the trail turns due south to wind along the nose of the ridge. You are approaching the area opposite Blue Ledge. The trail is covered with the tall white pine that rim the entire gorge here. The route is up and down along the ledge, past a pine point that affords a small glimpse of the crest of Blue Ledge on the opposite shore. The crest rises higher than your perch on the north shore. You will have walked for no more than an hour, but pause to enjoy sounds from the promontory overlooking the Hudson: the wind in the tall pines and the din of the rapids. With the exception of the Harris Rift west of the confluence with the Boreas, the most violent of the Hudson's rapids are the ones you hear. They churn and boil the river both above and below Blue Ledge.

Now the trail drops rapidly to the Hudson, past rattlesnake fern, boulders and ledges, right down to the sandy banks. Blue Ledge rises 300 feet above you on the opposite shore. The blue cliffs are surrounded with other ledges colored gray and green and even various hues of orange and salmon. Pines and cedars cling to tiny crevices in the cliff faces. The marvelous colors and the variously eroded bands reflect Blue Ledge's geological structure: a series of banded gneiss beneath bands of schist interstratified with gneiss and limestone.

Short informal paths head both east and west along the riverbank. Cedars rim the shoreline, which is barely flat enough for a picnic site, though it is obvious that several places have attracted campers. The Hudson is only 150 feet wide just below the cliffs. Huge rocks break the water into swirling rapids and crests of foam, both upstream and downstream. The deep pools for swimming are deceptive, for the Hudson can have a mighty current. Be careful if you do enjoy the cooling waters.

In spring, in high water, you may glimpse a kayak or rubber raft shooting the rapids. Eagles and hawks are often sighted riding the updrafts above Blue Ledge. And, of course, this is one of the few places in the Adirondacks where in spring you can expect to see ravens.

Allow at least a full day for the trip to Blue Ledge even though you will spend no more than three hours of it walking. The drive in and out may take another hour and a half, and you will want plenty of time to picnic and admire the cliffs.

Blue Ledge

Vanderwhacker Mountain

Distance (round trip): 5.8 miles
Vertical rise: 1,700 feet
Hiking time: 5 hours
Map: USGS 15' Newcomb

Vanderwhacker Mountain stands alone, the only peak in a rough rectangle of Wild Forest land outlined by the Hudson River on the south, west, and a portion of the north, and the Boreas River on the east. Neither river is visible from the summit of Vanderwhacker, but the broad expanse they define separates the mountain from any other that approaches its height. Enormous Vanderwhacker sits in isolated splendor, offering commanding views of distant summits.

The recent reopening of Vanderwhacker's tower once again gives the hiker spectacular views north to the High Peaks. For several years past, the combination of the closed tower and the wooded summit meant that hikers had to scramble to obtain even a limited view, but Vanderwhacker is so wonderful that it was worth it.

Vanderwhacker is very steep, rising sharply 1,700 feet from the surrounding valleys. The trail generally follows a long narrow ridge that leads to the small summit cone. The 2.9-mile climb is strenuous enough to make a good one-day hike.

To find the trailhead, drive north from North Creek on NY 28N, which is also called the Theodore Roosevelt Highway. A sign beside a deserted frame building 14.6 miles north of NY 28 relates the events of September 4, 1901, when then-Vice President Theodore Roosevelt heard that President William McKinley was on his deathbed. Roosevelt stopped at the inn here on his wild dash from Mount Marcy, where he had been vacationing, to North Creek, where he caught a train to Buffalo to be sworn in as President of the United States.

You cross the Boreas River at 16.2 miles, and if you are not in a hurry, you might enjoy walking .5 mile south on an informal path that follows the eastern shore of that river past rapids and a small falls.

Drive beyond the bridge another .1 mile to a dirt road on the west. It is marked as the trail to Vandershacker. A sign indicates it is 4.2 miles to Vanderwhacker, but that is incorrect. The dirt road makes fairly good driv-

View from Vanderwhacker

ing; just use caution. A parking area is on the left near the start, and many camping places are tucked beneath the tall pines lining the road. Huge hemlock stand out in the dense mixed forest off to the sides. The dirt road is so beautiful that you might enjoy walking along this stretch. Particularly good camping spots are 1.1 miles in and 1.5 miles in, near Vanderwhacker Brook. Just beyond, you cross the railroad track from Tahawus mine, which trains use at irregular intervals, so look before you cross. The road continues west, more interesting than many trails in the Adirondacks. Beyond the tracks it climbs a small spruce-covered bank bordered with bunchberry, blueberry, and pipsissiwa. The road turns at a gravel pit and reaches a fork, 2.6 miles from the highway. The way left leads to a private club at Moose Pond. Your route is to the right, as designated by a red, hand-painted sign. Park 100 yards from the fork beside another camping place, with water nearby. The trail heads west from this spot, following the old road to the fire ranger's cabin. The road is barred, so you begin the hike here.

The trail's beginning is marked for snowmobiles, with orange disks, and for hikers, with red disks. One footpath immediately forks left, following a line of unused telephone poles, but it quickly rejoins the road. Deep moss paves the roadway, which has a corduroy base. You cross a stream on a slippery log bridge and then practically skate across another stream on a second slimy log. You cross the stream or its tributaries a half-dozen times in the early part of the walk. On the third crossing, the bridge is out, but that usually presents no problem. After a pleasant fifteen-minute walk close to the tiny stream, a spruce bog appears through the trees. Giant spruce, as well as some enormous skeletons of dead spruce, dot the old beaver flow, which is filled with sphagnum and lush ferns. Deadfalls bar the way as you round the flow's western end.

Cross the stream that feeds the flow by hopping across a series of stones. Beyond, the beaver meadow continues on your left, and you can now see the mountain ahead.

Within a half-hour the roadway begins rising gently. At the next stream crossing you may elect to ford the stream rather than challenge the slippery logs of the old bridge. At 1.2 miles the trail forks, with the snowmobile trail heading left. At this point you can almost see the fire observer's abandoned cabins 200 yards straight ahead. Take the trail to the cabins.

You have 1.4 miles left to walk, but 1400 feet still to climb. The trail starts immediately up the steep slope, leaving the meadow via a narrow footpath between the two cabins. The route shows little use, but it is not difficult to follow. Few trail markers guide the way.

Brilliant birch light the hardwood forest that clings to the steep slopes. Your route seems to traverse the steepest slope, crossing a sheer face with an incredible drop to your left.

By the time you reach the ridge, a fifteen-minute climb, you are sure to be out of breath. The route now alternates between relatively level stretches and steep rises along the obvious ridge, which drops off now on both sides. After twenty-five minutes you descend a small draw, cross to a ridge on the north, and begin climbing again, this time on bedrock. The soil is so thin it has washed away.

You continue climbing a moderately steep pitch through a narrow-

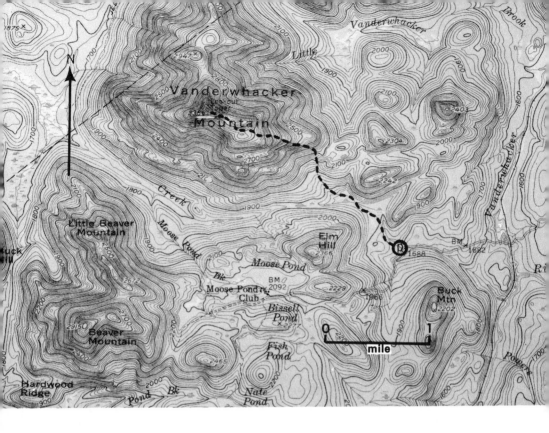

walled corridor edged with scrub spruce and balsam. Soft mosses line the corridor and host golden thread, bunchberry, and sorrel. For a time you sense there is higher ground on your right, but the mountain continues to drop steeply away from the trail on your left. The narrow passageway is really pretty, and it even smells good. You walk through it for a good twenty minutes. Gradually the woods are more open. After one more pitch, where you feel you are almost walking on a knife-edge, Moose Pond becomes visible down on the left through the trees. Note the spot, for the top of the cliff on the left was blown clear during the 1950 hurricane. It is still difficult to push through

deadfalls to the cliff edge, but you can find an opening that provides the best views south. The tower is only five minutes farther up the ridge.

When you reach the summit, your first impression of the view north is of the looming, massive hulk of Santanoni and the enormous spread of the MacIntyre Mountains.

You can see west to Kempshall and the mountains that line Long Lake and through the south to Blue Mountain. At your feet below lies the village of Newcomb, identified by the town's water tower, with Lake Harris to the west of it. Santanoni, with its long, curved slide, is beyond Newcomb, and to the left of Santanoni lie the Seward Mountains, with Couchsachraga and

Little Santanoni between. The summit of Ampersand is barely visible to the left of Santanoni, and to its right on the horizon lies Sawtooth Mountain. Henderson is to the right of Santanoni, and beyond it flat-topped Mac-Naughton and Wallface, with its cliff bordering Indian Pass and leading up to the broad sweep of the MacIntyre Mountains. Continuing to the right, the cone of Colden is impressive behind Mount Adams, whose rock outcrops can be seen with field glasses.

Next is Redfield, with Marcy peeping over it and then Skylight and Haystack on the horizon. In the foreground, the North River Mountains lead up to Allen and on to Haystack.

Farther east range Colvin and Nippletop, then the cleft of Hunters Pass, with Dix, Hough, and McComb rising behind Boreas Mountain. You feel you are on top of the world, surveying the broad valley to the north and the sweep up to the Adirondacks' most impressive range.

To the east, you can spot Texas Ridge and Hoffman Notch with Hoffman Mountain beyond. Pharoah Mountain can be seen over Hoffman's right flank.

To the south, you can see all the way to Indian Lake and the mountains on its western shore. Immediately below the tower lies Moose Pond and, spotting clockwise (west) from Moose Pond, you can identify Little Beaver Mountain in the foreground, and Beaver and Split Rock ponds. Directly over them lies Panther Mountain, with Wakely to the west. Panther defines the western side of Squaw Brook Valley, which you look straight through from this angle. Snowy Mountain outlines its eastern side. Next is Indian Lake, and to the east, or left, lies the heart-shaped summit of Humphrey, the Puffer, and finally Bullhead. Between the latter two, and closer, is one of the rare views of the chimney on Chimney Mountain. The dominant mountain in the south-south-east is Moxham, which appears like the back of a closed fist, its string of summits ranging off to the left.

With the tower open, you can easily identify the mountains to the south-east. Gore, with its tower, is clearly defined a little east of south over Moose Pond. The mountains edging Lake George can even be discerned from here on a really clear day.

Return by the same route; remember that the roadway is not too well marked. You will have to look carefully near several of the stream crossings to be sure you are following the proper route.

Goodnow Mountain

Distance (round trip): 3 miles
Vertical rise: 1,050 feet
Hiking time: 2 hours
Map: USGS 15' Newcomb
Fire Tower; closed Tuesday, Wednesday

Goodnow is a nice little mountain just south of the High Peaks with a great view. It is accessible to state campsites and close to a nature center and a swimming lake. In short, it is the best way to become acquainted with the region near Newcomb, which has many attractions for hikers.

Goodnow Mountain is also owned by Syracuse University and although the DEC no longer maintains the fire tower there, the University still allows access to the mountain. The tower closing does limit the mountain's views, though you can still enjoy the wonderful ones north to the High Peaks from the exposed rocks from the tower site.

Goodnow lies south of NY 28N. The trailhead is 3.4 miles west of the Newcomb Town Hall and 10.4 miles east of the intersection of NY 28N and NY 30 in Long Lake village. Closer at hand, the trailhead is just west of the Syracuse University Ecology Center and 1.4 miles west of the Huntington Nature Preserve. You might want to add to the day's outing

a walk through the preserve on the labeled nature trail, which takes you past marshes, bogs, and forest sites.

The trail to Goodnow, marked with red disks and older red blazes, follows an old logging road through a clearing into second growth forest. The road becomes fairly steep almost immediately, winding beneath a new telephone line. An unmarked turn right takes you away from the line, but the road quickly swings back east to rejoin it.

Logging has greatly disturbed the surroundings, and the roadway is worn to bedrock. Corduroy patches cover a few mud holes. There is little special on the first part of the trail, except in spring when carpets of dogtooth violets mass beneath the stubby growth.

Within fifty minutes the trail levels off in the col west of the summit. Here there is a shed and a covered springhouse with good cold water. The trail, now only a footpath, turns east up the narrow ridge. The route is handsome through an enclosing cover of spruce and balsam. An opening gives a view north to Rich Lake at just about the point an unmarked footpath from NY 28N intersects the trail. Shortly, the tower comes into view at the end of the evergreen-covered tunnel that traverses the last pitch to the summit. The climb, of just over a thousand feet, should take no more than an hour and fifteen minutes.

Goodnow surveys the southern panorama of the High Peaks and the most impressive part of the view is to the northeast, through Indian Pass (see Hike 49). Wallface and the MacIntyre Mountains clearly define the pass. Following along to the right, east, Avalanche Pass is also outlined, with the MacIntyre peaks on the left and Colden on the right. Next, Marcy,

Skylight, and Haystack define the horizon, with Marcy almost hidden behind Redfield and Skylight. The jagged crest of Sawteeth leads up to a part of the series of peaks that Adirondackers call the Range Trail. That route connects the summits of Basin, Saddleback, Gothics, Armstrong, and Upper and Lower Wolfjaw. Here the eastern peaks of the Range Trail lead around to Giant, which is barely visible. To the right of Giant, Colvin, Nippletop, and Dix are easily spotted.

A little north of east lies Boreas Mountain, and south of east is Vanderwhacker, both with fire towers. Goodnow River flows south along the western edge of the mountain, and beyond its flow lie the little-known and rugged slopes of Dun Brook

Along the trail at Goodnow

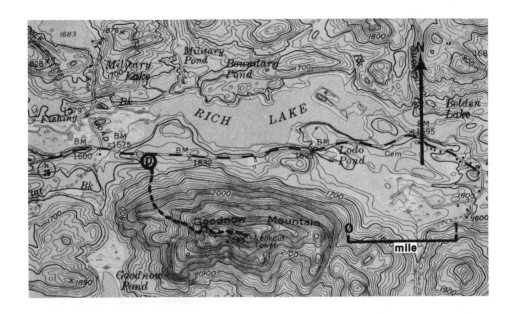

Mountain and the Fishing Brook Range.

Following around to the south, Snowy, 21 miles away on the shore of Indian Lake, is unmistakable. In the south, beyond the small hills that rim the Hudson River Valley, Humphrey, Puffer, and Bullhead range east on the horizon, with the mine cut on Gore making that mountain most distinctive in the south-southeast.

Looking back north, Mount Adams, topped by a tower, rises south of the MacIntyre Mountains. To the left, west, of Indian Pass you can see Henderson and then Santanoni. To the west of Santanoni, and over several intervening hills, lie Couchsachraga and Little Santanoni mountains. Farther left, the Seward Mountains define the northern horizon. To the northwest, Kempshall Mountain lies between you and Long Lake.

Harris Lake, with its state campsite, is visible in the northeastern foreground, just beyond Newcomb. Due north, below Goodnow, is Rich Lake.

After your return, a forty-five minute walk, drive east 1.5 miles toward Newcomb and turn left on Nature Center Road. Park on the right near the highway for the nature trail, which is south of the highway. On the left, .1 mile farther, there is parking for Rich Lake. It is just a short walk west to its sandy shores, where the swimming is great. No camping is allowed, but this .1-mile-long path is a good canoe access. The northern cedar that rim the lake frame handsomely a view of Goodnow and the tower.

Santanoni Preserve

Distance (round trip): 10.2 miles
Vertical rise: minimal
Hiking time: 4 hours
Maps. USGS 15' Newcomb, USGS 15' Santanoni
High Peaks Wilderness Area

Picture yourself camping near or canoeing on a remote lake surrounded by beautiful mountains and having the spot almost to yourself. You can arrange to do it in the Santanoni Preserve, and you do not even have to carry your own canoe.

Santanoni Preserve was once a huge private estate. After it was acquired by the state, it was opened to the public but with restrictions that protect the privacy of all who now enjoy it. Camping is limited to a couple of lean-tos and a few isolated and primitive tent sites around the shores of Newcomb Lake. Free permits limit the number of campers, but the camping spots are rarely full. In spring and fall it is possible to enjoy the handsome lake in almost complete solitude. Best of all, the boathouse that once served the estate now houses boats and canoes that can be rented for a very nominal sum. Make arrangements when you register with the preserve caretaker. Hikers and campers must register with the caretaker, who is on duty seven days a week from 8:00 A.M. to 6:00 P.M.

To maintain the wilderness feeling, no motorized vehicles are permitted in Santanoni. Hunting, in season, is permitted, subject to the usual state regulations. Fishing for both brook and lake trout is limited to artificial lures only, with a minimum size of twelve and twenty-one inches, respectively, and a day limit of three brook trout and one lake trout.

Day hikers and canoeists can easily make the 5.1-mile walk to the estate boathouse in two hours. The trail follows the old estate road that is broad and fairly level and still used by the caretaker. You should plan a fairly early start in order to spend a full day on the lake, and then walk out after a picnic supper. That way you can enjoy birding both in early morning and late evening, when it is best.

Campers find walking with a pack takes a bit longer. They may resent the fact that they are carrying packs when the road appears to be suitable for vehicular traffic; in fact the road is in such good shape that bicyclists can and do use it.

To reach the entrance to the preserve from the east, use either Blue Ridge Road from the Adirondack Northway (Exit 29 off I-87), or NY 28N

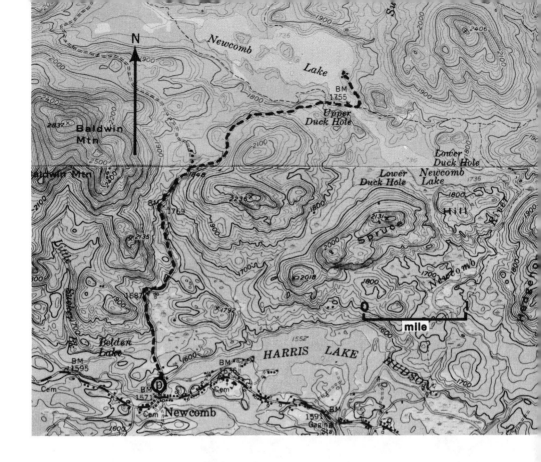

northwest from North Creek. It is about a forty-minute drive along either road to their intersection. Continue on NY 28N west, passing the Harris Lake Campsite in 3.1 miles and crossing the Hudson River in 3.4 miles. The entrance to the preserve is in Newcomb, 5.2 miles from the intersection. If you are driving from the south or west along NY 30, turn east onto NY 28N at Long Lake, and drive 14.7 miles to the entrance. Drive north along the entrance road across the Hudson to the gatehouse near a farmhouse, one of the oldest buildings in the village of Newcomb. Dark brown shingles with red trim and fieldstone distinguish all the estate's buildings, including the magnificent home that still stands on the shore of Newcomb Lake.

A sign near the parking area tells the estate's history. The late Robert C. Pruyn, one of the state's wealthier foresters, assembled the Santanoni Preserve from several smaller parcels in the late 1800s and early 1900s. He used the property until 1953, when it was sold to the Melville family. Through efforts of the Nature Conservancy, the DEC, the Federal Bureau of Outdoor Recreation, and anonymous donors, the land was acquired and given to the state to manage as a wilderness retreat.

From the entrance many foot and

View to Santanoni across Newcomb Lake

horse trails emanate into the preserve and on into the High Peaks area. All routes begin along the estate road.

A parklike area greets you just beyond the gatehouse, a forest of large hemlock, spruce, tamarack, cedar and birch. Down on your right you can spot a beaver flow through a spruce thicket. Within a half-hour you pass the shingled barns and silo of an old farmsite. Stone walls still edge the fields, which lead east to an open flow. The meadow beside the flow is a good place to watch for birds.

The roadway winds past other fieldstone buildings through woods to open fields, across which you can see a small hill to the north; you will circle it to reach the lake. Watch for hawks and owls near the fields. If you make the walk in spring, say late May, you should be able to spot a dozen different warblers. They migrate into the area before the leaves are fully out, making it easy to spot them in the mature forests that edge the road.

The road follows a stream on the right for a time, crossing it on a beautiful stone bridge, passing a wet meadow, and rising a gentle incline to a fork 2.1 miles and less than an hour's walk from the gate. The way left heads to Moose Ponds, but you keep straight on the principal road toward Newcomb Lake, 2.7 miles away. The road begins a very pleasant and gentle descent around the hillside. In very little time you see the lake through the trees. Keep circling, now to the east, above the lake, crossing two stone bridges. At 3.7 miles, a red-marked trail heads left through the woods to numbered campsites on the lake's southern shore. The road now descends to a promontory where a picnic table overlooks the lake. Beyond, the bridge carries you over a narrow neck of the lake. The bridge separates the flows called the Upper and Lower Duck Holes from the western principal part of the lake. Continue along the road, which turns west, paralleling the lakeshore for .4 mile to the estate and boathouse.

The high open forest along the eastern shores appears undisturbed by any logging. Most of the western shoreline and all of the islands are densely covered with cedars. The islands range in size from .3 mile long to tree-covered boulders. Even if you are not a fisherman, you will enjoy exploring the lake's bays and coves. You can easily spend nearly four hours paddling around Newcomb Lake and the Duck Holes, all of which abound with birdlife. The shoreline is partly edged with boulders, often with huge pine capping the rocky promontories, and the lake bottom is generally sandy and perfect for swimming. Standing at the boathouse, you can see Moose Mountain in the west, with Baldwin on the left and Santanoni peaking over the trees on your right. As you move out into the western end of the lake, Santanoni becomes most impressive with its long, thin, curved slide glistening in the sunlight.

You will certainly want to poke about the buildings of the estate. They are massive log structures connected by wide porches and covered breezeways, which seem to attract the slightest winds from the lake. The doors, inlaid with rustic logs in a variety of geometric patterns, are truly fascinating. Huge fieldstone fireplaces warmed every room of this lodge, which was typical of the Adirondacks' retreats built in the late nineteenth and early twentieth century by those whose wealth permitted "camping" in such a grand style.

The return seems a bit steeper than the trip in because of the height-of-land on the shoulder of the hill, less than halfway back to the gatehouse. It is mostly an illusion, for the road never rises more than 200 feet above the level of the lake. Maybe the fact that you notice a climb and the length of the trip out reflects displeasure at leaving so beautiful a spot.

Hoffman Notch

Distance (one way): 7.5 miles
Vertical rise: 300 feet
Hiking time: 6 hours
Map: USGS 15' Schroon Lake
Hoffman Notch Wilderness Area

The Hoffman Notch trail is a beautiful and little-used route though a high mountain pass. Handsome streams, waterfalls, and upland marshes edge the trail its entire length. You can walk into the Notch from either end of the trail and then simply retrace your route, but if you want a full day of great hiking, walk it all at once, traveling from south to north. The logistics of leaving cars at both ends is time-consuming, but not impossible.

The northern trailhead, where you leave your second vehicle, is on the south side of Blue Ridge Road, the western spur of the road at Interchange 29 of the Adirondack Northway (I-87). Here, Blue Ridge Road follows The Branch, which flows south from Elk Lake and then east to the Schroon River. In 2.5 miles you reach the small settlement of Blue Ridge, where lodgings and campsites on private property overlook a set of falls you will certainly want to stop to view. Continuing west, you pass the marked turn for Elk Lake Road in 1.8 miles and 1.5 miles farther come to a small parking area just beyond the bridge over The Branch. Here an

abandoned road heads south along The Branch. Although there are no signposts, the road and the continuing route south are marked by new yellow DEC disks.

Finding the southern trailhead is an adventure in itself. From the Northway, exit onto the parallel highway, NY 9, and drive to Schroon Lake village, about halfway between Interchanges 27 and 28. There take Hoffman Road west, climbing steeply away from the highways. In just over 5 miles it crosses Trout Brook, just beyond which a road forks left to Olmstedville. Less than .2 mile farther, Potash Road forks right. You could turn here, but natives warn that its condition can be marginal. Instead, turn right at the Loch Mueller sign, .8 mile beyond. Loch Mueller Road intersects Potash and continues north past the Dimick Farm (fresh eggs and asparagus in season) to a farmhouse beneath a giant pine.

Pause a moment here to enjoy the view north through Hoffman Notch, to search for bluebirds in the old apple orchard, and to read the sign affixed to the pine: "On this spot in 1845, a sapling of 12 years was transplanted by me. I have watched and protected it in my advancing years. It has given me rest and comfort. Woodsman spare that tree, touch not a single branch. In youth it sheltered me and I'll protect it now. Signed, Paschal P. Warren, June 1, 1920, age 87."

Your route north follows some of the roads early settlers used as they moved into the mountains to harvest the virgin timber and farm the rugged countryside. This isolated and remote valley has been settled since the early nineteenth century.

Continue another 200 yards into a draw and turn right about 100 yards up its far side. The spot is poorly marked but leads into a large open field that serves as the parking area for the trailhead as well as for fishermen who try their luck in the branches of Trout Brook.

Walking from south to north through the Notch you have less of a climb and also gain an enhanced sense of the transition from a southern Adirondack forest to a northern one. The hemlock at the southern edge of the Notch give way to balsam on the north. It also puts the greatest excitement as well as risk of getting wet near the hike's end, where there are several brook crossings. The streams are certainly more beautiful in high water. I think it is worth risking wet feet toward the trail's end just to make sure there is enough water in the flow that plunges from Washburn Ridge, partway along and not far from the trail. The fall is spectacular.

The lovely high meadow where you park offers another fine view of the Notch. Fire rings show that campers have used the clearing. No signs specifically indicate the trail, but if you head into the woods on the north side of the parking area, beside a

"Wilderness" sign, you discover the first of the new yellow DEC trail disks. If you are observant you may also notice here a faint, blue-marked trail heading northwest toward Bailey Pond.

Your route is downhill on an abandoned logging road through a tall and impressive forest with some good-sized white birch. In a hemlock swale the road has been dug out to a depth of several feet. Within fifteen minutes, listen for the West Branch of Trout Brook, which you soon cross on a snowmobile bridge that may not last many more years. In low water the bridge is not needed.

Continue, now uphill, through a lovely forest of pine and birch with a good ground covering of blooming plants. A second bridge and a section of corduroy mark the gentle climb to a very tiny clearing, which has enough clues, apple trees for instance, to indicate that an early settler lived here.

The woods road continues climbing gently through maple and large popple to a fork. Bear right on the fork clearly marked with yellow disks. The road descends a second time and then turns to follow a stream coming in from your left. You are now in a big, deep valley, and only a narrow footpath is worn along the route of the abandoned road. You cross the stream twice within 150 feet.

You are now walking in one of the most stately mixed forests in the Adirondacks, making you wonder if it has even been logged. Huge yellow birch, tall hemlock and ash, and a few large beech stand out. Continuing through a deep, wet glen to the left of the stream, the roadway is filled with lush ferns and wildflowers. You recross the stream on a very slippery log bridge, pass a section of cor-

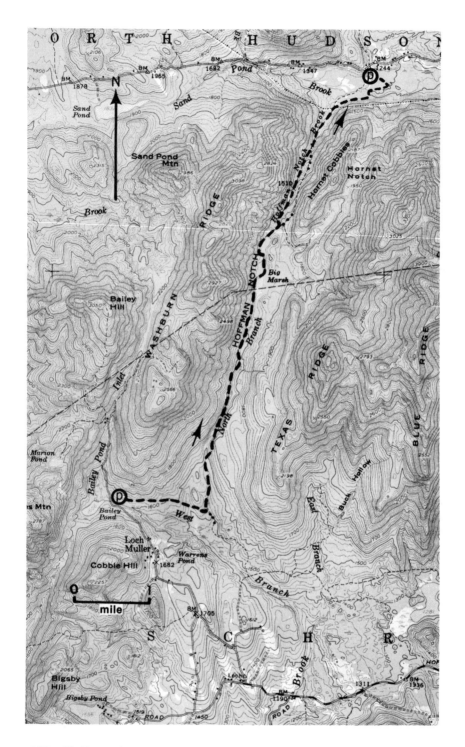

duroy, and finally hear a larger stream. Flowing from the Notch, it is the North Branch of Trout Brook.

You can walk to the North Branch in forty minutes. As you turn north along the brook signs point to Big Marsh. Almost no footpath shows on a little-used route that forks right across a bridge over the brook. It is marked for Big Rogers, the local name for Big Pond. Notice the bear scratch high on the balsam beside the bridge. Bear often sharpen their claws by scraping them on the trunks of trees. The scratches you see on this walk indicate this is bear country and big bear at that.

Your route is now almost due north beside the North Branch, but you cross many small streams that flow from Washburn Ridge on your left. The valley is almost level, and your route is joyously accompanied by the many small riffles and falls in the brook beside you. Big boulders fill the valley, which a magnificent mix of maple and hemlock shade.

Beside the third intermittent stream crossing, stop to notice a huge yellow birch. Its diameter at chest height exceeds five feet. Next you pass a giant rounded boulder shaped like the back of a sleeping dinosaur and capped with moss and polypody ferns. At one point, a glacial drummond lies between you and the stream, but most of the time you walk close to it.

For this first hour or so, you have probably been traveling quickly and easily. Now reduce your pace so you can appreciate the details of the deepening valley. There is so much to see. The hillside above the stream on your right, east, rises directly and steeply from the brook. Ledges on the left now crowd the road, and for a time the valley floor is little more than 100 feet across, so there is

scarcely room to walk. The trail continues for .5 mile as a narrow footpath through a rich forest floor, threading its way between a jumble of boulders and ledges.

You finally become aware that you are climbing into the Notch. For a time the valley is more open, filled here with giant spruce and pine, through which you can glimpse the top of Texas Ridge on your right.

After an hour and a half—or more if you've kept a leisurely pace—and a distance of just over 3 miles, the trail climbs above an alder meadow. Giant spruce edge the flow and through them you sense you are seeing the end of the Notch in the distant north. Leave the trail to step out into the sphagnum bog filled with spruce and hemlock stumps and many signs of old beaver work. Again look for bear scratches on the spruce.

The trail, carpeted with violets, continues close to the bog's edge, over which are more views of Texas Ridge. As the valley narrows again, you climb over small ledges beside the marshy stream. You are nearly at the top of the Notch. Look for a giant tree, felled on your left beside the trail. A typical 13½-foot section has been removed from the butt end, but the rest, stretching over 100 feet, has been left to decay, so that a fair-sized birch and several small evergreens grow from its rotted remains.

Erratics and boulders fill the valley, and a balsam thicket crowds a patch of royal fern close to the bog. After a bit more than two hours of walking, a distance of about 4 miles, you see the waters of Big Marsh, which is just over halfway through the Notch. It takes about ten minutes to walk along the marsh to find a picnic rock with a view of the hills to the east.

Cliffs and ledges extend almost to

the water's edge, and huge boulders ring the marsh, where an open flow of shallow water reflects the surrounding hills as well as the tall pine and white birch that border the marsh. Texas Ridge rises to the south, and the steep knob to the north is Hornet Cobbles. East, opposite your perch, is the valley cut by a stream flowing from the flanks of the Blue Ridge Range. The peak of Hoffman Mountain rises above that valley.

As you continue the valley broadens. Turn away from the marsh to hug the western side, crossing several intermittent streams. The trail is very narrow, with frequent and necessary markers. It takes at least twenty minutes to cross the rest of the Notch and begin the descent, where the old roadway becomes apparent again.

Within thirty minutes you are really descending and can begin to hear Hoffman Notch Brook, which accompanies you most of the remaining distance. You first approach the brook near a wonderful little waterfall. A bridge here has washed away, so you must devise an alternate method of crossing. In summer, hopping stones to continue on the trail is no problem. In high water, stay on the left and bushwhack along the stream to pick up the trail again in about .2 mile. Actually the bushwhack route is more interesting than the trail, for you stay within the deepest part of the hemlock-shrouded gorge, walking close to the rapids and little falls. The route is rugged, the drop is steep, and the ravine is very deep, but the trek is beautiful. Within fifteen minutes you should see yellow markers again. The bridge on which the trail used to recross here is also washed out.

Good-sized cliffs and ledges rise on your left, and you occasionally glimpse Hornet Cobbles, which seems to loom incredibly steeply above the trail on the right. When you reach an old logging clearing in a grove of maple saplings, less than an hour's walk from Big Marsh, begin looking carefully to your left. Shortly, you should catch sight of a 100-foot ledge topped with cedars and birch, over which a stream of water shoots, splitting into several cascades, dropping to pools on ledges on the dark black rock face, and then splitting again into a multitude of fine sprays.

If you are tempted to scramble up the talus slope for a better look at the falls, watch out for the horse nettles that cover the hillside and beware of poison ivy. This may be one of the most remote sites reached by that companion of man.

Continuing north beside the stream, you pass a waterfall right beside a giant boulder, an erratic over thirty feet in diameter and more than fifteen feet high. Many other boulders fill the valley. Giant cedars grow among the hemlock, which make the stream so dark photographing is impossible. The valley narrows again, so that it is now scarcely 100 yards across. That horse and oxcarts once traveled this route defies belief . . .

Gradually the brook levels, its route becoming more sinuous but its shores still edged with impressive erratics. Gravel improvements indicate the road's recent use. Trees become smaller, and you pass a small gravel pit, some abandoned and rusted machinery, and many signs of a logging camp. Your route is now high above the stream, which is still lovely

View of Hoffman Notch and Hoffman Mountain

in the deep gorge below you. The browns, turquoises, and greens of lichens color its light grey rocks.

After walking an hour and a half from the Notch, you reach a sign that says you have left the Hoffman Notch Wilderness Area. Land ahead is private, but the state has obtained an easement for the trail. Hunting, fishing, and camping are not permitted.

The trail meets the stream at a spot that could be difficult to ford in high water. In early spring or after a rain, you will surely get wet. In low water, one good-sized jump may be all that is needed. The trail continues level, staying east of the stream on a soft-packed, open roadway, but still within the sound of water. You should arrive at a broad cleared swath below a power line within two hours of leaving Big Marsh.

No sign indicates the trail across the field, and the obvious route straight ahead to the continuing roadway is not the right choice! Walk east in the power line clearing at least 150 yards, then enter the woods on the north below the ledge on which the first of the huge stanchions for the power line is mounted. The spot is poorly marked. It is the beginning of a new route that has been cut and marked with the yellow disks to avoid a beaver flow that flooded the old road and most of the lowlands between you and Blue Ridge Road, your final destination. The trail heads east and almost parallels the power line, staying just below the edge of the trees, and then swings north again to traverse the flooded lands and cross Hoffman Notch Brook on a rickety bridge perched on top of an untended beaver dam. Someone, man or beaver, has work to do. The trail intersects the road again with 200 yards to the bridge and climbs quickly to the highway.

Deeper, more rugged and dramatic mountain passes exist in the Adirondacks but none are more remote or untouched by civilization. The trail is not particularly difficult, and it is ranked by experienced Adirondackers among the best of the wilderness treks.

Boreas Mountain

Distance (round trip): 7.2 miles
Vertical rise: 2,076 feet
Hiking time: 4 hours
Map: USGS 15' Mount Marcy, USGS 15' Schroon Lake

Facing each other on opposite sides of Elk Lake, both Boreas and Sunrise mountains have spectacular views of the southern sides of the eastern High Peaks. You may still climb Boreas, but because the tower on its summit has been closed, that mountain's magnificent panorama must now be enjoyed in pieces through openings in the trees. A worse fate has befallen Sunrise, which has an unrestricted view toward Mount Marcy from open rock ledges. The trail to its summit, like that of Boreas's, crosses private property. Careless and unthinking hikers have littered the trail and otherwise abused the private land, forcing its owners to limit hikers to guests of the Elk Lake Lodge and groups who have obtained special permission.

Even if you are climbing only Boreas, the Elk Lake Lodge is an elegant place to stay. Guests may canoe around the bays and islands of Elk Lake, surrounded by a sweep of mountains that includes Mount Marcy, Nippletop, and Dix. Hikers find it a delightful base for exploring the area. The regulations governing the use of Elk Lake lands are simple: no

camping, hunting, fishing, or building of fires. The trailhead for Boreas is just outside the gate of the Elk Lake Lodge property, but still on private land. When you hike Boreas, be sure to respect those lands so all may continue to enjoy the mountain.

Now, to the pleasure of the mountain. From many peaks near the periphery of the Adirondacks, the distant horizon has been defined by some aspect of the eastern High Peaks. The hikes in this guide have you approaching the inner mountain range that holds the Adirondacks' highest peaks as you would approach a great sculptural work of art, looking at it from different angles, tracing its lines and curves, examining its shapes and masses, watching the play of light and shadow cast by sun and clouds, pausing to enjoy the brilliance of the white slash of mountain slides or the sparkle reflected from high mountain streams.

When you climb the eastern High Peaks, the views from the summits within this crowded cluster of mountains make you feel on top of the world, but few of these vistas rival those from the peaks immediately

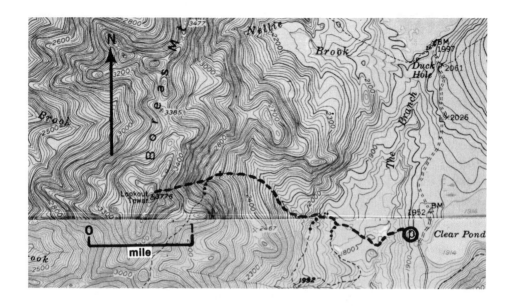

surrounding the Adirondacks' highest
range. Circling this sculptural mass,
you find that the most spectacular of
all views is from the south, from
Boreas and Sunrise, looking to the
steepest faces, the deepest mountain
passes, and the greatest expanse of
bare rock and precipitous slides.

From one of the openings between
the trees on Boreas you see northeast
across Elk Lake to a range that
traces the outline of a bracket
against the horizon. Hough is the
apex, flanked by Dix and McComb
mountains, each of which has enormous vertical slides. Farther north,
the flanks of Dix and Nippletop form
Hunters Pass. From Boreas you see
right through the pass to Giant Mountain, marked by the slides surrounding its cirque. North, left, of Nippletop
is the row of mountains flanking the
east side of the Ausable valley with
Blake Mountain and Mount Colvin
clearly identified.

On the north side of the Ausable

valley, you see Sawteeth with the
rocky face of Gothics right behind.
You cannot help but be impressed by
its rocky countenance. Continuing
left, the tops of Saddleback and
Basin lead to the impressive cluster
of Skylight, Marcy, and Haystack.
Both Saddleback and Basin have
deep slashes of open rock. The latter
group is most easily seen from the
top of a rock west of the abandoned
tower. From there also you can just
barely see the MacIntyre Mountains.
Through another small opening west
of the tower the North River Mountains are visible over Boreas Ponds.
To the right and beyond these mountains is Santanoni, with its distinctive
scar. Behind Santanoni and to the
north, right, are Seward and Seymour.
Next north is Redfield with Allen
before it and Ampersand peeping over
a cut to Redfield's left.

This is considered the best view of
the mountains that border the
Ausable valley and on the north. Un-

fortunately, the southern landmarks, once visible from the tower, cannot be enjoyed. That view included Pharaoh Mountain on the southeast and Blue Mountain on the southwest.

Unhappily, the trail to these views is not among the Adirondacks' best; over 2 miles of the route are through recently logged lands using a segment of a network of rocky logging roads.

To reach the trailhead, exit from the Adirondack Northway (I-87) at Interchange 29, and turn left, west, on Blue Ridge Road toward Newcomb. In 4 miles, bear north on dirt Elk Lake Road and park at the designated spot in 3.2 miles.

Red trail markers lead you across the private land on a narrow footpath, west and downhill .3 mile toward The Branch. The trail crosses The Branch on a sturdy hikers' log bridge at the edge of an alder bed to join an old logging road. In the next mile the trail winds through level terrain, circling a spruce bog. After following the trail for twenty minutes you should come to a sign indicating that Boreas is 2.5 miles away. You can spot the summit of Boreas through the trees above the swamp bordering the road.

Bunchberry edge the road as it approaches another spruce bog. Cross a small stream on a log bridge and continue on the level through the grasses of an older beaver flow. Beyond the meadow, bear left on the road, which is now obvious again. Beaver must have flooded it in the recent past. What a rush of water it must have taken to wash out the next stretch of road, which is rutted into deep gullies! Tall maples edge the way for a short stretch, but you soon emerge in an open field. A second logging road crosses at right angles, but you continue straight to the field's far side and up through the woods. There is now a stream on your right.

Unfortunately the red trail markers are often hidden by new growth. Most of the time there is no question about the direction to take, and usually you will find a marker if you search for it. However, the maze of logging roads here sometimes confuses the road along which the trail is routed. The first of the hidden markers is at the edge of a dense thicket of cherry trees beyond the field. After thirty-five minutes of walking, at about 1.3 miles, the trail makes a well-marked left turn up a slide to intersect another logging road. Here go left, or north.

For the next mile you climb gently but steadily through an uninteresting stretch of logged lands. You meet another confusing intersection within five minutes. Go straight across the remains of a washed-out bridge, passing a gravel pit on your right and staying on the left side of a field.

The stream is now on your left, and through an opening you have another glimpse of the tower on the summit, which does not appear much closer. In fifteen minutes more, or 1.9 miles from the start, the trail turns left to another logging road to cross the stream you have been following. The red trail marker is obscured but a red disk has been placed conspicuously in the middle of the bridge. The continuing roadway is terribly washed out, with the footpath threading between wheel ruts nearly two feet deep. Again you see the mountain above a field ahead of you. You go straight through the field, ignoring a left fork. The road climbs more steeply for .4 mile and ends in a field that contains the abandoned cabin for the fire observer.

The stream behind the cabin is a

230 *Boreas Mountain*

good place to stop for water. The trail plunges into the woods left of the cabin and immediately across the creek begins up the mountain. Nearly 1,000 feet remain to climb in the last .9 mile. The forest is cooler and less disturbed but still composed of fairly small trees. The route is a steep, steady climb through balsam and spruce. You cross a small stream on the remains of a washed-out bridge .3 mile from the cabin clearing and recross the stream shortly in a deep draw edged with birch and mountain ash. The third time you cross the stream it has dwindled to barely a trickle.

Within thirty minutes from the cabin you climb quite steeply through a rocky ravine where the trail is washed. The grade levels briefly before leading into an incredibly steep pitch, but fifteen minutes of hard hiking ("climbing" might be more exact) brings you to a forested spot where blue sky shows through the trees in all directions. After a series of small switchbacks the light breeze alerts you that you are approaching a ridge of the mountain. As you come over the ridge in a meadow of tall ferns, turn left to head up the narrow spine toward the summit. Within a couple of minutes you will see the tower on a knoll on your left.

The tower is closed and its support cables are loose. Stairs lean against the lower landing, but they are without bolts, so consider them unsafe. Stay with the views through the trees.

On the descent you should have no problem with any directions. All the logging roads seem to funnel toward the route you are following.

View from Boreas

Giant Mountain

Distance (one way): 6.6 miles
Vertical rise: 3,000 feet
Hiking time: 6 hours
Maps: USGS 15' Mount Marcy, USGS 15' Elizabethtown
Giant Mountain Wilderness Area

Giant is in every way an appropriate name for the mountain between Pleasant Valley south of Elizabethtown and the East Branch of the Ausable south of Keene Valley. Several trails lead to its summit, and although the route chosen here, from the west, presents the greatest vertical rise of any hike described in this guide, trails from Pleasant Valley on Giant's east side require another thousand feet of climbing. Giant is indeed a giant. The summit commands the best view from the east of the High Peaks, while overlooking almost all of the Champlain Valley and, on south, to the mountains beside Lake George. The climb from Chapel Pond on the west is challenging, and you can descend via the trail along Roaring Brook, also on the west, for a hike as varied as you could wish. If you pause for a picnic lunch on Giant's summit, the day's outing should take at least 7 hours.

If you plan to hike the two trails as described here, two cars are advisable. You can walk along NY 73 between the Chapel Pond and roaring Brook trailheads in less than a half-hour, but the highway is very busy

and apt to be dangerous for pedestrians. If you decide simply to retrace your route, I suggest using the Chapel Pond trail. The unfolding views on that trail far exceed any along the Roaring Brook route. The trip is fairly strenuous, so be sure you carry enough water. The summit is exposed, so also carry extra clothing.

To reach the trailheads, take Exit 30 off the Adirondack Northway (I-87) and head northwest on NY 73, following signs for Keene Valley. Chapel Pond is 3.6 miles beyond the road that forks right toward Elizabethtown. The Roaring Brook trailhead, where your hike ends, is 1.4 miles farther, opposite the southern entrance to the Ausable Club.

After parking at Chapel Pond, and if you can tear yourself away from the views of the cliffs that rise from the pond, as well as those on the shoulder of Giant, walk south 250 yards to the trailhead, which is concealed in a marsh on the east side of the road. An inconspicuous sign denotes the route to Giant via the Ridge Trail.

Orange Adirondack Trail Improvement Society (ATIS) markers indicate the way. You begin to climb immediately after crossing an intermittent stream. Rocks are tumbled everywhere. At .3 mile the trail angles left and a sign points right to a spring that is not dependable in dry weather. New birch railings guide you to a recently rerouted stretch of trail. Follow the prescribed route, which zigzags across the steep slope. A steeper climb is possible but it hastens erosion. The sparse birch cover tells of raging forest fires, and there is no ground cover to hold the thin soil. The mountainside is amazingly bare, brown, and sterile below the tree cover.

Within fifteen minutes, as you traverse back toward the highway, a glimpse of Round Mountain serves as a gauge on how rapidly you are climbing. In .5 mile you reach a rubble-filled wash and continue under overhanging ledges. The wash was once the outlet of the Giant's Washbowl, a tiny pond on the mountainside. After walking less than a half-hour, you reach an unmarked fork where a footpath leads 50 feet to the left to the edge of a cliff that drops directly to the highway by Chapel Pond. Notice how the cliffs that overhang the western side of the pond have already shrunk below you. The tops of Armstrong and the Wolf-jaws are visible to the west.

Continue on the right fork, almost on the cliff edge, to a second lookout and then turn away from the cliff to drop a few feet to a trail junction .7 mile from the highway. The left fork leads to Saint Huberts, but you continue straight beside the Giant's Washbowl. Pause to enjoy the reflections of the Giant's cliffs. The route heads northeast into a spruce and hemlock grove, which indicates the limits of the fires up the mountain.

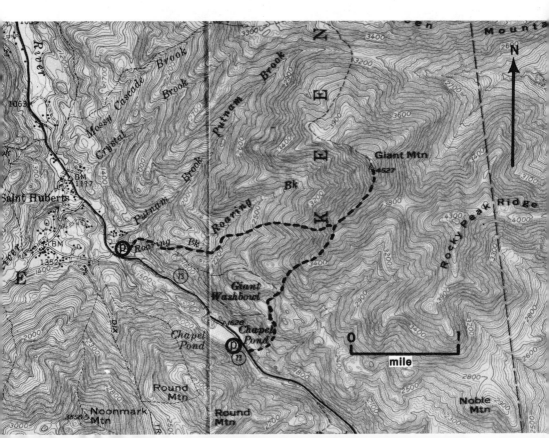

234 *Giant Mountain*

The trail continues through deep woods with huge cedars for .2 mile to a second marked junction where the fork left also heads towards Saint Huberts, via Roaring Brook.

Bearing right, you start up a steep pitch, and the cover quickly thins. After about an hour of climbing, a slide at 1.2 miles yields views across the valley to Round Mountain and Noonmark. You now scramble up bare rock to a second lookout southwest toward Hough and both South and East Dix mountains. The peaks covered by the Range Trail are now visible beyond the Ausable valley.

For the twenty minutes you need to ascend the sheer rock face, cairns guide you along the right. The climb continues between view spots, each providing needed respite. Gothics becomes clearly distinguished between Sawteeth and Wolfjaw. The opening south through the long valley shows Pharaoh Mountain's cone 24 miles away and the Tip of the Tongue and Black Mountain near Lake George 40 miles away.

Cairns direct the trail between the scrubby clumps of spruce, balsam, and blueberries that separate patches of open rock. You come to an overlook east toward Rocky Peak Ridge about the same time you see a false summit on Giant. Chapel Pond seems no bigger than a drop of water. The Ausable Club is visible in the western foreground, and the mountains on the north side of Johns Brook Valley appear above the mountains of the Range Trail.

You continue to scramble through low woods to another sheer slope of open rock. The views of only ten minutes before are even more dra-

View of Chapel Pond

matic, and now you begin to see straight through Hunters Pass, with Dix on the left and Dial on the right. Nippletop is still hidden behind Dial, but Hough, McComb, South Dix, and East Dix now range as separate peaks to the south. Colvin appears on the side of Ausable Lake, and the bare cone of Haystack is apparent between Gothics and Sawteeth.

The trail forks, the way right climbing over and the way left circling a little knob from which the southern end of Giant's summit ridge is visible. The trails rejoin at about 1.8 miles and just under two hours into your hike. You continue across a ridge, looking toward the Giant's cirque, the huge bowl slashed by recent slides, which make this mountain recognizable from such enormous distances.

Beyond a relatively level stretch, the trail rises to another intersection, 2.2 miles from Chapel Pond. The left fork leads down toward Saint Huberts, the way you will return. The right fork leads .7 mile and 700 feet to the summit, a climb you can make in a half-hour. You pass a slant rock shelter and then reach a level stretch around the top of the cirque, with a steep rock ledge on your right. The footpath is narrow, winding through trees scarcely taller than hikers' heads. The summit is still .3 mile ahead. One more steep pitch brings you to it. A couple hundred yards before the actual peak, another trail forks right, leading in .7 mile to the Rocky Peak Ridge.

Walk along the summit ridge to find overlooks for all directions. Right at your feet extends the new scar of the slide that washed from Giant's summit in a violent series of thunderstorms. Before you, across the deep, scarred valley enclosed by the Giant's arms, spread the Ausable valley with Gothics beyond, a little south of west, and Mount Marcy finally visible above it. Over the wooded slopes north of Gothics lies MacIntyre, with Colden barely visible between it and Marcy.

On the northern side of Johns Brook Valley, Big Slide is to the left of Cascade and Porter, which appear almost as two summits of the same mountain. To the right of MacIntyre on the distant horizon, MacNaughton, Street, and Nye form a ridge ending over Big Slide. To the right of Porter and Cascade, the long ridge with lots of rock is Pitchoff, and beyond it, the Sentinels and Whiteface are visible.

Now, as you look through Hunters Pass, the tower on Boreas is visible. To its right and 43 miles distant are the steep slopes of Puffer and the heart-shaped top of Humphrey to the left. Farther left, Snowy's peak is obvious, and continuing left, Panther and Wakely are visible with good binoculars.

Hurricane is obvious in the northeast, identified by its tower and rock summit. The eastern horizon is filled with the sweep of Lake Champlain; and of the distant Green Mountains, only Camel's Hump and Mount Mansfield are obvious and easily identified. The mountains of Vermont seem to range forever, to both the north and south.

Retrace your route .7 mile to the trail to Saint Huberts. The route is steep enough so that you may need twenty-five minutes to reach the junction. Take the right fork, which heads into deep woods, traversing the steep slopes of Giant, dropping like a rock. The slopes you cross are sometimes pitched at a sixty-degree angle, so even the traverse route is steep. No open places distract you as you keep your eyes on the trail to ensure safe footing.

Thirty minutes from the junction the trail levels out, but you must walk a bit farther before the trees become noticeably taller. As you enter a valley you sense you are near the edge of the glacial cirque, but new growth conceals it from view. The steep descent continues for the better part of an hour on this trail, covering nearly 1.5 miles before reaching a muddy seep within a majestic hemlock grove. From here you can hear the water of Roaring Brook. You cross two streams flowing from your left in .2 mile, and reach a trail junction in another .1 mile. The route left is through the Giant's Nubble. You turn right and shortly cross the brook on the pure white rocks amidst signs of terrifying amounts of water and fallen debris. The rubble from the slide is now uphill above you. A trail to the right heads up the mountain but is quickly obliterated by the slide. You turn left to follow the valley of Roaring Brook, walking through the prettiest wooded section on the hike, a hemlock grove of tall, straight, towering trees.

A path forks left 3.3 miles from the summit, back to the top of Roaring Brook Falls, a place of beauty and danger. The trail continues on a contour around a deep ravine, running first through magnificient hemlock and then past huge birch, and finally dropping to the valley floor. The entire 3.6-mile descent, with time to pause and study the slide and enjoy the falls, takes at least two hours and a half.

Indian Pass

Distance (one way): 10.6 miles
Vertical rise: 674 feet
Hiking time: 7 hours
Maps: USGS 15' Mount Marcy, USGS 15' Santanoni
High Peaks Wilderness Area

In 1836 Professor Ebenezer Emmons was appointed chief geologist in charge of studying the Adirondacks. In the course of this study he visited the "Adirondack Pass" we now know as Indian Pass. Of it he wrote that "in this country there is no object of the kind on a scale so vast and imposing as this. We look upon the Falls of Niagara with awe and a feeling of our insignificance; but much more are we impressed with the great and sublime in the view of the simple and naked rock of the Adirondack Pass." Later nineteenth-century explorers discovered many more dramatic natural features, but Indian Pass remains the most incredibly wild and dramatic spot in the eastern United States.

Indian Pass bisects the Adirondack High Peaks. You can hike through it in one day, if you arrange to leave a car at both the north and south trailheads. I suggest you walk the pass from north to south for both aesthetic and historic reasons. The route is one to anticipate and savor, so set aside ample time to appreciate the marvelous sights and sounds you will encounter.

To heighten the drama read Alfred Billings Street's nineteenth-century classic *The Indian Pass* before you go. He used every passionate and romantic adjective to describe the pass's awe-inspiring rocks, cliffs, and vistas. For example, a typical summer thunderstorm became a dialogue between the echoing voices of the mountains. For all the excesses of his nineteenth-century prose, you will discover that the pass remains the "magnificent spectacle" he described.

The quirks of sound and echoes that astounded Street will amaze you, for the voices of other hikers seem to reflect from many improbable sources. According to Street, Indians called the pass, He-no-do-as-da, the path of the thunder, or Os-ten-wanne, Great Rock, or Otne-yar-heh, the Stonish Giants.

The southern trailhead, where your hike ends, is the Upper works Trailhead north of Tahawus, the site of National Lead Company's titanium mine. From Exit 29 of the Adirondack Northway (I-87), drive west 13.5 miles on Blue Ridge Road to an intersection marked Tahawus and turn right, or north. From Long Lake on NY 30, take

NY 28N east 15.5 miles through Newcomb and turn north at the marked intersection. Just south of the entrance to the mine, a road forks left 3.7 miles to the Upper Works Trailhead.

To reach the northern trailhead, drive to the end of Heart Lake Road which runs south from NY 73 at the hamlet of North Elba, 11.2 miles west of Keene and 3.2 miles east of Lake Placid. Park by the Adirondac Loj, which is owned and managed by the Adirondack Mountain Club. The club charges a nominal parking fee.

Walk north on Heart Lake Road from the Loj parking lot 100 yards to the trailhead. The red-marked trail circles north of the Loj, swings south beside the Natural History Museum, and continues south along the shore of Heart Lake, following a dirt road which gives access to lean-tos and campsites on Loj property.

Within .2 mile you pass a trail that forks right to head up Mount Jo. That trail, which is described excellently in Dr. Edwin Ketchledge's *Guide to the Natural History of Mt. Jo,* is short and spectacular. First-time visitors to the High Peaks will find it an excellent introduction. From Mount Jo, the view across Heart Lake to the MacIntyre Mountains is most beautiful.

In less than fifteen minutes, .5 mile from the start, you reach the end of the lake, where a side trail forks left to circle it. Continue straight, passing the sign-in box for the trail, through a birch and cedar second-growth forest over rolling country. Within .1 mile you reach the boundary of state land. For the next 1.5 miles the walking is easy on a good hard-packed trail. Enormous spruce and good-sized balsam dot the hardwood forest of beech, maple, and birch. A rich forest floor supports a wide variety of wildflowers and ferns. In summer the red berries of twisted stalk and the blue berries of clintonia stand out beside the trail. Openings to the right through the trees give hints of the outline of the valley of Indian Pass Brook. While some guidebooks pay scant attention to these first 2 miles, you should not, for you are walking in a very fine forest.

In addition to red trail markers, yellow markers with red numbers at .5 mile intervals measure your progress from the Loj. You can easily reach the 2-mile marker within an hour. In another .1 mile, on the far side of a stream crossing, a loop trail heads right, past Rock Falls and a lean-to. This spur is little more than 200 yards longer than the main trail, so take it and enjoy walking beside Indian Pass Brook with its white stone base and views of the falls that drop into a deep pool from a chute through a deep cleft in the bedrock. Returning to the main trail requires scrambling up a short pitch, but the entire detour, .3 mile long, should take no more than fifteen minutes to walk.

Where you return to the main trail, a benchmark marks the elevation as 2,160 feet. Turn right, south, passing an intermittent stream and then a second stream in a small gorge. Beyond a rocky section you encounter a mud hole, and you pass the 3-mile marker in the midst of a big stretch of mud and corduroy.

There are interesting ledges on your left as the walking continues easy and level. Along this stretch you may encounter a howler, or widowmaker, a treetop leaning on a second tree and rubbing against it to create weird shrieking sounds.

Through openings to the right you should be able to glimpse the shoulders of Street and Nye moun-

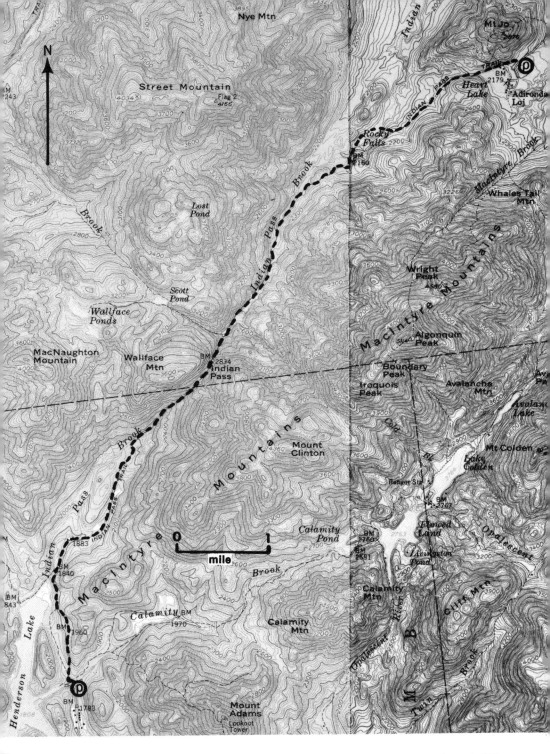

tains and the unnamed mountain that conceals Lost Pond near its summit. You cross one and then another creek, where ledges on surrounding hills begin to enclose the pass. As the valley narrows you reach the Scott's Clearing lean-to, 4 miles from the Loj. Ford the creek in front of the lean-to by hopping rocks. The trail then turns right, and within a few minutes you enter the meadow of Scott's Clearing, which today is filled with raspberries, barrel staves and iron artifacts, and spectacular white birch.

In another .3 mile, a blue-marked trail heads west to Wallface and Scott ponds. Just beyond, a marvelous rock dam creates a flow over which there is a view of Wallface Mountain and Indian Pass. An ancient beaver house stands in the pond, and signs of beaver work abound. A low water-level trail continues toward Indian Pass, but it can be wet even in a dry summer. I suggest you walk an alternate route, which circuits a small hill whose cliff face drops directly to the pond. To find it, angle left at the east end of the dam, almost as if to parallel the trail from the lean-to, and walk to the brook. For about 100 yards the trail follows the brook, whose rock base is strangely colored steel gray. It then swings up a draw; the footing is rough among the rocks and roots. Rounding the top of the draw, the trail crosses a height-of-land in a small ravine, turns toward the valley, and starts down through a steep cleft that cuts the cliff wall.

When you return to the level of the flow again, you become aware of how narrow the valley is. A rock wall is now visible on the east. You cross a stream that enters from the left at 4.7 miles. The next section of trail lies too close to Indian Pass Brook, and

footing is apt to be wet until you cross a second brook, .2 mile farther. Both streams flow from Algonquin Pass. At 5.1 miles, after about two and a half hours of walking, you intersect a yellow-marked trail that heads east for 3.3 miles to Lake Colden.

Just beyond that trail junction you have a good view of cliffs on an unnamed knob, but then the pass becomes progressively narrower, and vertical cliffs form walls on both sides of the stream. You cross Indian Pass Brook on a gravely wash, and then recross it to follow a smaller flow from the pass. Just beyond you see the outlet of Scott Pond, which flows from the west.

The trail now enters the narrow cleft of Indian Pass and begins to climb rapidly. A faint footpath winds up and over boulders and moss-covered ledges, following the small cold brook that flows from the pass. Steep cliffs face the flanks of MacIntyre to form the pass's eastern wall. Here the pass itself is scarcely 100 feet wide and filled with the rubble of ancient slides. You may often have to use your hands to help yourself along. The dark, moss-covered canyon with overhanging cliffs ends all too soon. This entrance to the pass is but .4-mile long. It should take twenty minutes to scramble up the 400-foot rise into the pass.

As you reach the end of the ravine, Wallface begins to loom high up on your right, its sheer, vertical cliff cut jaggedly. The pass opens wide, and you climb a few feet on the east side, overlooking a precipitous mass of boulders so rugged the trail could not possibly be routed through the deepest part. As you walk the short distance of the height-of-land, watch for the holes and the mouths of caves among the slabs. On a hot summer day fog and mist rise in cool drafts from these crevices, where ice often persists well into July. The sharply angular tops of the larger boulders support lichens and mosses and even large spruce and birch. Rising above it all, Wallface creates a dramatic backdrop for the wild scene.

The pass developed as a northeast-trending fault at the same time as many other Adirondack fault valleys from pressures created by the Taconic uplift, But while many of these faults are filled with long, thin lakes, rocks and boulders fallen from the cliff of Wallface and the flanks of MacIntyre have filled the pass to its present level.

By the route you have taken it is nearly 5.8 miles to the height-of-land in the pass, a point denoted by a DEC trail marker. As you continue south, the temperature rises noticeably when the trail leads a few feet up a ridge on the east side of the pass. As you make a short descent, the sheer cliffs, columns, and hanging ledges on Wallface seem even higher. You walk through a small meadow, and within ten minutes reach a clearing with a fireplace. This is a good stopping spot for viewing the highest part of the cliffs, which rise nearly 1,000 feet above you.

To continue south, find and cross a small stream. It, like the brook on the north, rises from a spring in the height of the pass. The northern brook makes its way to the West Branch of the Ausable, which empties into Lake Champlain. The one you have just met, confusingly also called Indian Pass Brook, flows south into Lake Henderson, whose outlet, Calamity Brook, joins the Hudson River.

Just beyond the meadow an enormous fallen slab of cliff blocks the trail. You wind around it, climbing slightly before beginning the final descent, which is along a ridge above and on the east side of the gorge. The south side of the pass is drier and more open than the north. Its sides are precipitously steep below you. After a half-hour walk, for it takes that long to enjoy this .4-mile segment, you reach a small footpath that heads right through the edge of forest to a huge boulder, Summit Rock, which marks the southern edge of Indian Pass. It overlooks the broad sweep of the pass as it falls off toward Lake Henderson, with Henderson and Santanoni mountains behind. The sight rivals the majestic grandeur of the vista back toward the cliffs on Wallface. You will stand on the outcrop like the tiny figures of the Hudson River School painters, overlooking an awe-inspiring view, completely overwhelmed by the scale of the rocks and forests around you.

A steep descent of 500 feet over .5 mile to the southern Indian Pass Brook follows. Within a few minutes you reach the first ladder, a necessary convenience because of the cliffs that rim the pass. The jumble of boulders, caves, and overhanging cliffs continues. Then, in a spot not well marked, the trail turns right, east, toward the gorge around a ledge, at the beginning of a very steep sliding descent into the valley. Lovely views accompany you on the precipitous route.

By the time you reach a second ladder, this one broken, the valley has become quite broad. The terrain continues to be rugged. A few openings between tree-capped boulders offer dramatic views of Wallface, which seems to loom even higher than it did before. You continue to look down in-

to the depths of the cleft on your right, with everything on a much larger scale than it was along the northern entrance to the pass.

You pass a waterfall just before you actually reach and cross the brook. Here you have your last view back of the cliffs on Wallface. It will probably take you at least a half-hour to cover the .5-mile descent from Summit Rock.

The stream crossing marks a real change in the route, for the trail now enters deep mature woods. The descent is gentle for a short time, until you reach a boggy section of trail. Cross it, on slippery logs, looking for turtlehead as you go.

You cross the wash of an intermittent stream, which affords views back east to the ridge that makes up the foothills of the MacIntyre Mountains. The trail crosses a larger stream, the outlet of Wallface Ponds, and then continues beneath ledges on the west side of the valley to the Wallface lean-to, 1.2 miles and at least a half-hour from the stream crossing.

A washed-out bridge is all there is for crossing a small stream just below the lean-to. Within twenty minutes the trail angles left up a small rise, where it meets a freshly painted but ambiguous sign, on which is written in elegant script only the word "Bridge." Turn left from the trail to follow a freshly cut, narrow footpath 100 yards east to a beautiful new bridge over Indian Pass Brook. A ten-foot-tall crib of boulders supports the bridge's west end, while a single boulder supports the east end. Beyond, the footpath turns south beside the stream and leads to an old clear-

Summit Rock and Wallface
in Indian Pass

ing with another bridge sign and an incorrect mileage marker where the trail forks. A blue-marked trail heads back east toward Colden. It is .3-mile to the Henderson lean-to, and 2 miles from the clearing to the Upper Works Trailhead. The trail stays near the stream as far as the lean-to, which is less than 100 yards from the boundary of private lands. The red-marked trail continues through private lands. Permission to cross has been granted hikers, but the lands are posted against fishing, hunting, trapping, and camping.

At a major intersection .1 mile south of the boundary, a trail turns right, west, toward Duck Hole and Corrys, west of Ampersand.

Here you pick up a yellow-marked trail heading south along logging roads improved with gravel. Because the surrounding land is private, you never really see Lake Henderson. After a dull, relatively level stretch you cross the Hudson River, just below the outlet of Lake Henderson. In another five minutes you walk downhill to the trailhead and your waiting car.

It takes a full day to enjoy the 10.6-mile walk, but there is still more to see. Immediately south of the Upper Works Trailhead, a row of deserted houses marks the 1833 settlement of Adirondac where the workers of the McIntyre Iron Works were housed.

A mile south of the trailhead stands the stone tower of the mine's blast furnace, erected in 1854. A beauty of the precise angles of the tower's cut stone will remind you of European castles. The tower, nearly forty-eight feet tall, now bears a crown of cedar and huge birch.

The iron ore was "discovered" in 1826 by a party who made the trip through Indian Pass from North Elba, led by an Indian guide, Lewis Elijah, who knew the site of the ore bed. The group included my great-great-grandfather's brother, Duncan McMartin; David Henderson; a black manservant; and a dog called Wallace. Within a few years, a company formed by Henderson, McMartin, and Archibald McIntyre began mining and shipping out the high-grade iron ore. Unfortunately, high titanium content, which made ore separation difficult, and the problems of shipping the ore from its wilderness location brought an end to the iron mining operation after only a few years.

Driving south toward Newcomb, you cannot help but be aware of the successor company, National Lead, which now mines and ships titanium from pits deep in the earth near Lake Sanford. a short detour to the mine is worthwhile. A parking turnout is provided beside the road for those who wish to stop for samples of the ilmenite from which the titanium is processed, and heavy pieces of magnetite, which contain the iron ore. Above the spot marked as a "Mineral Collecting Area," you will find one of the Adironacks' more impressive views. Due east lie the North River Mountains, with Allen to their north, then Redfield leading up to Skylight, with Mount Marcy peeping behind. Just east of north lies Mount Adams, identified by its tower. Northwest, over the mine pit, stands Henderson, with Santanoni beyond.

If you continue on the mine road, you will reach the overlook where you may view the current operation. In a dozen years it has created a hole 3,000 feet long, 1,500 feet wide, and 300 feet deep in the spot where the mining village of Tahawus once existed.

When you return home you will want to relive the pleasures of the hike through Indian Pass by reading Arthur H. Masten's *The Story of Adirondac,* available in reprint. In it you will find a copy of the letter in which David Henderson wrote of his discovery trip through the Pass, as well as the history of the mine. And, you will want to relive the trip, for you will agree it is the most exciting walk in the eastern United States.

Algonquin Peak in the MacIntyre Mountains

Distance (round trip): 8 miles
Vertical rise: 2,936 feet
Hiking time: 6 hours
Map: USGS 15' Mount Marcy
High Peaks Wilderness Area

Algonquin Peak in the MacIntyre Mountains is, at 5,114 feet, the second highest mountain in New York State. But in all other respects, Algonquin is second to none. Standing in the midst of the noblest group of mountains in the Adirondacks, it offers an exciting climb and the best view from within the High Peaks.

The trailhead for Algonquin is an historic site at the end of Heart Lake Road, which heads south from NY 73 in North Elba, 11.2 miles west of Keene and 3.2 miles east of Lake Placid. When you first turn south toward Heart Lake, stop to enjoy the view of the High Peaks; the MacIntyre Mountains completely dominate the skyline.

This northern gateway to the High Peaks is owned and managed by the Adirondack Mountain Club, which maintains a parking lot at the end of Heart Lake Road. The club charges a nominal fee for parking. Public accommodation is available at the club's Loj, and many lean-tos and tent sites near the shores of Heart Lake may also be rented on a daily basis. The Loj was built near the site

of an imposing hotel the inventor Henry van Hoevenberg had constructed of massive logs in 1878-1880. Van Hoevenberg's fortune financed the lodge he planned to run with his fiancee, Josephine Scofield, for whom he named the mountain behind the lodge, Mount Jo. Disapproving parents and her untimely death brought an end to the marriage plans, and the forest fires of 1903 brought an end to the lodge. Donaldson's *A History of the Adirondacks* contains many fascinating details of the development of this northern gateway to the High Peaks.

The MacIntyre Mountains derived their name from Archibald McIntyre, Comptroller of the State of New York and partner in the McIntyre Iron Mine, south of Indian Pass. Algonquin Peak was named about 1880 by the surveyor Verplank Colvin after the tribe that once controlled most of New England, the Hudson River Valley, and the St. Lawrence River Valley. The tribe, which sided with the French in the French and English wars of the seventeenth century, was gradually overpowered by the Iroquois. Algonquin, according to Russell M.L. Carson in *Peaks and People of the Adirondacks,* "is there for a monument to an annihilated people, who were the original possessors of the Adirondack Wilderness." (Carson's book is a complete record of the names, early ascents, and trails on the Adirondacks' forty-six peaks over 4,000 feet in elevation.)

The trailhead and registration booth are located at the southeastern edge of the Loj parking lot. For the first mile you follow the newly constructed Van Hoevenberg Trail, which is the principle route to Mount Marcy, denoted with blue markers. The route begins down a small incline and crosses a marsh, an alder swamp, and then the outlet of Heart Lake on a log bridge. After climbing the side of a small hill, you enter state land, and within twenty minutes, or 1 mile, you come to a major trail junction. Here the blue-marked trail to Marcy Dam heads south, or left, and the MacIntyre trails, marked with yellow disks, continue straight ahead.

From the intersection it is 3 miles to the summit of Algonquin, with almost all the ascent yet to come. The Adirondack Mountain Club is proud of the work that has been done to repair sections of the trail and reroute worn areas. Waterbars, stairs, and stone work all help prevent erosion. As a result, the lower sections of the trail are easy to walk.

Within twenty minutes you come to a stretch where large stones have been placed through a muddy swale. A ski-touring trail forks left at 1.4 miles, toward Whales Tail Notch. The Whales Tail is a small knob directly northeast of MacIntyre's northern summit, Wright Peak. Continuing, you walk through a rich hardwood forest whose floor is punctuated by the blooming flowers of understory plants.

Gradually paper birch becomes the predominant tree. This indicates the extent of the fires that burned the mountainside and all the Heart Lake area in the early twentieth century. The spruce and balsam now establishing themselves beneath the birch are your clues to the length of time that has passed. You walk through the birch forest for nearly 1 mile, past ledges on the left, climbing moderately. You will hardly be aware of where you cross the old worn trail. At 2.3 miles, an hour and fifteen minutes into your walk, a sign points to the summit 1.6 miles away. The gullied wash leading back to your left is the abandoned trail.

A few minutes later you come to a sign pointing left, east, to a camping area. Just beyond, the trail crosses a brook not shown on the USGS map. In dry summers there is barely enough flow to fill your canteen, but this last source of water is clear and very cold. In wet seasons a crystal sheet of water falls over a high ledge, creating a charming resting spot.

As you climb again, the balsam become thicker, and ledges on the left are covered with a deep moss carpet. Within fifteen minutes, in a short level, you cross an almost dry stream. Then a jumble of old blowdowns edges a steep section of trail that zigzags through the scrub. In fifteen minutes more, at 2.9 miles, you pass a rock knob on your right, just off the trail. A sign warns you not to proceed farther without proper gear, a caution you should always heed while hiking in the High Peaks.

As you turn left away from the knob to scramble up a very steep section, you have views of a wooded

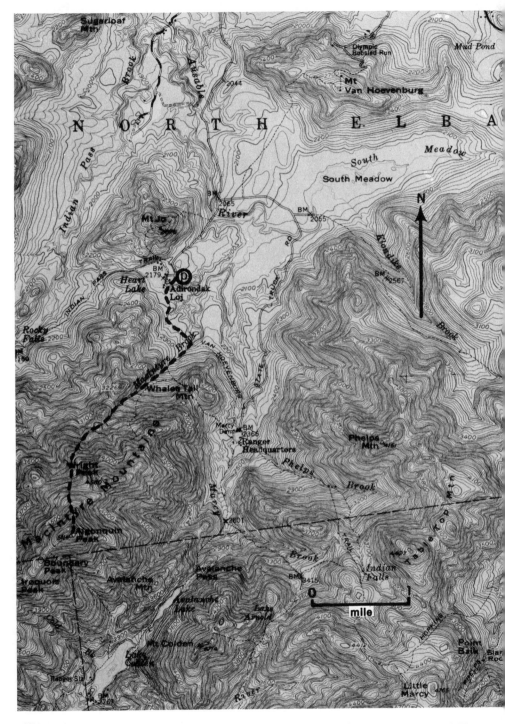

Algonquin Peak in the MacIntyre Mountains **247**

248 *Algonquin Peak in the MacIntyre Mountains*

summit, the first of many false summits you glimpse as you climb.

Two hours into your hike, at 3.1 miles, you reach another trail junction. The way left, marked with blue disks, leads in .5 mile to Wright Peak, 385 feet higher than your present location. Continue straight on the yellow-marked trail to begin one of the steepest climbs on a High Peaks trail, an ascent of 912 feet in .9 mile. It may take you a full hour to reach the summit from here.

The route is steep, over ledges, with water usually coursing over the bare rock that constitutes the trail. Scrubby spruce and balsam line the route and cling to the sphagnum that makes up the vertical bogs of the alpine summits. The shallow soil is home to many ground covers, including creeping white winterberry, golden thread, and bunchberry, here blossoming at the end of July, eight weeks later than in the Adirondack lowlands. When you reach a stretch of sheer rock trail, pause to look back, for you can now see the summit of Wright Peak, and you appear to be at about the same elevation. Openings permit views north to Whiteface and McKenzie and east to the precipitous rock face of Gothics. Again you have a view of a summit ahead, but it too is false. The blue leaves of dwarf bilberry and the blue-green and white almost needlelike leaves of bog rosemary show up in the mats of low scrub bushes along the trail. Huge blue crystals of labradorite are imbedded in the anorthosite that makes up the rock base of this and all the eastern High Peaks.

Forty minutes from the junction you reach treeline, with .4 mile left to

Colden from Algonquin

climb. A sign asks that you please stay on the marked trail so that you do not trample the fragile alpine vegetation. From here on, only arrows painted on bedrock or cairns mark the trail. The route is not hard to follow in good weather, but if clouds should roll in, a not uncommon event on high Adirondack summits, watch carefully for the arrows.

Another false summit looms ahead, but finally you climb over a small ledge and find the true summit. As you climb the open rock slabs, you begin to see the three-leafed cinquefoil of the alpine summits, and in summer you will be surprised to discover bottle gentian blooming at the same time as bunchberry. Adirondack High Peak summers are compressed into a short season.

After you settle in for a picnic, spread out your maps and orient yourself. The most impressive mountain view is southeast to Colden, the stripes of its slides radiating from the summit like the outflow from some gigantic moonscape eruption. Slides from Colden have changed the outlet of Avalanche Lake, which lies hidden between Algonquin and Colden. Colden's famous trap dyke, a narrow gorge carved out in the sheer rock dome, is clearly visible to the left of the major slides. This view of Colden is my favorite scene in the High Peaks, and one of the reasons is that the mountain was for a time called Mount McMartin, after my great-great-grandfather's brother, who was one of the founders of the McIntyre iron mine south of Indian Pass.

On the horizon left, east of Colden, lie Skylight, Gray Peak, and Marcy. Continuing left are Hough, the Dixes, and the mountains of the Range Trail, with Giant almost due east. Hurricane, Porter, and Cascade are visible around to the north, with Van Hoevenburg to the northeast. The Sentinel Range is visible over Van Hoevenburg, and to its left, west, lies Whiteface. You will have no trouble spotting the new Olympic Ski Jump at Lake Placid.

Moving around to the northwest, Street and Nye form a long wooded range that leads to Wallface in the west. The cliffs on Wallface clearly outline Indian Pass.

Starting again with Colden but this time moving right, or west, you should identify first Redfield. Below you lie Lake Colden and Flowed Land. South of Lake Colden and just to the right of Redfield you can see the cliffs on Cliff Mountain. Next comes a small peak, Little Nippletop, and then Calamity Mountain. Flowed Land points to the valley between Cliff and Calamity, through which Opalescent River, the outlet of Flowed Land, exits. Over Calamity Mountain and to the right you should see Henderson, with Santanoni the huge mountain behind, Seward and Seymour mark the western horizon behind Wallface, with the Sawtooth Mountains to its

north, followed by Ampersand.

You will need binoculars and exceptionally clear weather to see more distant peaks, but Blue Mountain and Vanderwhacker are possible to pick out as well as many of the outlying summits described in this guide.

Your return will occupy the better part of two hours and a half, with fifty minutes devoted to the first .9-mile descent. It is that steep! If you are making a midsummer trip, look for Milbert's Tortoise, an uncommon angle-wing butterfly often seen in large numbers on Algonquin.

Algonquin is a fairly strenuous climb, yet it is much easier to reach than the majority of the High Peaks, which require treks from interior backpacking locations. If the introduction to the eastern High Peaks has stimulated your interest in the Adirondacks' higher climbs, sample a few, but do not neglect the outlying mountains, for which few adequate guidebooks exist. You will find their climbs and views are more than comparable, but you will also discover a sense of wilderness that is becoming rare in the popular High Peaks.

Guidebooks from Backcountry Publications

Written for people of all ages and experience, these highly popular and carefully prepared books feature detailed trail directions, notes on points of interest, maps, and photographs.

About New York —

Discover the Adirondacks, 2: Walks, Waterways, and Winter Treks in the Southern Adirondacks, by Barbara McMartin. $7.95
Discover the Adirondacks, 1: From Indian Lake to the Hudson River, by Barbara McMartin. $6.95
Fifty Hikes in Central New York, by Bill Ehling. $8.95
Canoeing Central New York, by Bill Ehling. $8.95
20 Bicycle Tours in the Finger Lakes, by Mark Roth and Sally Walters. $6.95
20 Bicycle Tours In and Around New York City, by Dan Carlinsky and David Heim. $6.95
25 Ski Tours in the Adirondacks, by Almy and Anne Coggeshall. $5.95
25 Ski Tours in Central New York, by Bill Ehling. $5.95

For Hikers —

Fifty Hikes in Connecticut (1984), by Gerry and Sue Hardy. $8.95
Fifty Hikes in Vermont, by Ruth and Paul Sadlier. $7.95
Fifty Hikes in Massachusetts, by John Brady and Brian White. $8.95
Fifty Hikes in the White Mountains, by Dan Doan. $8.95
Fifty More Hikes in New Hampshire, by Dan Doan. $8.95
Fifty Hikes in Maine, by John Gibson. $8.95
Fifty More Hikes in Maine, by Cloe Catlett. $8.95
Fifty Hikes in Eastern Pennsylvania, by Carolyn Hoffman. $8.95
Fifty Hikes in Western Pennsylvania, by Tom Thwaites. $8.95

Available from bookstores, certain sporting goods stores, or the publisher. For complete descriptions of these and all our *hiking, skiing, walking, canoeing,* and *bicycling* guides for the Northeast and Mid-Atlantic states, write to: Backcountry Publications, P.O. Box 175, Woodstock VT 05091.